Java Deep Learning Cookbook

Train neural networks for classification, NLP, and
reinforcement learning using Deeplearning4j

Rahul Raj

BIRMINGHAM - MUMBAI

Java Deep Learning Cookbook

Copyright © 2019 Packt Publishing

Commissioning Editor: Sunith Shetty
Acquisition Editor: Meeta Rajani
Content Development Editor: Ronn Kurien
Senior Editor: Rahul Dsouza
Technical Editor: Dinesh Pawar
Copy Editor: Safis Editing
Project Coordinator: Vaidehi Sawant
Proofreader: Safis Editing
Indexer: Rekha Nair
Production Designer: Arvindkumar Gupta

First published: November 2019

Production reference: 1081119

Published by Packt Publishing Ltd.
Livery Place
35 Livery Street
Birmingham
B3 2PB, UK.

ISBN 978-1-78899-520-7

www.packt.com

To my wife, Sharanya, for being my loving partner throughout our joint life journey.
To my mother, Soubhagyalekshmi, and my father, Rajasekharan, for their love, continuous
support, sacrifices, and inspiration.

– Rahul Raj

Packt.com

Subscribe to our online digital library for full access to over 7,000 books and videos, as well as industry leading tools to help you plan your personal development and advance your career. For more information, please visit our website.

Why subscribe?

- Spend less time learning and more time coding with practical eBooks and Videos from over 4,000 industry professionals

- Improve your learning with Skill Plans built especially for you

- Get a free eBook or video every month

- Fully searchable for easy access to vital information

- Copy and paste, print, and bookmark content

Did you know that Packt offers eBook versions of every book published, with PDF and ePub files available? You can upgrade to the eBook version at www.packt.com and as a print book customer, you are entitled to a discount on the eBook copy. Get in touch with us at customercare@packtpub.com for more details.

At www.packt.com, you can also read a collection of free technical articles, sign up for a range of free newsletters, and receive exclusive discounts and offers on Packt books and eBooks.

Contributors

About the author

Rahul Raj has more than 7 years of IT industry experience in software development, business analysis, client communication, and consulting on medium-/large-scale projects in multiple domains. Currently, he works as a lead software engineer in a top software development firm. He has extensive experience in development activities comprising requirement analysis, design, coding, implementation, code review, testing, user training, and enhancements. He has written a number of articles about neural networks in Java and they are featured by DL4J/ official Java community channels. He is also a certified machine learning professional, certified by Vskills, the largest government certification body in India.

I want to thank the people who have been close to me and have supported me, especially my wife, Sharanya, and my parents.

About the reviewers

Cristian Stancalau has an MSc and BSc in computer science and engineering from Babes-Bolyai University, where he has worked as an assistant lecturer since 2018. Currently, he works as chief software architect, focused on enterprise code review. Previously, he cofounded and led a video technology start-up as technical director. Cristian has proven mentoring and teaching expertise in both the commercial and academic sectors, advising on Java technologies and product architecture.

I would like to thank Packt for the opportunity to perform the technical review for Java Deep Learning Cookbook. Reading it was a real pleasure for me and I am sure it will also be for its readers.

Aristides Villarreal Bravo is a Java developer, a member of the NetBeans Dream Team, and a Java User Groups leader. He lives in Panama. He has organized and participated in various conferences and seminars related to Java, Java EE, NetBeans, the NetBeans platform, free software, and mobile devices. He is the author of the jmoordb framework, and tutorials and blogs about Java, NetBeans, and web development. He has participated in several interviews about topics such as NetBeans, NetBeans DZone, and JavaHispano. He is a developer of plugins for NetBeans.

I want to thank my parents and brothers for their unconditional support (Nivia, Aristides, Secundino, and Victor).

Packt is searching for authors like you

If you're interested in becoming an author for Packt, please visit `authors.packtpub.com` and apply today. We have worked with thousands of developers and tech professionals, just like you, to help them share their insight with the global tech community. You can make a general application, apply for a specific hot topic that we are recruiting an author for, or submit your own idea.

Table of Contents

Preface

Deep learning has helped many industries/companies to solve big challenges, enhance their products, and strengthen their infrastructure. The advantage of deep learning is that you neither have to design decision-making algorithms nor make decisions regarding important dataset features. Your neural network is capable of doing both. We have seen enough theoretical books that leave the audience all at sea having explained complex concepts. It is also important to know how/when you can apply what you have learned, especially in relation to enterprise. This is a concern for advanced technologies such as deep learning. You may have undertaken capstone projects, but you also want to take your knowledge to the next level.

Of course, there are best practices in enterprise development that we may not cover in this book. We don't want readers to question themselves about the purpose of developing an application if it is too tedious to deploy in production. We want something very straightforward, targeting the largest developer community in the world. We have used **DL4J** (short for **Deeplearning4j**) throughout this book to demonstrate examples for the same reason. It has DataVec for **ETL** (short for **Extract, Transform, and Load**), ND4J as a scientific computation library, and a DL4J core library to develop and deploy neural network models in production. There are cases where DL4J outperforms some of the major deep learning libraries on the market. We are not degrading other libraries, as it all depends on what you want to do with them. You may also try accommodating multiple libraries in different phases if you don't want to bother switching to multiple technical stacks.

Who this book is for

In order to get the most out of this book, we recommend that readers have basic knowledge of deep learning and data analytics. It is also preferable for readers to have basic knowledge of MLP (multilayer perceptrons) or feed forward networks, recurrent neural networks, LSTM, word vector representations, and some level of debugging skills to interpret the errors from the error stack. As this book targets Java and the DL4J library, readers should also have sound knowledge of Java and DL4J. This book is not suitable for anyone who is new to programming or who doesn't have basic knowledge of deep learning.

What this book covers

Chapter 1, *Introduction to Deep Learning in Java*, provides a brief introduction to deep learning using DL4J.

Chapter 2, *Data Extraction, Transformation, and Loading*, discusses the ETL process for handling data for neural networks with the help of examples.

Chapter 3, *Building Deep Neural Networks for Binary Classification*, demonstrates how to develop a deep neural network in DL4J in order to solve binary classification problems.

Chapter 4, *Building Convolutional Neural Networks*, explains how to develop a convolutional neural network in DL4J in order to solve image classification problems.

Chapter 5, *Implementing Natural Language Processing*, discusses how to develop NLP applications using DL4J.

Chapter 6, *Constructing LSTM Networks for Time Series*, demonstrates a time series application on a PhysioNet dataset with single-class output using DL4J.

Chapter 7, *Constructing LSTM Neural Networks for Sequence Classification*, demonstrates a time series application on a UCI synthetic control dataset with multi-class output using DL4J.

Chapter 8, *Performing Anomaly Detection on Unsupervised Data*, explains how to develop an unsupervised anomaly detection application using DL4J.

Chapter 9, *Using RL4J for Reinforcement Learning*, explains how to develop a reinforcement learning agent that can learn to play the *Malmo* game using RL4J.

Chapter 10, *Developing Applications in a Distributed Environment*, covers how to develop distributed deep learning applications using DL4J.

Chapter 11, *Applying Transfer Learning to Network Models*, demonstrates how to apply transfer learning to DL4J applications.

Chapter 12, *Benchmarking and Neural Network Optimization*, discusses various benchmarking approaches and neural network optimization techniques that can be applied to your deep learning application.

To get the most out of this book

Readers are expected to have basic knowledge of deep learning, reinforcement learning, and data analytics. Basic knowledge of deep learning will help you understand the neural network design and the various hyperparameters used in the examples. Basic data analytics skills and an understanding of data requirements will help you to explore DataVec better, while some prior knowledge of the basics of reinforcement learning will help you while working through Chapter 9, *Using RL4J for Reinforcement Learning*. We will also be discussing distributed neural networks in Chapter 10, *Developing Applications in a Distributed Environment*, for which basic knowledge of Apache Spark is preferred.

Download the example code files

You can download the example code files for this book from your account at www.packt.com. If you purchased this book elsewhere, you can visit www.packtpub.com/support and register to have the files emailed directly to you.

You can download the code files by following these steps:

1. Log in or register at www.packt.com.
2. Select the **Support** tab.
3. Click on **Code Downloads**.
4. Enter the name of the book in the **Search** box and follow the onscreen instructions.

Once the file is downloaded, please make sure that you unzip or extract the folder using the latest version of:

- WinRAR/7-Zip for Windows
- Zipeg/iZip/UnRarX for Mac
- 7-Zip/PeaZip for Linux

The code bundle for the book is also hosted on GitHub at https://github.com/ PacktPublishing/Java-Deep-Learning-Cookbook. In case there's an update to the code, it will be updated on the existing GitHub repository.

We also have other code bundles from our rich catalog of books and videos available at https://github.com/PacktPublishing/. Check them out!

Download the color images

We also provide a PDF file that has color images of the screenshots/diagrams used in this book. You can download it here: `https://static.packt-cdn.com/downloads/9781788995207_ColorImages.pdf`.

Conventions used

There are a number of text conventions used throughout this book.

`CodeInText`: Indicates code words in text, database table names, folder names, filenames, file extensions, pathnames, dummy URLs, user input, and Twitter handles. Here is an example: "Create a `CSVRecordReader` to hold customer churn data."

A block of code is set as follows:

```
File file = new File("Churn_Modelling.csv");
recordReader.initialize(new FileSplit(file));
```

Any command-line input or output is written as follows:

```
mvn clean install
```

Bold: Indicates a new term, an important word, or words that you see on screen. For example, words in menus or dialog boxes appear in the text like this. Here is an example: "We just need to click on the **Model** tab on the left-hand sidebar."

 Warnings or important notes appear like this.

 Tips and tricks appear like this.

Sections

In this book, you will find several headings that appear frequently (*Getting ready*, *How to do it...*, *How it works...*, *There's more...*, and *See also*).

To give clear instructions on how to complete a recipe, use these sections as follows:

Getting ready

This section tells you what to expect in the recipe and describes how to set up any software or any preliminary settings required for the recipe.

How to do it...

This section contains the steps required to follow the recipe.

How it works...

This section usually consists of a detailed explanation of what happened in the previous section.

There's more...

This section consists of additional information about the recipe in order to make you more knowledgeable about the recipe.

See also

This section provides helpful links to other useful information for the recipe.

Get in touch

Feedback from our readers is always welcome.

General feedback: If you have questions about any aspect of this book, mention the book title in the subject of your message and email us at `customercare@packtpub.com`.

Errata: Although we have taken every care to ensure the accuracy of our content, mistakes do happen. If you have found a mistake in this book, we would be grateful if you would report this to us. Please visit `www.packtpub.com/support/errata`, selecting your book, clicking on the Errata Submission Form link, and entering the details.

Piracy: If you come across any illegal copies of our works in any form on the internet, we would be grateful if you would provide us with the location address or website name. Please contact us at `copyright@packt.com` with a link to the material.

If you are interested in becoming an author: If there is a topic that you have expertise in, and you are interested in either writing or contributing to a book, please visit authors.packtpub.com.

Reviews

Please leave a review. Once you have read and used this book, why not leave a review on the site that you purchased it from? Potential readers can then see and use your unbiased opinion to make purchase decisions, we at Packt can understand what you think about our products, and our authors can see your feedback on their book. Thank you!

For more information about Packt, please visit packt.com.

Introduction to Deep Learning in Java

Let's discuss various deep learning libraries so as to pick the best for the purpose at hand. This is a context-dependent decision and will vary according to the situation. In this chapter, we will start with a brief introduction to deep learning and explore how DL4J is a good choice for solving deep learning puzzles. We will also discuss how to set up DL4J in your workspace.

In this chapter, we will cover the following recipes:

- Deep learning intuition
- Determining the right network type to solve deep learning problems
- Determining the right activation function
- Combating overfitting problems
- Determining the right batch size and learning rates
- Configuring Maven for DL4J
- Configuring DL4J for a GPU-accelerated environment
- Troubleshooting installation issues

Technical requirements

You'll need the following to get the most out of this cookbook:

- Java SE 7, or higher, installed
- Basic core Java knowledge
- DL4J basics
- Maven basics
- Basic data analytical skills

- Deep learning/machine learning basics
- OS command basics (Linux/Windows)
- IntelliJ IDEA IDE (this is a very easy and hassle-free way of managing code; however, you're free to try another IDE, such as Eclipse)
- Spring Boot basics (to integrate DL4J with Spring Boot for use with web applications)

We use DL4J version 1.0.0-beta3 throughout this book except for `Chapter 7`, *Constructing an LSTM Neural Network for Sequence Classification*, where we used the current latest version, 1.0.0-beta4, to avoid bugs.

Deep learning intuition

If you're a newbie to deep learning, you may be wondering how exactly it is differs from machine learning; or is it the same? Deep learning is a subset of the larger domain of machine learning. Let's think about this in the context of an automobile image classification problem:

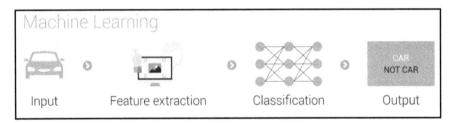

As you can see in the preceding diagram, we need to perform feature extraction ourselves as legacy machine learning algorithms cannot do that on their own. They might be super-efficient with accurate results, but they cannot learn signals from data. In fact, they don't learn on their own and still rely on human effort:

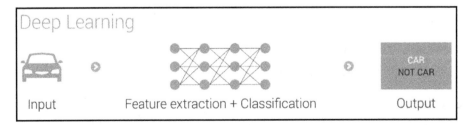

On the other hand, deep learning algorithms learn to perform tasks on their own. Neural networks under the hood are based on the concept of deep learning and it trains on their own to optimize the results. However, the final decision process is hidden and cannot be tracked. The intent of deep learning is to imitate the functioning of a human brain.

Backpropagation

The backbone of a neural network is the backpropagation algorithm. Refer to the sample neural network structure shown as follows:

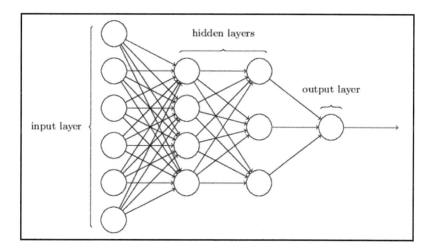

For any neural network, data flows from the input layer to the output layer during the forward pass. Each circle in the diagram represents a neuron. Every layer has a number of neurons present. Our data will pass through the neurons across layers. The input needs to be in a numerical format to support computational operations in neurons. Each neuron in the neural network is assigned a weight (matrix) and an activation function. Using the input data, weight matrix, and an activation function, a probabilistic value is generated at each neuron. The error (that is, a deviation from the actual value) is calculated at the output layer using a loss function. We utilize the loss score during the backward pass (that is, from the output layer to the input layer) by reassigning weights to the neurons to reduce the loss score. During this stage, some output layer neurons will be assigned with high weights and vice versa depending upon the loss score results. This process will continue backward as far as the input layer by updating the weights of neurons. In a nutshell, we are tracking the rate of change of loss with respect to the change in weights across all neurons. This entire cycle (a forward and backward pass) is called an epoch. We perform multiple epochs during a training session. A neural network will tend to optimize the results after every training epoch.

Multilayer Perceptron (MLP)

An MLP is a standard feed-forward neural network with at least three layers: an input layer, a hidden layer, and an output layer. Hidden layers come after the input layer in the structure. Deep neural networks have two or more hidden layers in the structure, while an MLP has only one.

Convolutional Neural Network (CNN)

CNNs are generally used for image classification problems, but can also be exposed in **Natural Language Processing** (**NLP**), in conjunction with word vectors, because of their proven results. Unlike a regular neural network, a CNN will have additional layers such as convolutional layers and subsampling layers. Convolutional layers take input data (such as images) and apply convolution operations on top of them. You can think of it as applying a function to the input. Convolutional layers act as filters that pass a feature of interest to the upcoming subsampling layer. A feature of interest can be anything (for example, a fur, shade and so on in the case of an image) that can be used to identify the image. In the subsampling layer, the input from convolutional layers is further smoothed. So, we end up with a much smaller image resolution and reduced color contrast, preserving only the important information. The input is then passed on to fully connected layers. Fully connected layers resemble regular feed-forward neural networks.

Recurrent Neural Network (RNN)

An RNN is a neural network that can process sequential data. In a regular feed-forward neural network, the current input is considered for neurons in the next layer. On the other hand, an RNN can accept previously received inputs as well. It can also use memory to memorize previous inputs. So, it is capable of preserving long-term dependencies throughout the training session. RNN is a popular choice for NLP tasks such as speech recognition. In practice, a slightly variant structure called **Long Short-Term Memory** (**LSTM**) is used as a better alternative to RNN.

Why is DL4J important for deep learning?

The following points will help you understand why DL4J is important for deep learning:

- DL4J provides commercial support. It is the first commercial-grade, open source, deep learning library in Java.
- Writing training code is simple and precise. DL4J supports Plug and Play mode, which means switching between hardware (CPU to GPU) is just a matter of changing the Maven dependencies and no modifications are needed on the code.
- DL4J uses ND4J as its backend. ND4J is a computation library that can run twice as fast as NumPy (a computation library in Python) in large matrix operations. DL4J exhibits faster training times in GPU environments compared to other Python counterparts.
- DL4J supports training on a cluster of machines that are running in CPU/GPU using Apache Spark. DL4J brings in automated parallelism in distributed training. This means that DL4J bypasses the need for extra libraries by setting up worker nodes and connections.
- DL4J is a good production-oriented deep learning library. As a JVM-based library, DL4J applications can be easily integrated/deployed with existing corporate applications that are running in Java/Scala.

Determining the right network type to solve deep learning problems

It is crucial to identify the right neural network type to solve a business problem efficiently. A standard neural network can be a best fit for most use cases and can produce approximate results. However, in some scenarios, the core neural network architecture needs to be changed in order to accommodate the features (input) and to produce the desired results. In the following recipe, we will walk through key steps to decide the best network architecture for a deep learning problem with the help of known use cases.

How to do it...

1. Determine the problem type.
2. Determine the type of data engaged in the system.

How it works...

To solve use cases effectively, we need to use the right neural network architecture by determining the problem type. The following are globally some use cases and respective problem types to consider for step 1:

- **Fraud detection problems**: We want to differentiate between legitimate and suspicious transactions so as to separate unusual activities from the entire activity list. The intent is to reduce false-positive (that is, incorrectly tagging legitimate transactions as fraud) cases. Hence, this is an anomaly detection problem.

- **Prediction problems**: Prediction problems can be classification or regression problems. For labeled classified data, we can have discrete labels. We need to model data against those discrete labels. On the other hand, regression models don't have discrete labels.

- **Recommendation problems**: You would need to build a recommender system (a recommendation engine) to recommend products or content to customers. Recommendation engines can also be applied to an agent performing tasks such as gaming, autonomous driving, robotic movements, and more. Recommendation engines implement reinforcement learning and can be enhanced further by introducing deep learning into it.

We also need to know the type of data that is consumed by the neural network. Here are some use cases and respective data types for step 2:

- **Fraud detection problems**: Transactions usually happen over a number of time steps. So, we need to continuously collect transaction data over time. This is an example of time series data. Each time sequence represents a new transaction sequence. These time sequences can be regular or irregular. For instance, if you have credit card transaction data to analyze, then you have labeled data. You can also have unlabeled data in the case of user metadata from production logs. We can have supervised/unsupervised datasets for fraud detection analysis, for example. Take a look at the following CSV supervised dataset:

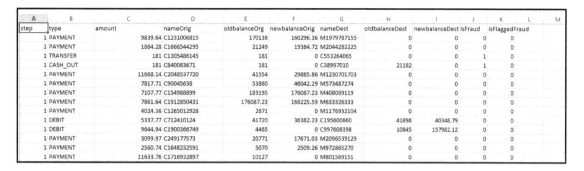

step	type	amount	nameOrig	oldbalanceOrg	newbalanceOrig	nameDest	oldbalanceDest	newbalanceDest	isFraud	isFlaggedFraud
1	PAYMENT	9839.64	C1231006815	170136	160296.36	M1979787155	0	0	0	0
1	PAYMENT	1864.28	C1666544295	21249	19384.72	M2044282225	0	0	0	0
1	TRANSFER	181	C1305486145	181	0	C553264065	0	0	1	0
1	CASH_OUT	181	C840083671	181	0	C38997010	21182	0	1	0
1	PAYMENT	11668.14	C2048537720	41554	29885.86	M1230701703	0	0	0	0
1	PAYMENT	7817.71	C90045638	53860	46042.29	M573487274	0	0	0	0
1	PAYMENT	7107.77	C154988899	183195	176087.23	M408069119	0	0	0	0
1	PAYMENT	7861.64	C1912850431	176087.23	168225.59	M633326333	0	0	0	0
1	PAYMENT	4024.36	C1265012928	2671	0	M1176932104	0	0	0	0
1	DEBIT	5337.77	C712410124	41720	36382.23	C195660860	41898	40348.79	0	0
1	DEBIT	9644.94	C1900366749	4465	0	C997608398	10845	157982.12	0	0
1	PAYMENT	3099.97	C249177573	20771	17671.03	M2096539129	0	0	0	0
1	PAYMENT	2560.74	C1648232591	5070	2509.26	M972865270	0	0	0	0
1	PAYMENT	11633.76	C1716932897	10127	0	M801569151	0	0	0	0

In the preceding screenshot, features such as `amount`, `oldBalanceOrg`, and so on make sense and each record has a label indicating whether the particular observation is fraudulent or not.

On the other hand, an unsupervised dataset will not give you any clue about input features. It doesn't have any labels either, as shown in the following CSV data:

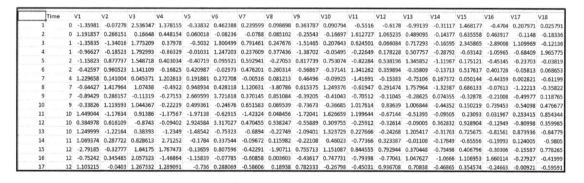

	Time	V1	V2	V3	V4	V5	V6	V7	V8	V9	V10	V11	V12	V13	V14	V15	V16	V17	V18
1	0	-1.35981	-0.07278	2.536347	1.378155	-0.33832	0.462388	0.239599	0.098698	0.363787	0.090794	-0.5516	-0.6178	-0.99139	-0.31117	1.468177	-0.4704	0.207971	0.025791
2	0	1.191857	0.266151	0.16648	0.448154	0.060018	-0.08236	-0.0788	0.085102	-0.25543	-0.16697	1.612727	1.065235	0.489095	-0.14377	0.635558	0.463917	-0.1148	-0.18336
3	1	-1.35835	-1.34016	1.773209	0.37978	-0.5032	1.800499	0.791461	0.247676	-1.51465	0.207643	0.624501	0.066084	0.717293	-0.16595	2.345865	-2.89008	1.109969	-0.12136
4	1	-0.96627	-0.18523	1.792993	-0.86329	-0.01031	1.247203	0.237609	0.377436	-1.38702	-0.05495	-0.22649	0.178228	0.507757	-0.28792	-0.63142	-1.05965	-0.68409	1.965775
5	2	-1.15823	0.877737	1.548718	0.403034	-0.40719	0.095921	0.592941	-0.27053	0.817739	0.753074	-0.82284	0.538196	1.345852	-1.11967	0.175121	-0.45145	-0.23703	-0.03819
6	2	-0.42597	0.960523	1.141109	-0.16825	0.420987	-0.02973	0.476201	0.260314	-0.56867	-0.37141	1.341262	0.359894	-0.35809	-0.13713	0.517617	0.401726	-0.05813	0.068653
7	4	1.229658	0.141004	0.045371	1.202613	0.191881	0.272708	-0.00516	0.081213	0.46496	-0.09925	-1.41691	-0.15383	-0.75106	0.167372	0.050144	-0.44359	0.002821	-0.61199
8	7	-0.64427	1.417964	1.07438	-0.4922	0.948934	0.428118	1.120631	-3.80786	0.615375	1.249376	-0.61947	0.291474	1.757964	-1.32387	0.686133	-0.07613	-1.22213	-0.35822
9	7	-0.89429	0.286157	-0.11319	-0.27153	2.669599	3.721818	0.370145	0.851084	-0.39205	-0.41043	-0.70512	-0.11045	-0.28625	0.074355	-0.32878	-0.21008	-0.49977	0.118765
10	9	-0.33826	1.119593	1.044367	-0.22219	0.499361	-0.24676	0.651583	0.069539	-0.73673	-0.36685	1.017614	0.83639	1.006844	-0.44352	0.150219	0.739453	-0.54098	0.476677
11	10	1.449044	-1.17634	0.91386	-1.37567	-1.97138	-0.62915	-1.42324	0.048456	-1.72041	1.626659	1.199644	-0.67144	-0.51395	-0.09505	0.23093	0.031967	0.253415	0.854344
12	10	0.384978	0.616109	-0.8743	-0.09402	2.924584	3.317027	0.470455	0.538247	-0.55889	0.309755	-0.25912	-0.32614	-0.09005	0.362832	0.928904	-0.12949	-0.80998	0.359985
13	10	1.249999	-1.22164	0.38393	-1.2349	-1.48542	-0.75323	-0.6894	-0.22749	-2.09401	1.323729	0.227666	-0.24268	1.205417	-0.31763	0.725675	-0.81561	0.873936	-0.84779
14	11	1.069374	0.287722	0.828613	2.71252	-0.1784	0.337544	-0.09672	0.115982	-0.22108	0.46023	-0.77366	0.323387	-0.01108	-0.17849	-0.65556	-0.19993	0.124005	-0.9805
15	12	-2.79185	-0.32777	1.64175	1.767473	-0.13659	0.807596	-0.42291	-1.90711	0.755713	1.151087	0.844555	0.792944	0.370448	-0.73498	0.406796	-0.30306	-0.15587	0.778265
16	12	-0.75242	0.345485	2.057323	-1.46864	-1.15839	-0.07785	-0.60858	0.003603	-0.43617	0.747731	-0.79398	-0.77041	1.047627	-1.0666	1.106953	1.660114	-0.27927	-0.41999
17	12	1.103215	-0.0403	1.267332	1.289091	-0.736	0.288069	-0.58606	0.18938	0.782333	-0.26798	-0.45031	0.936708	0.70838	-0.46865	0.354574	-0.24663	-0.00921	-0.59591

As you can see, the feature labels (top row) follow a numbered naming convention without any clue as to its significance for fraud detection outcomes. We can also have time series data where transactions are logged over a series of time steps.

- **Prediction problems**: Historical data collected from organizations can be used to train neural networks. These are usually simple file types such as a CSV/text files. Data can be obtained as records. For a stock market prediction problem, the data type would be a time series. A dog breed prediction problem requires feeding in dog images for network training. Stock price prediction is an example of a regression problem. Stock price datasets usually are time series data where stock prices are measured over a series as follows:

A_data.csv	20-Sep-2019 at 9:56 PM	56 KB	Comm...
AAL_data.csv	20-Sep-2019 at 9:56 PM	59 KB	Comm...
AAP_data.csv	20-Sep-2019 at 9:56 PM	62 KB	Comm...
AAPL_data.csv	20-Sep-2019 at 9:56 PM	67 KB	Comm...
ABBV_data.csv	20-Sep-2019 at 9:56 PM	61 KB	Comm...
ABC_data.csv	20-Sep-2019 at 9:56 PM	60 KB	Comm...
ABT_data.csv	20-Sep-2019 at 9:56 PM	59 KB	Comm...
ACN_data.csv	20-Sep-2019 at 9:56 PM	61 KB	Comm...
ADBE_data.csv	20-Sep-2019 at 9:56 PM	62 KB	Comm...
ADI_data.csv	20-Sep-2019 at 9:56 PM	59 KB	Comm...
ADM_data.csv	20-Sep-2019 at 9:56 PM	59 KB	Comm...
ADP_data.csv	20-Sep-2019 at 9:56 PM	60 KB	Comm...
ADS_data.csv	20-Sep-2019 at 9:56 PM	63 KB	Comm...
ADSK_data.csv	20-Sep-2019 at 9:56 PM	61 KB	Comm...
AEE_data.csv	20-Sep-2019 at 9:56 PM	59 KB	Comm...
AEP_data.csv	20-Sep-2019 at 9:56 PM	59 KB	Comm...
AES_data.csv	20-Sep-2019 at 9:56 PM	59 KB	Comm...

In most stock price datasets, there are multiple files. Each one of them represents a company stock market. And each file will have stock prices recorded over a series of time steps, as shown here:

Name
▼ ■ individual_stocks_5yr
■ A_data.csv
■ AAL_data.csv
■ AAP_data.csv
■ AAPL_data.csv
■ ABBV_data.csv
■ ABC_data.csv
■ ABT_data.csv
■ ACN_data.csv
■ ADBE_data.csv
■ ADI_data.csv
■ ADM_data.csv
■ ADP_data.csv
■ ADS_data.csv
■ ADSK_data.csv
■ AEE_data.csv
■ AEP_data.csv
■ AES_data.csv
■ AET_data.csv

	A	B	C	D	E	F	G
1	date	open	high	low	close	volume	Name
2	08/02/13	45.07	45.35	45	45.08	1824755	A
3	11/02/13	45.17	45.18	44.45	44.6	2915405	A
4	12/02/13	44.81	44.95	44.5	44.62	2373731	A
5	13/02/13	44.81	45.24	44.68	44.75	2052338	A
6	14/02/13	44.72	44.78	44.36	44.58	3826245	A
7	15/02/13	43.48	44.24	42.21	42.25	14657315	A
8	19/02/13	42.21	43.12	42.21	43.01	4116141	A
9	20/02/13	42.84	42.85	42.225	42.24	3873183	A
10	21/02/13	42.14	42.14	41.47	41.63	3415149	A
11	22/02/13	41.83	42.07	41.58	41.8	3354862	A
12	25/02/13	42.09	42.22	41.29	41.29	3622460	A
13	26/02/13	40.62	41.29	40.19	40.97	6185811	A
14	27/02/13	40.99	41.905	40.83	41.73	3564385	A
15	28/02/13	41.78	42.06	41.45	41.48	3464202	A
16	01/03/13	41.18	41.98	40.73	41.93	3089323	A
17	04/03/13	41.75	42.18	41.52	42.03	2435306	A
18	05/03/13	42.35	43.19	42.34	42.66	3289188	A
19	06/03/13	43	43.52	42.9	43.24	2996908	A
20	07/03/13	43.3	43.48	42.81	43.25	2414186	A
21	08/03/13	43.5	43.52	43.02	43.03	3256301	A
22	11/03/13	42.99	43.01	41.73	42.81	5472837	A

- **Recommendation problems**: For a product recommendation system, explicit data might be customer reviews posted on a website and implicit data might be the customer activity history, such as product search or purchase history. We will use unlabeled data to feed the neural network. Recommender systems can also solve games or learn a job that requires skills. Agents (trained to perform tasks during reinforcement learning) can take real-time data in the form of image frames or any text data (unsupervised) to learn what actions to make depending on their states.

There's more...

The following are possible deep learning solutions to the problem types previously discussed:

- **Fraud detection problems**: The optimal solution varies according to the data. We previously mentioned two data sources. One was credit card transactions and the other was user metadata based on their login/logoff activities. In the first case, we have labeled data and have a transaction sequence to analyze.

Recurrent networks may be best suited to sequencing data. You can add LSTM (https://deeplearning4j.org/api/latest/org/deeplearning4j/nn/layers/recurrent/LSTM.html) recurrent layers, and DL4J has an implementation for that. For the second case, we have unlabeled data and the best choice would be a variational (https://deeplearning4j.org/api/latest/org/deeplearning4j/nn/layers/variational/VariationalAutoencoder.html) autoencoder to compress unlabeled data.

- **Prediction problems**: For classification problems that use CSV records, a feed-forward neural network will do. For time series data, the best choice would be recurrent networks because of the nature of sequential data. For image classification problems, you would need a CNN (https://deeplearning4j.org/api/latest/org/deeplearning4j/nn/conf/layers/ConvolutionLayer.Builder.html).

- **Recommendation problems**: We can employ **Reinforcement Learning** (**RL**) to solve recommendation problems. RL is very often used for such use cases and might be a better option. RL4J was specifically developed for this purpose. We will introduce RL4J in Chapter 9, *Using RL4J for Reinforcement Learning*, as it would be an advanced topic at this point. We can also go for simpler options such as feed-forward networks RNNs) with a different approach. We can feed an unlabeled data sequence to recurrent or convolutional layers as per the data type (image/text/video). Once the recommended content/product is classified, you can apply further logic to pull random products from the list based on customer preferences.

In order to choose the right network type, you need to understand the type of data and the problem it tries to solve. The most basic neural network that you could construct is a feed-forward network or a multilayer perceptron. You can create multilayer network architectures using NeuralNetConfiguration in DL4J.

Refer to the following sample neural network configuration in DL4J:

```
MultiLayerConfiguration configuration = new
NeuralNetConfiguration.Builder()
 .weightInit(WeightInit.RELU_UNIFORM)
 .updater(new Nesterovs(0.008,0.9))
 .list()
 .layer(new
DenseLayer.Builder().nIn(layerOneInputNeurons).nOut(layerOneOutputNeurons).
activation(Activation.RELU).dropOut(dropOutRatio).build())
 .layer(new
DenseLayer.Builder().nIn(layerTwoInputNeurons).nOut(layerTwoOutputNeurons).
activation(Activation.RELU).dropOut(0.9).build())
 .layer(new OutputLayer.Builder(new LossMCXENT(weightsArray))
```

```
.nIn(layerThreeInputNeurons).nOut(numberOfLabels).activation(Activation.SOF
TMAX).build())
  .backprop(true).pretrain(false)
  .build();
```

We specify activation functions for every layer in a neural network, and `nIn()` and `nOut()` represent the number of connections in/out of the layer of neurons. The purpose of the `dropOut()` function is to deal with network performance optimization. We mentioned it in Chapter 3, *Building Deep Neural Networks for Binary Classification*. Essentially, we are ignoring some neurons at random to avoid blindly memorizing patterns during training. Activation functions will be discussed in the *Determining the right activation function* recipe in this chapter. Other attributes control how weights are distributed between neurons and how to deal with errors calculated across each epoch.

Let's focus on a specific decision-making process: choosing the right network type. Sometimes, it is better to use a custom architecture to yield better results. For example, you can perform sentence classification using word vectors combined with a CNN. DL4J offers the ComputationGraph (`https://deeplearning4j.org/api/latest/org/deeplearning4j/nn/graph/ComputationGraph.html`) implementation to accommodate CNN architecture.

`ComputationGraph` allows an arbitrary (custom) neural network architecture. Here is how it is defined in DL4J:

```
public ComputationGraph(ComputationGraphConfiguration configuration) {
  this.configuration = configuration;
  this.numInputArrays = configuration.getNetworkInputs().size();
  this.numOutputArrays = configuration.getNetworkOutputs().size();
  this.inputs = new INDArray[numInputArrays];
  this.labels = new INDArray[numOutputArrays];
  this.defaultConfiguration = configuration.getDefaultConfiguration();
//Additional source is omitted from here. Refer to
https://github.com/deeplearning4j/deeplearning4j
}
```

Implementing a CNN is just like constructing network layers for a feed-forward network:

```
public class ConvolutionLayer extends FeedForwardLayer
```

A CNN has `ConvolutionalLayer` and `SubsamplingLayer` apart from `DenseLayer` and `OutputLayer`.

Determining the right activation function

The purpose of an activation function is to introduce non-linearity into a neural network. Non-linearity helps a neural network to learn more complex patterns. We will discuss some important activation functions, and their respective DL4J implementations.

The following are the activation functions that we will consider:

- Tanh
- Sigmoid
- ReLU (short for **Rectified Linear Unit**)
- Leaky ReLU
- Softmax

In this recipe, we will walk through the key steps to decide the right activation functions for a neural network.

How to do it...

1. **Choose an activation function according to the network layers**: We need to know the activation functions to be used for the input/hidden layers and output layers. Use ReLU for input/hidden layers preferably.
2. **Choose the right activation function to handle data impurities**: Inspect the data that you feed to the neural network. Do you have inputs with a majority of negative values observing dead neurons? Choose the appropriate activation functions accordingly. Use Leaky ReLU if dead neurons are observed during training.
3. **Choose the right activation function to handle overfitting**: Observe the evaluation metrics and their variation for each training period. Understand gradient behavior and how well your model performs on new unseen data.
4. **Choose the right activation function as per the expected output of your use case**: Examine the desired outcome of your network as a first step. For example, the SOFTMAX function can be used when you need to measure the probability of the occurrence of the output class. It is used in the output layer. For any input/hidden layers, ReLU is what you need for most cases. If you're not sure about what to use, just start experimenting with ReLU; if that doesn't improve your expectations, then try other activation functions.

How it works...

For step 1, ReLU is most commonly used because of its non-linear behavior. The output layer activation function depends on the expected output behavior. Step 4 targets this too.

For step 2, Leaky ReLU is an improved version of ReLU and is used to avoid the zero gradient problem. However, you might observe a performance drop. We use Leaky ReLU if dead neurons are observed during training. Dead neurons are referred to as neurons with a zero gradient for all possible inputs, which makes them useless for training.

For step 3, the tanh and sigmoid activation functions are similar and are used in feed-forward networks. If you use these activation functions, then make sure you add regularization to network layers to avoid the vanishing gradient problem. These are generally used for classifier problems.

There's more...

The ReLU activation function is non-linear, hence, the backpropagation of errors can easily be performed. Backpropagation is the backbone of neural networks. This is the learning algorithm that computes gradient descent with respect to weights across neurons. The following are ReLU variations currently supported in DL4J:

- `ReLU`: The standard ReLU activation function:

  ```
  public static final Activation RELU
  ```

- `ReLU6`: ReLU activation, which is capped at 6, where 6 is an arbitrary choice:

  ```
  public static final Activation RELU6
  ```

- `RReLU`: The randomized ReLU activation function:

  ```
  public static final Activation RRELU
  ```

- `ThresholdedReLU`: Threshold ReLU:

  ```
  public static final Activation THRESHOLDEDRELU
  ```

There are a few more implementations, such as **SeLU** (short for the **Scaled Exponential Linear Unit**), which is similar to the ReLU activation function but has a slope for negative values.

Combating overfitting problems

As we know, overfitting is a major challenge that machine learning developers face. It becomes a big challenge when the neural network architecture is complex and training data is huge. While mentioning overfitting, we're not ignoring the chances of underfitting at all. We will keep overfitting and underfitting in the same category. Let's discuss how we can combat overfitting problems.

The following are possible reasons for overfitting, including but not limited to:

- Too many feature variables compared to the number of data records
- A complex neural network model

Self-evidently, overfitting reduces the generalization power of the network and the network will fit noise instead of a signal when this happens. In this recipe, we will walk through key steps to prevent overfitting problems.

How to do it...

1. Use KFoldIterator to perform k-fold cross-validation-based resampling:

```
KFoldIterator kFoldIterator = new KFoldIterator(k, dataSet);
```

2. Construct a simpler neural network architecture.
3. Use enough train data to train the neural network.

How it works...

In step 1, k is the arbitrary number of choice and dataSet is the dataset object that represents your training data. We perform k-fold cross-validation to optimize the model evaluation process.

Complex neural network architectures can cause the network to tend to memorize patterns. Hence, your neural network will have a hard time generalizing unseen data. For example, it's better and more efficient to have a few hidden layers rather than hundreds of hidden layers. That's the relevance of step 2.

Fairly large training data will encourage the network to learn better and a batch-wise evaluation of test data will increase the generalization power of the network. That's the relevance of step 3. Although there are multiple types of data iterator and various ways to introduce batch size in an iterator in DL4J, the following is a more conventional definition for `RecordReaderDataSetIterator`:

```
public RecordReaderDataSetIterator(RecordReader recordReader,
  WritableConverter converter,
  int batchSize,
  int labelIndexFrom,
  int labelIndexTo,
  int numPossibleLabels,
  int maxNumBatches,
  boolean regression)
```

There's more...

When you perform k-fold cross-validation, data is divided into *k* number of subsets. For every subset, we perform evaluation by keeping one of the subsets for testing and the remaining *k-1* subsets for training. We will repeat this *k* number of times. Effectively, we use the entire data for training with no data loss, as opposed to wasting some of the data on testing.

Underfitting is handled here. However, note that we perform the evaluation *k* number of times only.

When you perform batch training, the entire dataset is divided as per the batch size. If your dataset has 1,000 records and the batch size is 8, then you have 125 training batches.

You need to note the training-to-testing ratio as well. According to that ratio, every batch will be divided into a training set and testing set. Then the evaluation will be performed accordingly. For 8-fold cross-validation, you evaluate the model 8 times, but for a batch size of 8, you perform 125 model evaluations.

 Note the rigorous mode of evaluation here, which will help to improve the generalization power while increasing the chances of underfitting.

Determining the right batch size and learning rates

Although there is no specific batch size or learning rate that works for all models, we can find the best values for them by experimenting with multiple training instances. The primary step is to experiment with a set of batch size values and learning rates with the model. Observe the efficiency of the model by evaluating additional parameters such as Precision, Recall, and F1 Score. Test scores alone don't confirm the model's performance. Also, parameters such as Precision, Recall, and F1 Score vary according to the use case. You need to analyze your problem statement to get an idea about this. In this recipe, we will walk through key steps to determine the right batch size and learning rates.

How to do it...

1. Run the training instance multiple times and track the evaluation metrics.
2. Run experiments by increasing the learning rate and track the results.

How it works...

Consider the following experiments to illustrate step 1.

The following training was performed on 10,000 records with a batch size of 8 and a learning rate of 0.008:

```
15:47:10.115 [ADSI prefetch thread] DEBUG o.n.l.memory.abstracts.Nd4jWorkspace - Steps: 5
15:47:10.228 [main] DEBUG o.d.d.iterator.AsyncDataSetIterator - Manually destroying ADSI workspace
args =

========================Evaluation Metrics========================
# of classes:    2
Accuracy:        0.8505
Precision:       0.7785
Recall:          0.6934
F1 Score:        0.5321
Precision, recall & F1: reported for positive class (class 1 - "1") only
```

The following is the evaluation performed on the same dataset for a batch size of 50 and a learning rate of 0.008:

```
=======================Evaluation Metrics=======================
# of classes:    2
Accuracy:        0.8565
Precision:       0.8069
Recall:          0.6845
F1 Score:        0.5225
Precision, recall & F1: reported for positive class (class 1 - "1") only



========================Confusion Matrix========================
     0    1
```

To perform step 2, we increased the learning rate to 0.6, to observe the results. Note that a learning rate beyond a certain limit will not help efficiency in any way. Our job is to find that limit:

```
=======================Evaluation Metrics=======================
# of classes:    2
Accuracy:        0.8240
Precision:       0.8375
Recall:          0.5565
F1 Score:        0.2072
Precision, recall & F1: reported for positive class (class 1 - "1") only
```

You can observe that `Accuracy` is reduced to 82.40% and `F1 Score` is reduced to 20.7%. This indicates that `F1 Score` might be the evaluation parameter to be accounted for in this model. This is not true for all models, and we reach this conclusion after experimenting with a couple of batch sizes and learning rates. In a nutshell, you have to repeat the same process for your model's training and choose arbitrary values that yield the best results.

There's more...

When we increase the batch size, the number of iterations will eventually reduce, hence the number of evaluations will also be reduced. This can overfit the data for a large batch size. A batch size of 1 is as useless as a batch size based on an entire dataset. So, you need to experiment with values starting from a safe arbitrary point.

A very small learning rate will lead to a very small convergence rate to the target. This can also impact the training time. If the learning rate is very large, this will cause divergent behavior in the model. We need to increase the learning rate until we observe the evaluation metrics getting better. There is an implementation of a cyclic learning rate in the fast.ai and Keras libraries; however, a cyclic learning rate is not implemented in DL4J.

Configuring Maven for DL4J

We need to add DL4J/ND4J Maven dependencies to leverage DL4J capabilities. ND4J is a scientific computation library dedicated to DL4J. It is necessary to mention the ND4J backend dependency in your pom.xml file. In this recipe, we will add a CPU-specific Maven configuration in pom.xml.

Getting ready

Let's discuss the required Maven dependencies. We assume you have already done the following:

- JDK 1.7, or higher, is installed and the PATH variable is set.
- Maven is installed and the PATH variable is set.

 A 64-bit JVM is required to run DL4J.

Set the PATH variable for JDK and Maven:

- **On Linux**: Use the export command to add Maven and JDK to the PATH variable:

```
export PATH=/opt/apache-maven-3.x.x/bin:$PATH
export PATH=${PATH}:/usr/java/jdk1.x.x/bin
```

Replace the version number as per the installation.

- **On Windows**: Set **System Environment variables** from system **Properties**:

```
set PATH="C:/Program Files/Apache Software Foundation/apache-
maven-3.x.x/bin:%PATH%"
 set PATH="C:/Program Files/Java/jdk1.x.x/bin:%PATH%"
```

Replace the JDK version number as per the installation.

How to do it...

1. Add the DL4J core dependency:

```
<dependency>
 <groupId>org.deeplearning4j</groupId>
 <artifactId>deeplearning4j-core</artifactId>
 <version>1.0.0-beta3</version>
 </dependency>
```

2. Add the ND4J native dependency:

```
<dependency>
 <groupId>org.nd4j</groupId>
 <artifactId>nd4j-native-platform</artifactId>
 <version>1.0.0-beta3</version>
 </dependency>
```

3. Add the DataVec dependency to perform ETL (short for **Extract, Transform and Load**) operations:

```
<dependency>
 <groupId>org.datavec</groupId>
 <artifactId>datavec-api</artifactId>
 <version>1.0.0-beta3</version>
 </dependency>
```

4. Enable logging for debugging:

```
<dependency>
 <groupId>org.slf4j</groupId>
 <artifactId>slf4j-simple</artifactId>
 <version>1.7.25</version> //change to latest version
 </dependency>
```

Note that 1.0.0-beta 3 is the current DL4J release version at the time of writing this book, and is the official version used in this cookbook. Also, note that DL4J relies on an ND4J backend for hardware-specific implementations.

How it works...

After adding DL4J core dependency and ND4J dependencies, as mentioned in step 1 and step 2, we are able to create neural networks. In step 2, the ND4J maven configuration is mentioned as a necessary backend dependency for Deeplearnign4j. ND4J is the scientific computation library for Deeplearning4j.

ND4J is a scientific computing library written for Java, just like NumPy is for Python.

Step 3 is very crucial for the ETL process: that is, data extraction, transformation, and loading. So, we definitely need this as well in order to train the neural network using data.

Step 4 is optional but recommended, since logging will reducee the effort involved in debugging.

Configuring DL4J for a GPU-accelerated environment

For GPU-powered hardware, DL4J comes with a different API implementation. This is to ensure the GPU hardware is utilized effectively without wasting hardware resources. Resource optimization is a major concern for expensive GPU-powered applications in production. In this recipe, we will add a GPU-specific Maven configuration to pom.xml.

Getting ready

You will need the following in order to complete this recipe:

- JDK version 1.7, or higher, installed and added to the PATH variable
- Maven installed and added to the PATH variable
- NVIDIA-compatible hardware

- CUDA v9.2+ installed and configured
- **cuDNN** (short for **CUDA Deep Neural Network**) installed and configured

How to do it...

1. Download and install CUDA v9.2+ from the NVIDIA developer website URL: `https://developer.nvidia.com/cuda-downloads`.
2. Configure the CUDA dependencies. For Linux, go to a Terminal and edit the `.bashrc` file. Run the following commands and make sure you replace username and the CUDA version number as per your downloaded version:

```
nano /home/username/.bashrc
export PATH=/usr/local/cuda-9.2/bin${PATH:+:${PATH}}$

export
LD_LIBRARY_PATH=/usr/local/cuda-9.2/lib64${LD_LIBRARY_PATH:+:${LD_L
IBRARY_PATH}}

source .bashrc
```

3. Add the `lib64` directory to `PATH` for older DL4J versions.
4. Run the `nvcc --version` command to verify the CUDA installation.
5. Add Maven dependencies for the ND4J CUDA backend:

```
<dependency>
 <groupId>org.nd4j</groupId>
 <artifactId>nd4j-cuda-9.2</artifactId>
 <version>1.0.0-beta3</version>
 </dependency>
```

6. Add the DL4J CUDA Maven dependency:

```
<dependency>
 <groupId>org.deeplearning4j</groupId>
 <artifactId>deeplearning4j-cuda-9.2</artifactId>
 <version>1.0.0-beta3</version>
 </dependency>
```

7. Add cuDNN dependencies to use bundled CUDA and cuDNN:

```
<dependency>
 <groupId>org.bytedeco.javacpp-presets</groupId>
 <artifactId>cuda</artifactId>
```

```
<version>9.2-7.1-1.4.2</version>
<classifier>linux-x86_64-redist</classifier> //system specific
</dependency>
```

How it works...

We configured NVIDIA CUDA using steps 1 to 4. For more detailed OS-specific instructions, refer to the official NVIDIA CUDA website at `https://developer.nvidia.com/cuda-downloads`.

Depending on your OS, installation instructions will be displayed on the website. DL4J version 1.0.0-beta 3 currently supports CUDA installation versions 9.0, 9.2, and 10.0. For instance, if you need to install CUDA v10.0 for Ubuntu 16.04, you should navigate the CUDA website as shown here:

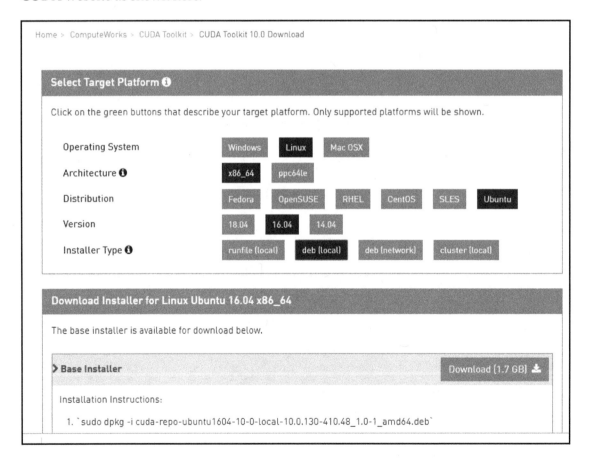

Note that step 3 is not applicable to newer versions of DL4J. For of 1.0.0-beta and later versions, the necessary CUDA libraries are bundled with DL4J. However, this is not applicable for step 7.

Additionally, before proceeding with steps 5 and 6, make sure that there are no redundant dependencies (such as CPU-specific dependencies) present in `pom.xml`.

DL4J supports CUDA, but performance can be further accelerated by adding a cuDNN library. cuDNN does not show up as a bundled package in DL4J. Hence, make sure you download and install NVIDIA cuDNN from the NVIDIA developer website. Once cuDNN is installed and configured, we can follow step 7 to add support for cuDNN in the DL4J application.

There's more...

For multi-GPU systems, you can consume all GPU resources by placing the following code in the main method of your application:

```
CudaEnvironment.getInstance().getConfiguration().allowMultiGPU(true);
```

This is a temporary workaround for initializing the ND4J backend in the case of multi-GPU hardware. In this way, we will not be limited to only a few GPU resources if more are available.

Troubleshooting installation issues

Though the DL4J setup doesn't seem complex, installation issues can still happen because of different OSes or applications installed on the system, and so on. CUDA installation issues are not within the scope of this book. Maven build issues that are due to unresolved dependencies can have multiple causes. If you are working for an organization with its own internal repositories and proxies, then you need to make relevant changes in the `pom.xml` file. These issues are also outside the scope of this book. In this recipe, we will walk through the steps to mitigate common installation issues with DL4J.

Getting ready

The following checks are mandatory before we proceed:

- Verify Java and Maven are installed and the PATH variables are configured.
- Verify the CUDA and cuDNN installations.
- Verify that the Maven build is successful and the dependencies are downloaded at ~/.m2/repository.

How to do it...

1. Enable logging levels to yield more information on errors:

```
Logger log = LoggerFactory.getLogger("YourClassFile.class");
 log.setLevel(Level.DEBUG);
```

2. Verify the JDK/Maven installation and configuration.
3. Check whether all the required dependencies are added in the pom.xml file.
4. Remove the contents of the Maven local repository and rebuild Maven to mitigate NoClassDefFoundError in DL4J. For Linux, this is as follows:

```
rm -rf ~/.m2/repository/org/deeplearning4j
 rm -rf ~/.m2/repository/org/datavec
 mvn clean install
```

5. Mitigate ClassNotFoundException in DL4J. You can try this if step 4 didn't help to resolve the issue. DL4J/ND4J/DataVec should have the same version. For CUDA-related error stacks, check the installation as well.

If adding the proper DL4J CUDA version doesn't fix this, then check your cuDNN installation.

How it works...

To mitigate exceptions such as ClassNotFoundException, the primary task is to verify we installed the JDK properly (step 2) and whether the environment variables we set up point to the right place. Step 3 is also important as the missing dependencies result in the same error.

In step 4, we are removing redundant dependencies that are present in the local repository and are attempting a fresh Maven build. Here is a sample for NoClassDefFoundError while trying to run a DL4J application:

```
root@instance-1:/home/Deeplearning4J# java -jar target/dl4j-1.0-
SNAPSHOT.jar
 09:28:22.171 [main] INFO org.nd4j.linalg.factory.Nd4jBackend - Loaded
[JCublasBackend] backend
 Exception in thread "main" java.lang.NoClassDefFoundError:
org/nd4j/linalg/api/complex/IComplexDouble
 at java.lang.Class.forName0(Native Method)
 at java.lang.Class.forName(Class.java:264)
 at org.nd4j.linalg.factory.Nd4j.initWithBackend(Nd4j.java:5529)
 at org.nd4j.linalg.factory.Nd4j.initContext(Nd4j.java:5477)
 at org.nd4j.linalg.factory.Nd4j.(Nd4j.java:210)
 at
org.datavec.image.transform.PipelineImageTransform.(PipelineImageTransform.
java:93)
 at
org.datavec.image.transform.PipelineImageTransform.(PipelineImageTransform.
java:85)
 at
org.datavec.image.transform.PipelineImageTransform.(PipelineImageTransform.
java:73)
 at examples.AnimalClassifier.main(AnimalClassifier.java:72)
 Caused by: java.lang.ClassNotFoundException:
org.nd4j.linalg.api.complex.IComplexDouble
```

One possible reason for NoClassDefFoundError could be the absence of required dependencies in the Maven local repository. So, we remove the repository contents and rebuild Maven to download the dependencies again. If any dependencies were not downloaded previously due to an interruption, it should happen now.

Here is an example of `ClassNotFoundException` during DL4J training:

```
14:28:37.549 [main] INFO  o.d.i.r.BaseImageRecordReader - ImageRecordReader: 4 label classes inferred using label g
enerator ParentPathLabelGenerator
14:28:37.557 [main] INFO  o.d.nn.multilayer.MultiLayerNetwork - Starting MultiLayerNetwork with WorkspaceModes set
to [training: ENABLED; inference: ENABLED], cacheMode set to [NONE]
14:28:37.595 [main] DEBUG o.n.j.handler.impl.CudaZeroHandler - Creating bucketID: 3
14:28:37.601 [main] DEBUG o.n.j.handler.impl.CudaZeroHandler - Creating bucketID: 4
14:28:37.640 [main] INFO  o.d.n.l.convolution.ConvolutionLayer - cuDNN not found: use cuDNN for better GPU performa
nce by including the deeplearning4j-cuda module. For more information, please refer to: https://deeplearning4j.org/
cudnn
java.lang.ClassNotFoundException: org.deeplearning4j.nn.layers.convolution.CudnnConvolutionHelper
        at java.net.URLClassLoader.findClass(URLClassLoader.java:381) ~[na:1.8.0_171]
        at java.lang.ClassLoader.loadClass(ClassLoader.java:424) ~[na:1.8.0_171]
        at sun.misc.Launcher$AppClassLoader.loadClass(Launcher.java:349) ~[na:1.8.0_171]
        at java.lang.ClassLoader.loadClass(ClassLoader.java:357) ~[na:1.8.0_171]
        at java.lang.Class.forName0(Native Method) ~[na:1.8.0_171]
        at java.lang.Class.forName(Class.java:264) ~[na:1.8.0_171]
        at org.deeplearning4j.nn.layers.convolution.ConvolutionLayer.initializeHelper(ConvolutionLayer.java:81) [dl
4j-1.0-SNAPSHOT.jar:na]
        at org.deeplearning4j.nn.layers.convolution.ConvolutionLayer.<init>(ConvolutionLayer.java:68) [dl4j-1.0-SNA
PSHOT.jar:na]
        at org.deeplearning4j.nn.conf.layers.ConvolutionLayer.instantiate(ConvolutionLayer.java:152) [dl4j-1.0-SNAP
SHOT.jar:na]
        at org.deeplearning4j.nn.multilayer.MultiLayerNetwork.init(MultiLayerNetwork.java:629) [dl4j-1.0-SNAPSHOT.j
ar:na]
        at org.deeplearning4j.nn.multilayer.MultiLayerNetwork.init(MultiLayerNetwork.java:530) [dl4j-1.0-SNAPSHOT.j
ar:na]
        at examples.AnimalClassifier.main(AnimalClassifier.java:121) [dl4j-1.0-SNAPSHOT.jar:na]
14:28:37.641 [main] DEBUG o.n.j.handler.impl.CudaZeroHandler - Creating bucketID: 5
14:28:37.646 [main] DEBUG o.n.j.handler.impl.CudaZeroHandler - Creating bucketID: 0
14:28:37.667 [main] DEBUG o.n.j.handler.impl.CudaZeroHandler - Creating bucketID: 2
14:28:38.040 [ADSI prefetch thread] DEBUG o.n.l.memory.abstracts.Nd4jWorkspace - Steps: 4
14:28:38.487 [main] INFO  o.d.o.l.ScoreIterationListener - Score at iteration 0 is 1.5323769998049381
14:28:42.981 [main] INFO  o.d.o.l.ScoreIterationListener - Score at iteration 100 is 1.4700070363395148
14:28:47.609 [main] INFO  o.d.o.l.ScoreIterationListener - Score at iteration 200 is 1.4696028415172688
14:28:52.409 [main] INFO  o.d.o.l.ScoreIterationListener - Score at iteration 300 is 1.3762216058284946
14:28:56.339 [main] DEBUG o.d.d.iterator.AsyncDataSetIterator - Manually destroying ADSI workspace
14:28:56.342 [ADSI prefetch thread] DEBUG o.n.l.memory.abstracts.Nd4jWorkspace - Steps: 4
14:28:57.108 [main] INFO  o.d.o.l.ScoreIterationListener - Score at iteration 400 is 1.498729275009222
14:29:01.682 [main] INFO  o.d.o.l.ScoreIterationListener - Score at iteration 500 is 1.4075598864086873
```

Again, this suggests version issues or redundant dependencies.

There's more...

In addition to the common runtime issues that were discussed previously, Windows users may face cuDNN-specific errors while training a CNN. The actual root cause could be different and is tagged under `UnsatisfiedLinkError`:

```
o.d.n.l.c.ConvolutionLayer - Could not load CudnnConvolutionHelper
java.lang.UnsatisfiedLinkError: no jnicudnn in java.library.path
  at java.lang.ClassLoader.loadLibrary(ClassLoader.java:1867)
~[na:1.8.0_102]
  at java.lang.Runtime.loadLibrary0(Runtime.java:870) ~[na:1.8.0_102]
  at java.lang.System.loadLibrary(System.java:1122) ~[na:1.8.0_102]
  at org.bytedeco.javacpp.Loader.loadLibrary(Loader.java:945)
~[javacpp-1.3.1.jar:1.3.1]
  at org.bytedeco.javacpp.Loader.load(Loader.java:750)
```

```
~[javacpp-1.3.1.jar:1.3.1]
  Caused by: java.lang.UnsatisfiedLinkError:
C:\Users\Jürgen.javacpp\cache\cuda-7.5-1.3-windows-
x86_64.jar\org\bytedeco\javacpp\windows-x86_64\jnicudnn.dll: Can't find
dependent libraries
  at java.lang.ClassLoader$NativeLibrary.load(Native Method) ~[na:1.8.0_102]
```

Perform the following steps to fix the issue:

1. Download the latest dependency walker here: https://github.com/lucasg/Dependencies/.

2. Add the following code to your DL4J main() method:

```
try {
 Loader.load(<module>.class);
 } catch (UnsatisfiedLinkError e) {
 String path = Loader.cacheResource(<module>.class, "windows-
x86_64/jni<module>.dll").getPath();
 new ProcessBuilder("c:/path/to/DependenciesGui.exe",
path).start().waitFor();
 }
```

3. Replace <module> with the name of the JavaCPP preset module that is experiencing the problem; for example, cudnn. For newer DL4J versions, the necessary CUDA libraries are bundled with DL4J. Hence, you should not face this issue.

If you feel like you might have found a bug or functional error with DL4J, then feel free to create an issue tracker at https://github.com/eclipse/deeplearning4j.

You're also welcome to initiate a discussion with the Deeplearning4j community here: https://gitter.im/deeplearning4j/deeplearning4j.

2
Data Extraction, Transformation, and Loading

Let's discuss the most important part of any machine learning puzzle: data preprocessing and normalization. *Garbage in, garbage out* would be the most appropriate statement for this situation. The more noise we let pass through, the more undesirable outputs we will receive. Therefore, you need to remove noise and keep signals at the same time.

Another challenge is handling various types of data. We need to convert raw datasets into a suitable format that a neural network can understand and perform scientific computations on. We need to convert data into a numeric vector so that it is understandable to the network and so that computations can be applied with ease. Remember that neural networks are constrained to only one type of data: vectors.

There has to be an approach regarding how data is loaded into a neural network. We cannot put 1 million data records onto a neural network at once – that would bring performance down. We are referring to training time when we mention performance here. To increase performance, we need to make use of data pipelines, batch training, and other sampling techniques.

DataVec is an input/output format system that can manage everything that we just mentioned. It solves the biggest headaches that every deep learning puzzle causes. DataVec supports all types of input data, such as text, images, CSV files, and videos. The DataVec library manages the data pipeline in DL4J.

In this chapter, we will learn how to perform ETL operations using DataVec. This is the first step in building a neural network in DL4J.

In this chapter, we will cover the following recipes:

- Reading and iterating through data
- Performing schema transformations
- Serializing transforms

- Building a transform process
- Executing a transform process
- Normalizing data for network efficiency

Technical requirements

Concrete implementations of the use cases that will be discussed in this chapter can be found at `https://github.com/PacktPublishing/Java-Deep-Learning-Cookbook/tree/master/02_Data_Extraction_Transform_and_Loading/sourceCode/cookbook-app/src/main/java/com/javadeeplearningcookbook/app`.

After cloning our GitHub repository, navigate to the `Java-Deep-Learning-Cookbook/02_Data_Extraction_Transform_and_Loading/sourceCode` directory. Then, import the `cookbook-app` project as a Maven project by importing the `pom.xml` file inside the `cookbook-app` directory.

The datasets that are required for this chapter are located in the `Chapter02` root directory (`Java-Deep-Learning-Cookbook/02_Data_Extraction_Transform_and_Loading/`). You may keep it in a different location, for example, your local directory, and then refer to it in the source code accordingly.

Reading and iterating through data

ETL is an important stage in neural network training since it involves data. Data extraction, transformation, and loading needs to be addressed before we proceed with neural network design. Bad data is a much worse situation than a less efficient neural network. We need to have a basic understanding of the following aspects as well:

- The type of data you are trying to process
- File-handling strategies

In this recipe, we will demonstrate how to read and iterate data using DataVec.

Getting ready

As a prerequisite, make sure that the required Maven dependencies have been added for DataVec in your `pom.xml` file, as we mentioned in previous chapter, *Configuring Maven for DL4J* recipe.

The following is the sample `pom.xml` file: `https://github.com/rahul-raj/Java-Deep-Learning-Cookbook/blob/master/02_Data_Extraction_Transform_and_Loading/sourceCode/cookbook-app/pom.xml`.

How to do it...

1. Manage a range of records using `FileSplit`:

```
String[] allowedFormats=new String[]{".JPEG"};
 FileSplit fileSplit = new FileSplit(new File("temp"),
allowedFormats,true)
```

 You can find the `FileSplit` example at `https://github.com/PacktPublishing/Java-Deep-Learning-Cookbook/blob/master/02_Data%20Extraction%2C%20Transform%20and%20Loading/sourceCode/cookbook-app/src/main/java/com/javadeeplearningcookbook/app/FileSplitExample.java`.

2. Manage the URI collection from a file using `CollectionInputSplit`:

```
FileSplit fileSplit = new FileSplit(new File("temp"));
 CollectionInputSplit collectionInputSplit = new
CollectionInputSplit(fileSplit.locations());
```

 You can find the `CollectionInputSplit` example at `https://github.com/PacktPublishing/Java-Deep-Learning-Cookbook/blob/master/02_Data%20Extraction%2C%20Transform%20and%20Loading/sourceCode/cookbook-app/src/main/java/com/javadeeplearningcookbook/app/CollectionInputSplitExample.java`.

3. Use `NumberedFileInputSplit` to manage data with numbered file formats:

```
NumberedFileInputSplit numberedFileInputSplit = new
NumberedFileInputSplit("numberedfiles/file%d.txt",1,4);
numberedFileInputSplit.locationsIterator().forEachRemaining(System.
out::println);
```

 You can find the `NumberedFileInputSplit` example at `https://github.com/PacktPublishing/Java-Deep-Learning-Cookbook/blob/master/02_Data%20Extraction%2C%20Transform%20and%20Loading/sourceCode/cookbook-app/src/main/java/com/javadeeplearningcookbook/app/NumberedFileInputSplitExample.java`.

4. Use `TransformSplit` to map the input URIs to the different output URIs:

```
TransformSplit.URITransform uriTransform = URI::normalize;

 List<URI> uriList = Arrays.asList(new
URI("file://storage/examples/./cats.txt"),
 new URI("file://storage/examples//dogs.txt"),
 new URI("file://storage/./examples/bear.txt"));

 TransformSplit transformSplit = new TransformSplit(new
CollectionInputSplit(uriList),uriTransform);
```

You can find the `TransformSplit` example at https://github.com/
PacktPublishing/Java-Deep-Learning-Cookbook/blob/master/02_
Data%20Extraction%2C%20Transform%20and%20Loading/sourceCode/
cookbook-app/src/main/java/com/javadeeplearningcookbook/app/
TransformSplitExample.java.

5. Perform URI string replacement using `TransformSplit`:

```
InputSplit transformSplit = TransformSplit.ofSearchReplace(new
CollectionInputSplit(inputFiles),"-in.csv","-out.csv");
```

6. Extract the CSV data for the neural network using `CSVRecordReader`:

```
RecordReader reader = new
CSVRecordReader(numOfRowsToSkip,deLimiter);
 recordReader.initialize(new FileSplit(file));
```

You can find the `CSVRecordReader` example at https://github.com/
PacktPublishing/Java-Deep-Learning-Cookbook/blob/master/02_
Data%20Extraction%2C%20Transform%20and%20Loading/sourceCode/
cookbook-app/src/main/java/com/javadeeplearningcookbook/app/
recordreaderexamples/CSVRecordReaderExample.java.

The dataset for this can be found at https://github.com/
PacktPublishing/Java-Deep-Learning-Cookbook/blob/master/02_
Data_Extraction_Transform_and_Loading/titanic.csv.

7. Extract image data for the neural network using `ImageRecordReader`:

```
ImageRecordReader imageRecordReader = new
ImageRecordReader(imageHeight,imageWidth,channels,parentPathLabelGe
nerator);
imageRecordReader.initialize(trainData,transform);
```

You can find the `ImageRecordReader` example at `https://github.com/PacktPublishing/Java-Deep-Learning-Cookbook/blob/master/02_Data%20Extraction%2C%20Transform%20and%20Loading/sourceCode/cookbook-app/src/main/java/com/javadeeplearningcookbook/app/recordreaderexamples/ImageRecordReaderExample.java`.

8. Transform and extract the data using `TransformProcessRecordReader`:

```
RecordReader recordReader = new
TransformProcessRecordReader(recordReader,transformProcess);
```

You can find the `TransformProcessRecordReader` example at `https://github.com/PacktPublishing/Java-Deep-Learning-Cookbook/blob/master/02_Data_Extraction_Transform_and_Loading/sourceCode/cookbook-app/src/main/java/com/javadeeplearningcookbook/app/recordreaderexamples/TransformProcessRecordReaderExample.java`

The dataset for this can be found at `https://github.com/PacktPublishing/Java-Deep-Learning-Cookbook/blob/master/02_Data_Extraction_Transform_and_Loading/transform-data.csv`.

9. Extract the sequence data using
`SequenceRecordReader` and `CodecRecordReader`:

```
RecordReader codecReader = new CodecRecordReader();
 codecReader.initialize(conf,split);
```

You can find the `CodecRecordReader` example at `https://github.com/PacktPublishing/Java-Deep-Learning-Cookbook/blob/master/02_Data%20Extraction%2C%20Transform%20and%20Loading/sourceCode/cookbook-app/src/main/java/com/javadeeplearningcookbook/app/recordreaderexamples/CodecReaderExample.java`.

The following code shows how to use `RegexSequenceRecordReader`:

```
RecordReader recordReader = new
RegexSequenceRecordReader((\d{2}/\d{2}/\d{2}) (\d{2}:\d{2}:\d{2})
([A-Z]) (.*)",skipNumLines);
 recordReader.initialize(new
NumberedFileInputSplit(path/log%d.txt));
```

You can find the `RegexSequenceRecordReader` example at `https://
github.com/PacktPublishing/Java-Deep-Learning-Cookbook/blob/
master/02_Data_Extraction_Transform_and_Loading/sourceCode/
cookbook-app/src/main/java/com/javadeeplearningcookbook/app/
recordreaderexamples/RegexSequenceRecordReaderExample.java`.

The dataset for this can be found at `https://github.com/
PacktPublishing/Java-Deep-Learning-Cookbook/blob/master/02_Data_
Extraction_Transform_and_Loading/logdata.zip`.

The following code shows how to use `CSVSequenceRecordReader`:

```
CSVSequenceRecordReader seqReader = new
CSVSequenceRecordReader(skipNumLines, delimiter);
  seqReader.initialize(new FileSplit(file));
```

You can find the `CSVSequenceRecordReader` example at `https://
github.com/PacktPublishing/Java-Deep-Learning-Cookbook/blob/
master/02_Data%20Extraction%2C%20Transform%20and%20Loading/
sourceCode/cookbook-app/src/main/java/com/
javadeeplearningcookbook/app/recordreaderexamples/
SequenceRecordReaderExample.java`.

The dataset for this can be found at `https://github.com/
PacktPublishing/Java-Deep-Learning-Cookbook/blob/master/02_Data_
Extraction_Transform_and_Loading/dataset.zip`.

10. Extract the JSON/XML/YAML data using `JacksonLineRecordReader`:

```
RecordReader recordReader = new
JacksonLineRecordReader(fieldSelection, new ObjectMapper(new
JsonFactory()));
  recordReader.initialize(new FileSplit(new File("json_file.txt")));
```

You can find the `JacksonLineRecordReader` example at `https://
github.com/PacktPublishing/Java-Deep-Learning-Cookbook/blob/
master/02_Data_Extraction_Transform_and_Loading/sourceCode/
cookbook-app/src/main/java/com/javadeeplearningcookbook/app/
recordreaderexamples/JacksonLineRecordReaderExample.java`.

The dataset for this can be found at `https://github.com/
PacktPublishing/Java-Deep-Learning-Cookbook/blob/master/02_Data_
Extraction_Transform_and_Loading/irisdata.txt`.

How it works...

Data can be spread across multiple files, subdirectories, or multiple clusters. We need a mechanism to extract and handle data in different ways due to various constraints, such as size. In distributed environments, a large amount of data can be stored as chunks in multiple clusters. DataVec uses InputSplit for this purpose.

In step 1, we looked at FileSplit, an InputSplit implementation that splits the root directory into files. FileSplit will recursively look for files inside the specified directory location. You can also pass an array of strings as a parameter to denote the allowed extensions:

- **Sample input**: A directory location with files:

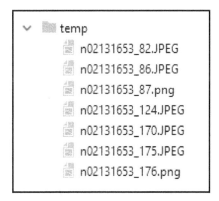

- **Sample output**: A list of URIs with the filter applied:

```
file:///D:/code/packt/Java-Deep-Learning-Cookbook/02_Data_Extraction_Transform_and_Loading/sourceCode/cookbook-app/temp/n02131653_124.JPEG
file:///D:/code/packt/Java-Deep-Learning-Cookbook/02_Data_Extraction_Transform_and_Loading/sourceCode/cookbook-app/temp/n02131653_170.JPEG
file:///D:/code/packt/Java-Deep-Learning-Cookbook/02_Data_Extraction_Transform_and_Loading/sourceCode/cookbook-app/temp/n02131653_175.JPEG
file:///D:/code/packt/Java-Deep-Learning-Cookbook/02_Data_Extraction_Transform_and_Loading/sourceCode/cookbook-app/temp/n02131653_82.JPEG
file:///D:/code/packt/Java-Deep-Learning-Cookbook/02_Data_Extraction_Transform_and_Loading/sourceCode/cookbook-app/temp/n02131653_86.JPEG
```

In the sample output, we removed any file paths that are not in `.jpeg` format. `CollectionInputSplit` would be useful here if you want to extract data from a list of URIs, like we did in step 2. In step 2, the `temp` directory has a list of files in it. We used `CollectionInputSplit` to generate a list of URIs from the files. While `FileSplit` is specifically for splitting the directory into files (a list of URIs), `CollectionInputSplit` is a simple `InputSplit` implementation that handles a collection of URI inputs. If we already have a list of URIs to process, then we can simply use `CollectionInputSplit` instead of `FileSplit`.

- **Sample input**: A directory location with files. Refer to the following screenshot (directory with image files as input):

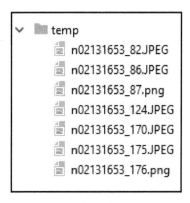

- **Sample output**: A list of URIs. Refer to the following list of URIs generated by `CollectionInputSplit` from the earlier mentioned input.

In step 3, `NumberedFileInputSplit` generates URIs based on the specified numbering format.

Note that we need to pass an appropriate regular expression pattern to generate filenames in a sequential format. Otherwise, it will throw runtime errors. A regular expression allows us to accept inputs in various numbered formats. `NumberedFileInputSplit` will generate a list of URIs that you can pass down the level in order to extract and process data. We added the `%d` regular expression at the end of file name to specify that numbering is present at the trailing end.

- **Sample input**: A directory location with files in a numbered naming format, for example, `file1.txt`, `file2.txt`, and `file3.txt`.
- **Sample output**: A list of URIs:

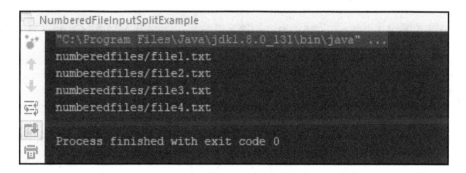

If you need to map input URIs to different output URIs, then you will need `TransformSplit`. We used it in step 4 to normalize/transform the data URI into the required format. It will be especially helpful if features and labels are kept at different locations. When step 4 is executed, the " . " string will be stripped from the URIs, which results in the following URIs:

- **Sample input**: A collection of URIs, just like what we saw in `CollectionInputSplit`. However, `TransformSplit` can accept erroneous URIs:

```
List<URI> uriList = Arrays.asList(new URI( str "file://storage/examples/./cats.txt"),
                                  new URI( str "file://storage/examples//dogs.txt"),
                                  new URI( str "file://storage/./examples/bear.txt"));
```

- **Sample output**: A list of URIs after formatting them:

After executing step 5, the $-$in.csv substrings in the URIs will be replaced with $-$out.csv.

CSVRecordReader is a simple CSV record reader for streaming CSV data. We can form data stream objects based on the delimiters and specify various other parameters, such as the number of lines to skip from the beginning. In step 6, we used CSVRecordReader for the same.

For the CSVRecordReader example, use the titanic.csv file that's included in this chapter's GitHub repository. You need to update the directory path in the code to be able to use it.

ImageRecordReader is an image record reader that's used for streaming image data.

In step 7, we read images from a local filesystem. Then, we scaled them and converted them according to a given height, width, and channels. We can also specify the labels that are to be tagged for the image data. In order to specify the labels for the image set, create a separate subdirectory under the root. Each of them represents a label.

In step 7, the first two parameters from the ImageRecordReader constructor represent the height and width to which images are to be scaled. We usually give a value of 3 for channels representing R, G, and B. parentPathLabelGenerator will define how to tag labels in images. trainData is the inputSplit we need in order to specify the range of records to load, while transform is the image transformation to be applied while loading images.

For the `ImageRecordReader` example, you can download some sample images from `ImageNet`. Each category of images will be represented by a subdirectory. For example, you can download dog images and put them under a subdirectory named "dog". You will need to provide the parent directory path where all the possible categories will be included.

The ImageNet website can be found at `http://www.image-net.org/`.

`TransformProcessRecordReader` requires a bit of explanation when it's used in the schema transformation process. `TransformProcessRecordReader` is the end product of applying schema transformation to a record reader. This will ensure that a defined transformation process is applied before it is fed to the training data.

In step 8, `transformProcess` defines an ordered list of transformations to be applied to the given dataset. This can be the removal of unwanted features, feature data type conversions, and so on. The intent is to make the data suitable for the neural network to process further. You will learn how to create a transformation process in the upcoming recipes in this chapter.

For the `TransformProcessRecordReader` example, use the `transform-data.csv` file that's included in this chapter's GitHub repository. You need to update the file path in code to be able to use it.

In step 9, we looked at some of the implementations of `SequenceRecordReader`. We use this record reader if we have a sequence of records to process. This record reader can be used locally as well as in distributed environments (such as Spark).

For the `SequenceRecordReader` example, you need to extract the `dataset.zip` file from this chapter's GitHub repository. After the extraction, you will see two subdirectories underneath: `features` and `labels`. In each of them, there is a sequence of files. You need to provide the absolute path to these two directories in the code.

`CodecRecordReader` is a record reader that handle multimedia datasets and can be used for the following purposes:

- H.264 (AVC) main profile decoder
- MP3 decoder/encoder
- Apple ProRes decoder and encoder

- H264 Baseline profile encoder
- Matroska (MKV) demuxer and muxer
- MP4 (ISO BMF, QuickTime) demuxer/muxer and tools
- MPEG 1/2 decoder
- MPEG PS/TS demuxer
- Java player applet parsing
- VP8 encoder
- MXF demuxer

`CodecRecordReader` makes use of jcodec as the underlying media parser.

For the `CodecRecordReader` example, you need to provide the directory location of a short video file in the code. This video file will be the input for the `CodecRecordReader` example.

`RegexSequenceRecordReader` will consider the entire file as a single sequence and will read it one line at a time. Then, it will split each of them using the specified regular expression. We can combine `RegexSequenceRecordReader` with `NumberedFileInputSplit` to read file sequences. In step 9, we used `RegexSequenceRecordReader` to read the transactional logs that were recorded over the time steps (time series data). In our dataset (`logdata.zip`), transactional logs are unsupervised data with no specification for features or labels.

For the `RegexSequenceRecordReader` example, you need to extract the `logdata.zip` file from this chapter's GitHub repository. After the extraction, you will see a sequence of transactional logs with a numbered file naming format. You need to provide the absolute path to the extracted directory in the code.

`CSVSequenceRecordReader` reads the sequences of data in CSV format. Each sequence represents a separate CSV file. Each line represents one time step.

In step 10, `JacksonLineRecordReader` will read the JSON/XML/YAML data line by line. It expects a valid JSON entry for each of the lines without a separator at the end. This follows the Hadoop convention of ensuring that the split works properly in a cluster environment. If the record spans multiple lines, the split won't work as expected and may result in calculation errors. Unlike `JacksonRecordReader`, `JacksonLineRecordReader` doesn't create the labels automatically and will require you to mention the configuration during training.

For the `JacksonLineRecordReader` example, you need to provide the directory location of `irisdata.txt`, which is located in this chapter's GitHub repository. In the `irisdata.txt` file, each line represents a JSON object.

There's more...

`JacksonRecordReader` is a record reader that uses the Jackson API. Just like `JacksonLineRecordReader`, it also supports JSON, XML, and YAML formats. For `JacksonRecordReader`, the user needs to provide a list of fields to read from the JSON/XML/YAML file. This may look complicated, but it allows us to parse the files under the following conditions:

- There is no consistent schema for the JSON/XML/YAML data. The order of output fields can be provided using the `FieldSelection` object.
- There are fields that are missing in some files but that can be provided using the `FieldSelection` object.

`JacksonRecordReader` can also be used with `PathLabelGenerator` to append the label based on the file path.

Performing schema transformations

Data transformation is an important data normalization process. It's a possibility that bad data occurs, such as duplicates, missing values, non-numeric features, and so on. We need to normalize them by applying schema transformation so that data can be processed in a neural network. A neural network can only process numeric features. In this recipe, we will demonstrate the schema creation process.

How to do it...

1. **Identify the outliers in the data**: For a small dataset with just a few features, we can spot outliers/noise via manual inspection. For a dataset with a large number of features, we can perform **Principal Component Analysis (PCA)**, as shown in the following code:

```
INDArray factor =
org.nd4j.linalg.dimensionalityreduction.PCA.pca_factor(inputFeature
```

```
   s, projectedDimension, normalize);
     INDArray reduced = inputFeatures.mmul(factor);
```

2. **Use a schema to define the structure of the data**: The following is an example of a basic schema for a customer churn dataset. You can download the dataset from `https://www.kaggle.com/barelydedicated/bank-customer-churn-modeling/downloads/bank-customer-churn-modeling.zip/1`:

```
Schema schema = new Schema.Builder()
.addColumnString("RowNumber")
.addColumnInteger("CustomerId")
.addColumnString("Surname")
.addColumnInteger("CreditScore")
.addColumnCategorical("Geography",
 Arrays.asList("France","Germany","Spain"))
.addColumnCategorical("Gender", Arrays.asList("Male","Female"))
.addColumnsInteger("Age", "Tenure")
.addColumnDouble("Balance")
.addColumnsInteger("NumOfProducts","HasCrCard","IsActiveMember")
.addColumnDouble("EstimatedSalary")
.build();
```

How it works...

Before we start schema creation, we need to examine all the features in our dataset. Then, we need to clear all the noisy features, such as name, where it is fair to assume that they have no effect on the produced outcome. If some features are unclear to you, just keep them as such and include them in the schema. If you remove a feature that happens to be a signal unknowingly, then you'll degrade the efficiency of the neural network. This process of removing outliers and keeping signals (valid features) is referred to in step 1. **Principal Component Analysis** (**PCA**) would be an ideal choice, and the same has been implemented in ND4J. The **PCA** class can perform dimensionality reduction in the case of a dataset with a large number of features where you want to reduce the number of features to reduce the complexity. Reducing the features just means removing irrelevant features (outliers/noise). In step 1, we generated a PCA factor matrix by calling `pca_factor()` with the following arguments:

- `inputFeatures`: Input features as a matrix
- `projectedDimension`: The number of features to project from the actual set of features (for example, 100 important features out of 1,000)
- `normalize`: A Boolean variable (true/false) indicating whether the features are to be normalized (zero mean)

Matrix multiplication is performed by calling the `mmul()` method and the end result. `reduced` is the feature matrix that we use after performing the dimensionality reduction based on the PCA factor. Note that you may need to perform multiple training sessions using input features (which are generated using the PCA factor) to understand signals.

In step 2, we used the customer churn dataset (the simple dataset that we used in the next chapter) to demonstrate the `Schema` creation process. The data types that are mentioned in the schema are for the respective features or labels. For example, if you want to add a schema definition for an integer feature, then it would be `addColumnInteger()`. Similarly, there are other `Schema` methods available that we can use to manage other data types.

Categorical variables can be added using `addColumnCategorical()`, as we mentioned in step 2. Here, we marked the categorical variables and the possible values were supplied. Even if we get a masked set of features, we can still construct their schema if the features are arranged in numbered format (for example, `column1`, `column2`, and similar).

There's more...

In a nutshell, here is what you need to do to build the schema for your datasets:

- Understand your data well. Identify the noise and signals.
- Capture features and labels. Identify categorical variables.
- Identify categorical features that one-hot encoding can be applied to.
- Pay attention to missing or bad data.
- Add features using type-specific methods such as `addColumnInteger()` and `addColumnsInteger()`, where the feature type is an integer. Apply the respective `Builder` method to other data types.
- Add categorical variables using `addColumnCategorical()`.
- Call the `build()` method to build the schema.

Note that you cannot skip/ignore any features from the dataset without specifying them in the schema. You need to remove the outlying features from the dataset, create a schema from the remaining features, and then move on to the transformation process for further processing. Alternatively, you can keep all the features aside, keep all the features in the schema, and then define the outliers during the transformation process.

When it comes to feature engineering/data analysis, DataVec comes up with its own analytic engine to perform data analysis on feature/target variables. For local executions, we can make use of `AnalyzeLocal` to return a data analysis object that holds information about each column in the dataset. Here is how you can create a data analysis object from a record reader object:

```
DataAnalysis analysis = AnalyzeLocal.analyze(mySchema, csvRecordReader);
 System.out.println(analysis);
```

You can also analyze your dataset for missing values and check whether it is schema-compliant by calling `analyzeQuality()`:

```
DataQualityAnalysis quality = AnalyzeLocal.analyzeQuality(mySchema,
csvRecordReader);
 System.out.println(quality);
```

For sequence data, you need to use `analyzeQualitySequence()` instead of `analyzeQuality()`. For data analysis on Spark, you can make use of the `AnalyzeSpark` utility class in place of `AnalyzeLocal`.

Building a transformation process

The next step after schema creation is to define a data transformation process by adding all the required transformations. We can manage an ordered list of transformations using `TransformProcess`. During the schema creation process, we only defined a structure for the data with all its existing features and didn't really perform transformation. Let's look at how we can transform the features in the datasets from a non-numeric format into a numeric format. Neural networks cannot understand raw data unless it is mapped to numeric vectors. In this recipe, we will build a transformation process from the given schema.

How to do it...

1. Add a list of transformations to `TransformProcess`. Consider the following example:

```
TransformProcess transformProcess = new
TransformProcess.Builder(schema)
 .removeColumns("RowNumber","CustomerId","Surname")
 .categoricalToInteger("Gender")
 .categoricalToOneHot("Geography")
```

```
.removeColumns("Geography[France]")
.build();
```

2. Create a record reader using `TransformProcessRecordReader` to extract and transform the data:

```
TransformProcessRecordReader transformProcessRecordReader = new
TransformProcessRecordReader(recordReader,transformProcess);
```

How it works...

In step 1, we added all the transformations that are needed for the dataset. `TransformProcess` defines an unordered list of all the transformations that we want to apply to the dataset. We removed any unnecessary features by calling `removeColumns()`. During schema creation, we marked the categorical features in the `Schema`. Now, we can actually decide on what kind of transformation is required for a particular categorical variable. Categorical variables can be converted into integers by calling `categoricalToInteger()`. Categorical variables can undergo one-hot encoding if we call `categoricalToOneHot()`. Note that the schema needs to be created prior to the transformation process. We need the schema to create a `TransformProcess`.

In step 2, we apply the transformations that were added before with the help of `TransformProcessRecordReader`. All we need to do is create the basic record reader object with the raw data and pass it to `TransformProcessRecordReader`, along with the defined transformation process.

There's more...

DataVec allows us to do much more within the transformation stage. Here are some of the other important transformation features that are available within `TransformProcess`:

- `addConstantColumn()`: Adds a new column in a dataset, where all the values in the column are identical and are as they were specified by the value. This method accepts three attributes: the new column name, the new column type, and the value.
- `appendStringColumnTransform()`: Appends a string to the specified column. This method accepts two attributes: the column to append to and the string value to append.

- `conditionalCopyValueTransform()`: Replaces the value in a column with the value specified in another column if a condition is satisfied. This method accepts three attributes: the column to replace the values, the column to refer to the values, and the condition to be used.
- `conditionalReplaceValueTransform()`: Replaces the value in a column with the specified value if a condition is satisfied. This method accepts three attributes: the column to replace the values, the value to be used as a replacement, and the condition to be used.
- `conditionalReplaceValueTransformWithDefault()`: Replaces the value in a column with the specified value if a condition is satisfied. Otherwise, it fills the column with another value. This method accepts four attributes: the column to replace the values, the value to be used if the condition is satisfied, the value to be used if the condition is not satisfied, and the condition to be used.
  We can use built-in conditions that have been written in DataVec with the transformation process or data cleaning process. We can use `NaNColumnCondition` to replace `NaN` values and `NullWritableColumnCondition` to replace null values, respectively.
- `stringToTimeTransform()`: Converts a string column into a time column. This targets date columns that are saved as a string/object in the dataset. This method accepts three attributes: the name of the column to be used, the time format to be followed, and the time zone.
- `reorderColumns()`: Reorders the columns using the newly defined order. We can provide the column names in the specified order as attributes to this method.
- `filter ()`: Defines a filter process based on the specified condition. If the condition is satisfied, remove the example or sequence; otherwise, keep the examples or sequence. This method accepts only a single attribute, which is the condition/filter to be applied. The `filter()` method is very useful for the data cleaning process. If we want to remove `NaN` values from a specified column, we can create a filter, as follows:

  ```
  Filter filter = new ConditionFilter(new
  NaNColumnCondition("columnName"));
  ```

  If we want to remove null values from a specified column, we can create a filter, as follows:

  ```
  Filter filter =  new ConditionFilter(new
  NullWritableColumnCondition("columnName"));
  ```

- `stringRemoveWhitespaceTransform()`: This method removes whitespace characters from the value of a column. This method accepts only a single attribute, which is the column from which whitespace is to be trimmed.
- `integerMathOp()`: This method is used to perform a mathematical operation on an integer column with a scalar value. Similar methods are available for types such as `double` and `long`. This method accepts three attributes: the integer column to apply the mathematical operation on, the mathematical operation itself, and the scalar value to be used for the mathematical operation.

 `TransformProcess` is not just meant for data handling – it can also be used to overcome memory bottlenecks by a margin.

Refer to the DL4J API documentation to find more powerful DataVec features for your data analysis tasks. There are other interesting operations supported in `TransformPorocess`, such as `reduce()` and `convertToString()`. If you're a data analyst, then you should know that many of the data normalization strategies can be applied during this stage. You can refer to the DL4J API documentation for more information on the normalization strategies that are available on `https://deeplearning4j.org/docs/latest/datavec-normalization`.

Serializing transforms

DataVec gives us the ability to serialize the transforms so that they're portable for production environments. In this recipe, we will serialize the transformation process.

How to do it...

1. Serialize the transforms into a human-readable format. We can transform to JSON using `TransformProcess` as follows:

```
String serializedTransformString = transformProcess.toJson()
```

We can transform to YAML using `TransformProcess` as follows:

```
String serializedTransformString = transformProcess.toYaml()
```

You can find an example of this at `https://github.com/PacktPublishing/Java-Deep-Learning-Cookbook/blob/master/02_Data_Extraction_Transform_and_Loading/sourceCode/cookbook-app/src/main/java/com/javadeeplearningcookbook/app/SerializationExample.java`.

2. Deserialize the transforms for JSON to `TransformProcess` as follows:

```
TransformProcess tp =
TransformProcess.fromJson(serializedTransformString)
```

You can do the same for YAML to `TransformProcess` as follows:

```
TransformProcess tp =
TransformProcess.fromYaml(serializedTransformString)
```

How it works...

In step 1, `toJson()` converts `TransformProcess` into a JSON string, while `toYaml()` converts `TransformProcess` into a YAML string.

Both of these methods can be used for the serialization of `TransformProcess`.

In step 2, `fromJson()` deserializes a JSON string into a `TransformProcess`, while `fromYaml()` deserializes a YAML string into a `TransformProcess`.

`serializedTransformString` is the JSON/YAML string that needs to be converted into a `TrasformProcess`.

This recipe is relevant while the application is being migrated to a different platform.

Executing a transform process

After the transformation process has been defined, we can execute it in a controlled pipeline. It can be executed using batch processing, or we can distribute the effort to a Spark cluster. Previously, we look at `TransformProcessRecordReader`, which automatically does the transformation in the background. We cannot feed and execute the data if the dataset is huge. Effort can be distributed to a Spark cluster for a larger dataset. You can also perform regular local execution. In this recipe, we will discuss how to execute a transform process locally as well as remotely.

How to do it...

1. Load the dataset into `RecordReader`. Load the CSV data in the case of `CSVRecordReader`:

```
RecordReader reader = new CSVRecordReader(0,',');
    reader.initialize(new FileSplit(file));
```

2. Execute the transforms in local using `LocalTransformExecutor`:

```
List<List<Writable>> transformed =
LocalTransformExecutor.execute(recordReader, transformProcess)
```

3. Execute the transforms in Spark using `SparkTransformExecutor`:

```
JavaRDD<List<Writable>> transformed =
SparkTransformExecutor.execute(inputRdd, transformProcess)
```

How it works...

In step 1, we load the dataset into a record reader object. For demonstration purposes, we used `CSVRecordReader`.

In step 2, the `execute()` method can only be used if `TransformProcess` returns non-sequential data. For local execution, it is assumed that you have loaded the dataset into a `RecordReader`.

For the `LocalTransformExecutor` example, please refer to the `LocalExecuteExample.java` file from this source:
https://github.com/PacktPublishing/Java-Deep-Learning-Cookbook/blob/master/02_Data_Extraction_Transform_and_Loading/sourceCode/cookbook-app/src/main/java/com/javadeeplearningcookbook/app/executorexamples/LocalExecuteExample.java.

 For the `LocalTransformExecutor` example, you need to provide a file path for `titanic.csv`. It is located in this chapter's GitHub directory.

In step 3, it is assumed that you have loaded the dataset into a JavaRDD object since we need to execute the DataVec transform process in a Spark cluster. Also, the `execute()` method can only be used if `TransformProcess` returns non-sequential data.

There's more...

If `TransformProcess` returns sequential data, then use the `executeSequence()` method instead:

```
List<List<List<Writable>>> transformed =
LocalTransformExecutor.executeSequence(sequenceRecordReader,
transformProcess)
```

If you need to join two record readers based on `joinCondition`, then you need the `executeJoin()` method:

```
List<List<Writable>> transformed =
LocalTransformExecutor.executeJoin(joinCondition, leftReader, rightReader)
```

The following is an overview of local/Spark executor methods:

- `execute()`: This applies the transformation to the record reader. `LocalTransformExecutor` takes the record reader as input, while `SparkTransformExecutor` needs the input data to be loaded into a JavaRDD object. This cannot be used for sequential data.
- `executeSequence()`: This applies the transformation to a sequence reader. However, the transform process should start with non-sequential data and then convert it into sequential data.
- `executeJoin()`: This method is used for joining two different input readers based on `joinCondition`.
- `executeSequenceToSeparate()`: This applies the transformation to a sequence reader. However, the transform process should start with sequential data and return non-sequential data.
- `executeSequenceToSequence()`: This applies the transformation to a sequence reader. However, the transform process should start with sequential data and return sequential data.

Normalizing data for network efficiency

Normalization makes a neural network's job much easier. It helps the neural network treat all the features the same, irrespective of their range of values. The main goal of normalization is to arrange the numeric values in a dataset on a common scale without actually disturbing the difference in the range of values. Not all datasets require a normalization strategy, but if they do have different numeric ranges, then it is a crucial step to perform normalization on the data. Normalization has a direct impact on the stability/accuracy of the model. ND4J has various preprocessors to handle normalization. In this recipe, we will normalize the data.

How to do it...

1. Create a dataset iterator from the data. Refer to the following demonstration for
   `RecordReaderDataSetIterator`:

   ```
   DataSetIterator iterator = new
   RecordReaderDataSetIterator(recordReader,batchSize);
   ```

2. Apply the normalization to the dataset by calling the `fit()` method of the normalizer implementation. Refer to the following demonstration for the `NormalizerStandardize` preprocessor:

   ```
   DataNormalization dataNormalization = new NormalizerStandardize();
   dataNormalization.fit(iterator);
   ```

3. Call `setPreprocessor()` to set the preprocessor for the dataset:

   ```
   iterator.setPreProcessor(dataNormalization);
   ```

How it works...

To start, you need to have an iterator to traverse and prepare the data. In step 1, we used the record reader data to create the dataset iterator. The purpose of the iterator is to have more control over the data and how it is presented to the neural network.

Once the appropriate normalization method has been identified (`NormalizerStandardize`, in step 2), we use `fit()` to apply the normalization to the dataset. `NormalizerStandardize` normalizes the data in such a way that feature values will have a zero mean and standard deviation of 1.

The example for this recipe can be found at `https://github.com/PacktPublishing/Java-Deep-Learning-Cookbook/blob/master/02_Data_Extraction_Transform_and_Loading/sourceCode/cookbook-app/src/main/java/com/javadeeplearningcookbook/app/NormalizationExample.java`.

- **Sample input**: A dataset iterator that holds feature variables (`INDArray` format). Iterators are created from the input data as mentioned in previous recipes.
- **Sample output**: Refer to the following snapshot for the normalized features (`INDArray` format) after applying normalization on the input data:

```
Before Applying Normalization
[main] INFO org.nd4j.linalg.factory.Nd4jBackend - Loaded [CpuBackend] backend
[main] INFO org.nd4j.nativeblas.NativeOpsHolder - Number of threads used for NativeOps: 4
[main] INFO org.nd4j.nativeblas.Nd4jBlas - Number of threads used for BLAS: 4
[main] INFO org.nd4j.linalg.api.ops.executioner.DefaultOpExecutioner - Backend used: [CPU]; OS: [Windows 10]
[main] INFO org.nd4j.linalg.api.ops.executioner.DefaultOpExecutioner - Cores: [8]; Memory: [1.8GB];
[main] INFO org.nd4j.linalg.api.ops.executioner.DefaultOpExecutioner - Blas vendor: [MKL]
[[   90.0000,        0,    1.0000],
 [   88.0000,        0,    1.0000]]
After Applying Normalization
[[    1.0759,   -1.0786,    0.5345],
 [    0.9815,   -1.0786,    0.5345]]
```

Note that we can't skip step 3 while applying normalization. If we don't perform step 3, the dataset won't be auto-normalized.

There's more...

Preprocessors normally have default range limits from 0 to 1. If you don't apply normalization to a dataset with a wide range of numeric values (when feature values that are too low and too high are present), then the neural network will tend to favor the feature values that have high numeric values. Hence, the accuracy of the neural network could be significantly reduced.

If values are spread across symmetric intervals such as (0,1), then all the feature values are considered equivalent during training. Hence, it also has an impact on the neural network's generalization.

The following are the preprocessors that are provided by ND4J:

- `NormalizerStandardize`: A preprocessor for datasets that normalizes feature values so that they have a *zero* mean and a standard deviation of 1.
- `MultiNormalizerStandardize`: A preprocessor for multi-datasets that normalizes feature values so that they have a zero mean and a standard deviation of 1.
- `NormalizerMinMaxScaler`: A preprocessor for datasets that normalizes feature values so that they lie between a minimum and maximum value that's been specified. The default range is 0 to 1.
- `MultiNormalizerMinMaxScaler`: A preprocessor for multi-datasets that normalizes feature values that lie between a minimum and maximum value that's been specified. The default range is 0 to 1.
- `ImagePreProcessingScaler`: A preprocessor for images with minimum and maximum scaling. The default ranges are (`miRange`, `maxRange`) − (0,1).
- `VGG16ImagePreProcessor`: A preprocessor specifically for the VGG16 network architecture. It computes the mean RGB value and subtracts it from each pixel on the training set.

Building Deep Neural Networks for Binary Classification

3

In this chapter, we are going to develop a **Deep Neural Network** (**DNN**) using the standard feedforward network architecture. We will add components and changes to the application while we progress through the recipes. Make sure to revisit Chapter 1, *Introduction to Deep Learning in Java*, and Chapter 2, *Data Extraction, Transformation, and Loading*, if you have not already done so. This is to ensure better understanding of the recipes in this chapter.

We will take an example of a customer retention prediction for the demonstration of the standard feedforward network. This is a crucial real-world problem that every business wants to solve. Businesses would like to invest more in happy customers, who tend to stay customers for longer periods of time. At the same time, predictions of losing customers will make businesses focus more on decisions that encourage customers not to take their business elsewhere.

Remember that a feedforward network doesn't really give you any hints about the actual features that decide the outcome. It just predicts whether a customer continues to patronize the organization or not. The actual feature signals are hidden, and it is left to the neural network to decide. If you want to record the actual feature signals that control the prediction outcome, then you could use an autoencoder for the task. Let's examine how to construct a feedforward network for our aforementioned use case.

In this chapter, we will cover the following recipes:

- Extracting data from CSV input
- Removing anomalies from the data
- Applying transformations to the data
- Designing input layers for the neural network model
- Designing hidden layers for the neural network model

- Designing output layers for the neural network model
- Training and evaluating the neural network model for CSV data
- Deploying the neural network model and using it as an API

Technical requirements

Make sure the following requirements are satisfied:

- JDK 8 is installed and added to PATH. Source code requires JDK 8 for execution.
- Maven is installed/added to PATH. We use Maven to build the application JAR file afterward.

Concrete implementation for the use case discussed in this chapter (Customer retention prediction) can be found at https://github.com/PacktPublishing/Java-Deep-Learning-Cookbook/blob/master/03_Building_Deep_Neural_Networks_for_Binary_classification/sourceCode/cookbookapp/src/main/java/com/javadeeplearningcookbook/examples/CustomerRetentionPredictionExample.java.

After cloning our GitHub repository, navigate to the Java-Deep-Learning-Cookbook/03_Building_Deep_Neural_Networks_for_Binary_classification/sourceCode directory. Then import the cookbookapp project into your IDE as a Maven project by importing pom.xml.

Dataset is already included in the resources directory (Churn_Modelling.csv) of the cookbookapp project.

However, the dataset can be downloaded at https://www.kaggle.com/barelydedicated/bank-customer-churn-modeling/downloads/bank-customer-churn-modeling.zip/1.

Extracting data from CSV input

ETL (short for **Extract, Transform and Load**) is the first stage prior to network training. Customer churn data is in CSV format. We need to extract it and put it in a record reader object to process further. In this recipe, we extract the data from a CSV file.

How to do it...

1. Create `CSVRecordReader` to hold customer churn data:

```
RecordReader recordReader = new CSVRecordReader(1,',');
```

2. Add data to `CSVRecordReader`:

```
File file = new File("Churn_Modelling.csv");
    recordReader.initialize(new FileSplit(file));
```

How it works...

The CSV data from the dataset has 14 features. Each row represents a customer/record, as shown in the following screenshot:

	A	B	C	D	E	F	G	H	I	J	K	L	M	N	O
1	RowNumber	Customer	Surname	CreditSco	Geograph	Gender	Age	Tenure	Balance	NumOfPr	HasCrCar	IsActiveM	Estimated	Exited	
2	1	15634602	Hargrave	619	France	Female	42	2	0	1	1	1	101348.9	1	
3	2	15647311	Hill	608	Spain	Female	41	1	83807.86	1	0	1	112542.6	0	
4	3	15619304	Onio	502	France	Female	42	8	159660.8	3	1	0	113931.6	1	
5	4	15701354	Boni	699	France	Female	39	1	0	2	0	0	93826.63	0	
6	5	15737888	Mitchell	850	Spain	Female	43	2	125510.8	1	1	1	79084.1	0	
7	6	15574012	Chu	645	Spain	Male	44	8	113755.8	2	1	0	149756.7	1	
8	7	15592531	Bartlett	822	France	Male	50	7	0	2	1	1	10062.8	0	
9	8	15656148	Obinna	376	Germany	Female	29	4	115046.7	4	1	0	119346.9	1	
10	9	15792365	He	501	France	Male	44	4	142051.1	2	0	1	74940.5	0	
11	10	15592389	H?	684	France	Male	27	2	134603.9	1	1	1	71725.73	0	
12	11	15767821	Bearce	528	France	Male	31	6	102016.7	2	0	0	80181.12	0	
13	12	15737173	Andrews	497	Spain	Male	24	3	0	2	1	0	76390.01	0	
14	13	15632264	Kay	476	France	Female	34	10	0	2	1	0	26260.98	0	
15	14	15691483	Chin	549	France	Female	25	5	0	2	0	1	190857.8	0	
16	15	15600882	Scott	635	Spain	Female	35	7	0	2	1	1	65951.65	0	
17	16	15643966	Goforth	616	Germany	Male	45	3	143129.4	2	0	1	64327.26	0	
18	17	15737452	Romeo	653	Germany	Male	58	1	132602.9	1	1	0	5097.67	1	
19	18	15788218	Henderso	549	Spain	Female	24	9	0	2	1	1	14406.41	0	
20	19	15661507	Muldrow	587	Spain	Male	45	6	0	1	0	0	158684.8	0	
21	20	15568982	Hao	726	France	Female	24	6	0	2	1	1	54724.03	0	
22	21	15577657	McDonald	732	France	Male	41	8	0	2	1	1	170886.2	0	
23	22	15597945	Dellucci	636	Spain	Female	32	8	0	2	1	0	138555.5	0	

Churn_Modelling   ⊕

Our dataset is a CSV file containing 10,000 customer records, where each record is labeled as to whether the customer left the business or not. Columns 0 to 13 represent input features. The 14th column, Exited, indicates the label or prediction outcome. We're dealing with a supervised model, and each prediction is labeled with 0 or 1, where 0 indicates a happy customer, and 1 indicates an unhappy customer who has left the business. The first row in the dataset is just feature labels, and we don't need them while processing the data. So, we have skipped the first line while we created the record reader instance in step 1. In step 1, 1 is the number of rows to be skipped on the dataset. Also, we have mentioned a comma delimiter (,) because we are using a CSV file. In step 2, we used FileSplit to mention the customer churn dataset file. We can also deal with multiple dataset files using other InputSplit implementations, such as CollectionInputSplit, NumberedFileInputSplit, and so on.

Removing anomalies from the data

For supervised datasets, manual inspection works fine for datasets with fewer features. As the feature count goes high, manual inspection becomes impractical. We need to perform feature selection techniques, such as chi-square test, random forest, and so on, to deal with the volume of features. We can also use an autoencoder to narrow down the relevant features. Remember that each feature should have a fair contribution toward the prediction outcomes. So, we need to remove noise features from the raw dataset and keep everything else as is, including any uncertain features. In this recipe, we will walk through the steps to identify anomalies in the data.

How to do it...

1. Leave out all the noise features before training the neural network. Remove noise features at the schema transformation stage:

```
TransformProcess transformProcess = new
TransformProcess.Builder(schema)
 .removeColumns("RowNumber","CustomerId","Surname")
 .build();
```

2. Identify the missing values using the DataVec analysis API:

```
DataQualityAnalysis analysis =
AnalyzeLocal.analyzeQuality(schema,recordReader);
 System.out.println(analysis);
```

3. Remove null values using a schema transformation:

```
Condition condition = new
NullWritableColumnCondition("columnName");
 TransformProcess transformProcess = new
TransformProcess.Builder(schema)
    .conditionalReplaceValueTransform("columnName",new
IntWritable(0),condition)
  .build();
```

4. Remove NaN values using a schema transformation:

```
Condition condition = new NaNColumnCondition("columnName");
 TransformProcess transformProcess = new
TransformProcess.Builder(schema)
    .conditionalReplaceValueTransform("columnName",new
IntWritable(0),condition)
  .build();
```

How it works...

If you recall our customer churn dataset, there are 14 features:

	A	B	C	D	E	F	G	H	I	J	K	L	M	N	O
1	RowNumber	Customer	Surname	CreditSco	Geograph	Gender	Age	Tenure	Balance	NumOfPr	HasCrCar	IsActiveM	Estimated	Exited	
2	1	15634602	Hargrave	619	France	Female	42	2	0	1	1	1	101348.9	1	
3	2	15647311	Hill	608	Spain	Female	41	1	83807.86	1	0	1	112542.6	0	
4	3	15619304	Onio	502	France	Female	42	8	159660.8	3	1	0	113931.6	1	
5	4	15701354	Boni	699	France	Female	39	1	0	2	0	0	93826.63	0	
6	5	15737888	Mitchell	850	France	Female	43	2	125510.8	1	1	1	79084.1	0	
7	6	15574012	Chu	645	Spain	Male	44	8	113755.8	2	1	0	149756.7	1	
8	7	15592531	Bartlett	822	France	Male	50	7	0	2	1	1	10062.8	0	
9	8	15656148	Obinna	376	Germany	Female	29	4	115046.7	4	1	0	119346.9	1	
10	9	15792365	He	501	France	Male	44	4	142051.1	2	0	1	74940.5	0	
11	10	15592389	H?	684	France	Male	27	2	134603.9	1	1	1	71725.73	0	
12	11	15767821	Bearce	528	France	Male	31	6	102016.7	2	0	0	80181.12	0	
13	12	15737173	Andrews	497	Spain	Male	24	3	0	2	1	0	76390.01	0	
14	13	15632264	Kay	476	France	Female	34	10	0	2	1	0	26260.98	0	
15	14	15691483	Chin	549	France	Female	25	5	0	2	0	0	190857.8	0	
16	15	15600882	Scott	635	Spain	Female	35	7	0	2	1	1	65951.65	0	
17	16	15643966	Goforth	616	Germany	Male	45	3	143129.4	2	0	1	64327.26	0	
18	17	15737452	Romeo	653	Germany	Male	58	1	132602.9	1	1	0	5097.67	1	
19	18	15788218	Henderso	549	Spain	Female	24	9	0	2	1	1	14406.41	0	
20	19	15661507	Muldrow	587	Spain	Male	45	6	0	1	0	0	158684.8	0	
21	20	15568982	Hao	726	France	Female	24	6	0	2	1	1	54724.03	0	
22	21	15577657	McDonald	732	France	Male	41	8	0	2	1	1	170886.2	0	
23	22	15597945	Dellucci	636	Spain	Female	32	8	0	2	1	0	138555.5	0	

Churn_Modelling ⊕

After performing step 1, you have 11 valid features remaining. The following marked features have zero significance on the prediction outcome. For example, the customer name doesn't influence whether a customer would leave the organization or not.

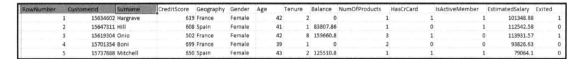

RowNumber	CustomerId	Surname	CreditScore	Geography	Gender	Age	Tenure	Balance	NumOfProducts	HasCrCard	IsActiveMember	EstimatedSalary	Exited
1	15634602	Hargrave	619	France	Female	42	2	0	1	1	1	101348.88	1
2	15647311	Hill	608	Spain	Female	41	1	83807.86	1	0	1	112542.58	0
3	15619304	Onio	502	France	Female	42	8	159660.8	3	1	0	113931.57	1
4	15701354	Boni	699	France	Female	39	1	0	2	0	0	93826.63	0
5	15737888	Mitchell	850	Spain	Female	43	2	125510.8	1	1	1	79084.1	0

In the above screenshot, we have marked the features that are not required for the training. These features can be removed from the dataset as it doesn't have any impact on outcome.

In step 1, we tagged the noise features (`RowNumber`, `Customerid`, and `Surname`) in our dataset for removal during the schema transformation process using the `removeColumns()` method.

The customer churn dataset used in this chapter has only 14 features. Also, the feature labels are meaningful. So, a manual inspection was just enough. In the case of a large number of features, you might need to consider using **PCA** (short for **Principal Component Analysis**), as explained in the previous chapter.

In step 2, we used the `AnalyzeLocal` utility class to find the missing values in the dataset by calling `analyzeQuality()`. You should see the following result when you print out the information in the `DataQualityAnalysis` object:

As you can see in the preceding screenshot, each of the features is analyzed for its quality (in terms of invalid/missing data), and the count is displayed for us to decide if we need to normalize it further. Since all features appeared to be OK, we can proceed further.

There are two ways in which missing values can be handled. Either we remove the entire record or replace them with a value. In most cases, we don't remove records; instead, we replace them with a value to indicate absence. We can do it during the transformation process using `conditionalReplaceValueTransform()` or `conditionalReplaceValueTransformWithDefault()`. In step 3/4, we removed missing or invalid values from the dataset. Note that the feature needs to be known beforehand. We cannot check the whole set of features for this purpose. At the moment, DataVec doesn't support this functionality. You may perform step 2 to identify features that need attention.

There's more...

We discussed earlier in this chapter how to use the `AnalyzeLocal` utility class to find out missing values. We can also perform extended data analysis using `AnalyzeLocal`. We can create a data analysis object that holds information on each column present in the dataset. It can be created by calling `analyze()`, as we discussed in the previous chapter. If you try to print out the information on the data analysis object, it will look like the following:

It will calculate the standard deviation, mean, and the min/max values for all the features in the dataset. The count of features is also calculated, which will be helpful toward identifying missing or invalid values in features.

```
sitive=10000,countMinValue=5,countMaxValue=233,count=10000, quantiles=[0.001 -> 368.55,0.01 -> 433.0


itive=10000,countMinValue=22,countMaxValue=2,count=10000, quantiles=[0.001 -> 18.0,0.01 -> 20.818487
sitive=10000,countMinValue=413,countMaxValue=490,count=10000, quantiles=[0.001 -> 0.0,0.01 -> 0.0,0.
=0,countPositive=10000,countMinValue=3617,countMaxValue=1,count=10000, quantiles=[0.001 -> 0.0,0.01
itive=10000,countMinValue=5084,countMaxValue=60,count=10000, quantiles=[0.001 -> 1.0,0.01 -> 1.0,0.1
tPositive=10000,countMinValue=2945,countMaxValue=7055,count=10000, quantiles=[0.001 -> 0.0,0.01 -> 0
ntPositive=10000,countMinValue=4849,countMaxValue=5151,count=10000, quantiles=[0.001 -> 0.0,0.01 ->
e=0,countPositive=10000,countMinValue=1,countMaxValue=1,count=10000, quantiles=[0.001 -> 231.5162499
ntPositive=10000,countMinValue=7963,countMaxValue=2037,count=10000, quantiles=[0.001 -> 0.0,0.01 ->
```

Both screenshots on the above indicate the data analysis results returned by calling `analyze()` method. For the customer churn dataset, we should have a total count of 10,000 for all features as the total number of records present in our dataset is 10,000.

Applying transformations to the data

Data transformation is a crucial data normalization procedure that must be done before we feed the data to a neural network. We need to transform non-numeric features to numeric values and handle missing values. In this recipe, we will perform schema transformation, and create dataset iterators after transformation.

How to do it...

1. Add features and labels into the schema:

```
Schema.Builder schemaBuilder = new Schema.Builder();
 schemaBuilder.addColumnString("RowNumber")
 schemaBuilder.addColumnInteger("CustomerId")
 schemaBuilder.addColumnString("Surname")
 schemaBuilder.addColumnInteger("CreditScore");
```

2. Identify and add categorical features to the schema:

```
schemaBuilder.addColumnCategorical("Geography",
Arrays.asList("France","Germany","Spain"))
 schemaBuilder.addColumnCategorical("Gender",
Arrays.asList("Male","Female"));
```

3. Remove noise features from the dataset:

```
Schema schema = schemaBuilder.build();
 TransformProcess.Builder transformProcessBuilder = new
TransformProcess.Builder(schema);
transformProcessBuilder.removeColumns("RowNumber","CustomerId","Sur
name");
```

4. Transform categorical variables:

```
transformProcessBuilder.categoricalToInteger("Gender");
```

5. Apply one-hot encoding by calling `categoricalToOneHot()`:

```
transformProcessBuilder.categoricalToInteger("Gender")
 transformProcessBuilder.categoricalToOneHot("Geography");
```

6. Remove the correlation dependency on the `Geography` feature by calling `removeColumns()`:

```
transformProcessBuilder.removeColumns("Geography[France]")
```

Here, we selected `France` as the correlation variable.

7. Extract the data and apply the transformation using `TransformProcessRecordReader`:

```
TransformProcess transformProcess =
transformProcessBuilder.build();
 TransformProcessRecordReader transformProcessRecordReader = new
TransformProcessRecordReader(recordReader,transformProcess);
```

8. Create a dataset iterator to train/test:

```
DataSetIterator dataSetIterator = new
RecordReaderDataSetIterator.Builder(transformProcessRecordReader,ba
tchSize) .classification(labelIndex,numClasses)
 .build();
```

9. Normalize the dataset:

```
DataNormalization dataNormalization = new NormalizerStandardize();
 dataNormalization.fit(dataSetIterator);
 dataSetIterator.setPreProcessor(dataNormalization);
```

10. Split the main dataset iterator to train and test iterators:

```
DataSetIteratorSplitter dataSetIteratorSplitter = new
DataSetIteratorSplitter(dataSetIterator,totalNoOfBatches,ratio);
```

11. Generate train/test iterators from `DataSetIteratorSplitter`:

```
DataSetIterator trainIterator =
dataSetIteratorSplitter.getTrainIterator();
 DataSetIterator testIterator =
dataSetIteratorSplitter.getTestIterator();
```

How it works...

All features and labels need to be added to the schema as mentioned in step 1 and step 2. If we don't do that, then DataVec will throw runtime errors during data extraction/loading.

```
Exception in thread "main" java.lang.IllegalStateException: Cannot execute transform: input writables list length (14) does not match expected number of elements (schema: 13).
    at org.datavec.api.transform.transform.column.RemoveColumnsTransform.map(RemoveColumnsTransform.java:129)
    at org.datavec.api.transform.TransformProcess.execute(TransformProcess.java:324)
    at org.datavec.api.records.reader.impl.transform.TransformProcessRecordReader.hasNext(TransformProcessRecordReader.java:132)
    at org.deeplearning4j.datasets.datavec.RecordReaderDataSetIterator.hasNext(RecordReaderDataSetIterator.java:434)
    at org.nd4j.linalg.dataset.api.preprocessor.AbstractDataSetNormalizer.fit(AbstractDataSetNormalizer.java:108)
    at com.javadeeplearningcookbook.examples.CustomerRetentionPredictionExample.main(CustomerRetentionPredictionExample.java:114)
```

In the preceding screenshot, the runtime exception is thrown by DataVec because of unmatched count of features. This will happen if we provide a different value for input neurons instead of the actual count of features in the dataset.

From the error description, it is clear that we have only added 13 features in the schema, which ended in a runtime error during execution. The first three features, named Rownumber, Customerid, and Surname, are to be added to the schema. Note that we need to tag these features in the schema, even though we found them to be noise features. You can also remove these features manually from the dataset. If you do that, you don't have to add them in the schema, and, thus, there is no need to handle them in the transformation stage

For large datasets, you may add all features from the dataset to the schema, unless your analysis identifies them as noise. Similarly, we need to add the other feature variables such as Age, Tenure, Balance, NumOfProducts, HasCrCard, IsActiveMember, EstimatedSalary, and Exited. Note the variable types while adding them to schema. For example, Balance and EstimatedSalary have floating point precision, so consider their datatype as double and use addColumnDouble() to add them to schema.

We have two features named gender and geography that require special treatment. These two features are non-numeric and their feature values represent categorical values compared to other fields in the dataset. Any non-numeric features need to transform numeric values so that the neural network can perform statistical computations on feature values. In step 2, we added categorical variables to the schema using addColumnCategorical(). We need to specify the categorical values in a list, and addColumnCategorical() will tag the integer values based on the feature values mentioned. For example, the Male and Female values in the categorical variable Gender will be tagged as 0 and 1 respectively. In step 2, we added the possible values for the categorical variables in a list. If your dataset has any other unknown value present for a categorical variable (other than the ones mentioned in the schema), DataVec will throw an error during execution.

In step 3, we marked the noise features for removal during the transformation process by calling removeColumns().

In step 4, we performed one-hot encoding for the Geography categorical variable. Geography has three categorical values, and hence it will take the 0, 1, and 2 values after the transformation. The ideal way of transforming non-numeric values is to convert them to a value of zero (0) and one (1). It would significantly ease the effort of the neural network. Also, the normal integer encoding is applicable only if there exists an ordinal relationship between the variables. The risk here is we're assuming that there exists natural ordering between the variables. Such an assumption can result in the neural network showing unpredictable behavior. So, we have removed the correlation variable in step 6. For the demonstration, we picked France as a correlation variable in step 6. However, you can choose any one among the three categorical values. This is to remove any correlation dependency that affects neural network performance and stability. After step 6, the resultant schema for the Geography feature will look like the following:

```
France, Germany, Spain
1,      0,       0
0,      1,       0
0,      0,       1
```

In step 8, we created dataset iterators from the record reader objects. Here are the attributes for the RecordReaderDataSetIterator builder method and their respective roles:

- labelIndex: The index location in the CSV data where our labels (outcomes) are located.
- numClasses: The number of labels (outcomes) from the dataset.
- batchSize: The block of data that passes through the neural network. If you specify a batch size of 10 and there are 10,000 records, then there will be 1,000 batches holding 10 records each.

Also, we have a binary classification problem here, and so we used the classification() method to specify the label index and number of labels.

For some of the features in the dataset, you might observe huge differences in the feature value ranges. Some of the features have small numeric values, while some have very large numeric values. These large/small values can be interpreted in the wrong way by the neural network. Neural networks can falsely assign high/low priority to these features and that results in wrong or fluctuating predictions. In order to avoid this situation, we have to normalize the dataset before feeding it to the neural network. Hence we performed normalization as in step 9.

In step 10, we used `DataSetIteratorSplitter` to split the main dataset for a training or test purpose.

The following are the parameters of `DataSetIteratorSplitter`:

- `totalNoOfBatches`: If you specify a batch size of 10 for 10,000 records, then you need to specify 1,000 as the total number of batches.
- `ratio`: This is the ratio at which the splitter splits the iterator set. If you specify 0.8, then it means 80% of data will be used for training and the remaining 20% will be used for testing/evaluation.

Designing input layers for the neural network model

Input layer design requires an understanding of how the data flows into the system. We have CSV data as input, and we need to inspect the features to decide on the input attributes. Layers are core components in neural network architecture. In this recipe, we will configure input layers for the neural network.

Getting ready

We need to decide the number of input neurons before designing the input layer. It can be derived from the feature shape. For instance, we have 13 input features (excluding the label). But after applying the transformation, we have a total of 11 feature columns present in the dataset. Noise features are removed and categorical variables are transformed during the schema transformation. So, the final transformed data will have 11 input features. There are no specific requirements for outgoing neurons from the input layer. If we assign the wrong number of incoming neurons at the input layer, we may end up with a runtime error:

```
Exception in thread "main" org.deeplearning4j.exception.DL4JInvalidInputException: Input size (11 columns; shape = [8, 11]) is invalid: does not match layer input size (layer # inputs
    at org.deeplearning4j.nn.layers.BaseLayer.preOutput(BaseLayer.java:301)
    at org.deeplearning4j.nn.layers.BaseLayer.activate(BaseLayer.java:320)
    at org.deeplearning4j.nn.layers.AbstractLayer.activate(AbstractLayer.java:255)
    at org.deeplearning4j.nn.multilayer.MultiLayerNetwork.ffToLayerActivationsInWs(MultiLayerNetwork.java:1057)
    at org.deeplearning4j.nn.multilayer.MultiLayerNetwork.computeGradientAndScore(MultiLayerNetwork.java:2629)
    at org.deeplearning4j.nn.multilayer.MultiLayerNetwork.computeGradientAndScore(MultiLayerNetwork.java:2557)
    at org.deeplearning4j.optimize.solvers.BaseOptimizer.gradientAndScore(BaseOptimizer.java:160)
    at org.deeplearning4j.optimize.solvers.StochasticGradientDescent.optimize(StochasticGradientDescent.java:63)
    at org.deeplearning4j.optimize.Solver.optimize(Solver.java:52)
    at org.deeplearning4j.nn.multilayer.MultiLayerNetwork.fitHelper(MultiLayerNetwork.java:1602)
```

The DL4J error stack is pretty much self-explanatory as to the possible reason. It points out the exact layer where it needs a fix (`layer0`, in the preceding example).

How to do it...

1. Define the neural network configuration using `MultiLayerConfiguration`:

```
MultiLayerConfiguration.Builder builder = new
NeuralNetConfiguration.Builder().weightInit(WeightInit.RELU_UNIFORM
)
  .updater(new Adam(0.015D))
  .list();
```

2. Define the input layer configuration using `DenseLayer`:

```
builder.layer(new
DenseLayer.Builder().nIn(incomingConnectionCount).nOut(outgoingConn
ectionCount).activation(Activation.RELU)
  .build())
  .build();
```

How it works...

We added layers to the network by calling the `layer()` method as mentioned in step 2. Input layers are added using `DenseLayer`. Also, we need to add an activation function for the input layer. We specified the activation function by calling the `activation()` method. We discussed activation functions in `Chapter 1`, *Introduction to Deep Learning in Java*. You can use one of the available activation functions in DL4J to the `activation()` method. The most generic activation function used is `RELU`. Here are roles of other methods in layer design:

- `nIn()`: This refers to the number of inputs for the layer. For an input layer, this is nothing but the number of input features.
- `nOut()`: This refers to number of outputs to next dense layer in neural network.

Designing hidden layers for the neural network model

Hidden layers are the heart of a neural network. The actual decision process happens there. The design of the hidden layers is based on hitting a level beyond which a neural network cannot be optimized further. This level can be defined as the optimal number of hidden layers that produce optimal results.

Hidden layers are the place where the neural network transforms the inputs into a different format that the output layer can consume and use to make predictions. In this recipe, we will design hidden layers for a neural network.

How to do it...

1. Determine the incoming/outgoing connections. Set the following:

```
incoming neurons = outgoing neurons from preceding layer.
 outgoing neurons = incoming neurons for the next hidden layer.
```

2. Configure hidden layers using `DenseLayer`:

```
builder.layer(new
DenseLayer.Builder().nIn(incomingConnectionCount).nOut(outgoingConn
ectionCount).activation(Activation.RELU).build());
```

How it works...

For step 1, if the neural network has only single hidden layer, then the number of neurons (inputs) in the hidden layer should be the same as the number of outgoing connections from the preceding layer. If you have multiple hidden layers, you will also need to confirm this for the preceding hidden layers.

After you make sure that the number of input neurons are the same as number of the outgoing neurons in the preceding layer, you can create hidden layers using `DenseLayer`. In step 2, we used `DenseLayer` to create hidden layers for the input layers. In practice, we need to evaluate the model multiple times to understand the network performance. There's no constant layer configuration that works well for all the models. Also, `RELU` is the preferred activation function for hidden layers, due to its nonlinear nature.

Designing output layers for the neural network model

Output layer design requires an understanding of the expected output. We have CSV data as input, and the output layer relies on the number of labels in the dataset. Output layers are the place where the actual prediction is formed based on the learning process that happened in the hidden layers.

In this recipe, we will design output layers for the neural network.

How to do it...

1. Determine the incoming/outgoing connections. Set the following:

```
incoming neurons = outgoing neurons from preceding hidden layer.
 outgoing neurons = number of labels
```

2. Configure the output layer for the neural network:

```
builder.layer(new OutputLayer.Builder(new
LossMCXENT(weightsArray)).nIn(incomingConnectionCount).nOut(labelCo
unt).activation(Activation.SOFTMAX).build())
```

How it works...

For step 1, we need to make sure that nOut() for the preceding layer should have the same number of neurons as nIn() for the output layer.

So, incomingConnectionCount should be the same as outgoingConnectionCount from the preceding layer.

We discussed the SOFTMAX activation function earlier in Chapter 1, *Introduction to Deep Learning in Java*. Our use case (customer churn) is an example for the binary classification model. We are looking for a probabilistic outcome, that is, the probability of a customer being labeled *happy* or *unhappy*, where 0 represents a happy customer and 1 represents an unhappy customer. This probability will be evaluated, and the neural network will train itself during the training process.

The proper activation function at the output layer would be SOFTMAX. This is because we need the probability of the occurrence of labels and the probabilities should sum to 1. SOFTMAX along with the log loss function produces good results for classification models. The introduction of weightsArray is to enforce a preference for a particular label among others in case of any data imbalance. In step 2, output layers are created using the OutputLayer class. The only difference is that OutputLayer expects an error function to calculate the error rate while making predictions. In our case, we used LossMCXENT, which is a multi-class cross entropy error function. Our customer churn example follows a binary classification model; however, we can still use this error function since we have two classes (labels) in our example. In step 2, labelCount would be 2.

Training and evaluating the neural network model for CSV data

During the training process, the neural network learns to perform the expected task. For every iteration/epoch, the neural network will evaluate its training knowledge. Accordingly, it will re-iterate the layers with updated gradient values to minimize the error produced at the output layer. Also, note that labels (0 and 1) are not uniformly distributed across the dataset. So, we might need to consider adding weights to the label that appears less in the dataset. This is highly recommended before we proceed with the actual training session. In this recipe, we will train the neural network and evaluate the resultant model.

How to do it...

1. Create an array to assign weights to minor labels:

```
INDArray weightsArray = Nd4j.create(new double[]{0.35, 0.65});
```

2. Modify `OutPutLayer` to evenly balance the labels in the dataset:

```
new OutputLayer.Builder(new
LossMCXENT(weightsArray)).nIn(incomingConnectionCount).nOut(labelCo
unt).activation(Activation.SOFTMAX))
.build();
```

3. Initialize the neural network and add the training listeners:

```
MultiLayerConfiguration configuration = builder.build();
    MultiLayerNetwork multiLayerNetwork = new
MultiLayerNetwork(configuration);
 multiLayerNetwork.init();
 multiLayerNetwork.setListeners(new
ScoreIterationListener(iterationCount));
```

4. Add the DL4J UI Maven dependency to analyze the training process:

```
<dependency>
 <groupId>org.deeplearning4j</groupId>
 <artifactId>deeplearning4j-ui_2.10</artifactId>
 <version>1.0.0-beta3</version>
 </dependency>
```

5. Start the UI server and add temporary storage to store the model information:

```
UIServer uiServer = UIServer.getInstance();
StatsStorage statsStorage = new InMemoryStatsStorage();
```

Replace `InMemoryStatsStorage` with `FileStatsStorage` (in case of memory restrictions):

```
multiLayerNetwork.setListeners(new ScoreIterationListener(100),
    new StatsListener(statsStorage));
```

6. Assign the temporary storage space to the UI server:

```
uiServer.attach(statsStorage);
```

7. Train the neural network by calling `fit()`:

```
multiLayerNetwork.fit(dataSetIteratorSplitter.getTrainIterator(),10
0);
```

8. Evaluate the model by calling `evaluate()`:

```
Evaluation evaluation =
multiLayerNetwork.evaluate(dataSetIteratorSplitter.getTestIterator(
),Arrays.asList("0","1"));
 System.out.println(evaluation.stats()); //printing the evaluation
metrics
```

How it works...

A neural network increases its efficiency when it improves its generalization power. A neural network should not just memorize a certain decision-making process in favor of a particular label. If it does, our outcomes will be biased and wrong. So, it is good to have a dataset where the labels are uniformly distributed. If they're not uniformly distributed, then we might have to adjust a few things while calculating the error rate. For this purpose, we introduced a `weightsArray` in step 1 and added to `OutputLayer` in step 2.

For `weightsArray = {0.35, 0.65}`, the network gives more priority to the outcomes of `1` (customer unhappy). As we discussed earlier in this chapter, the `Exited` column represents the label. If we observe the dataset, it is evident that outcomes labeled `0` (customer happy) have more records in the dataset compared to `1`. Hence, we need to assign additional priority to `1` to evenly balance the dataset. Unless we do that, our neural network may over fit and will be biased toward the `1` label.

In step 3, we added `ScoreIterationListener` to log the training process on the console. Note that `iterationCount` is the number of iterations in which it should log the network score. Remember, `iterationCount` is not the epoch. We say an epoch has happened when the entire dataset has traveled back and forth (backpropagation) once through the whole neural network.

In step 8, we used `dataSetIteratorSplitter` to obtain the training dataset iterator and trained our model on top of it. If you configured loggers properly, you should see the training instance is progressing as shown here:

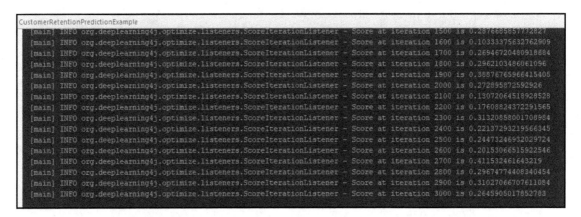

The score referred to in the screenshot is not the success rate; it is the error rate calculated by the error function for each iteration.

We configured the DL4J **user interface** (**UI**) in step 4, 5, and 6. DL4J provides a UI to visualize the current network status and training progress in your browser (real-time monitoring). This will help further tuning the neural network training. `StatsListener` will be responsible for triggering the UI monitoring while the training starts. The port number for UI server is `9000`. While the training is in progress, hit the UI server at `localhost:9000`. We should be able to see something like the following:

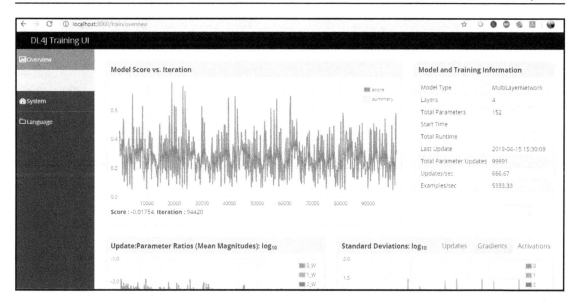

We can refer to the first graph seen in the **Overview** section for the **Model Score** analysis. The **Iteration** is plotted on the x axis, and the **Model Score** is on the y axis in the graph.

We can also further expand our research on how the **Activations**, **Gradients**, and the **Updates** parameters performed during the training process by inspecting the parameter values plotted on graphs:

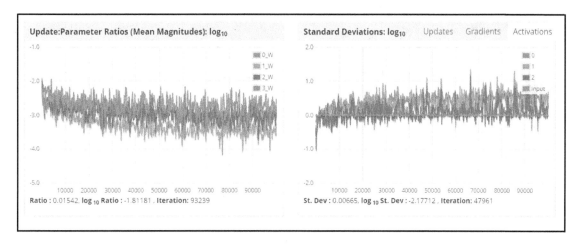

The x axis refers to the number of iterations in both the graphs. The y axis in the parameter update graph refers to the parameter update ratio, and the y axis in the activation/gradient graphs refers to the standard deviation.

It is possible to have layer-wise analysis. We just need to click on the **Model** tab on the left sidebar and choose the layer of choice for further analysis:

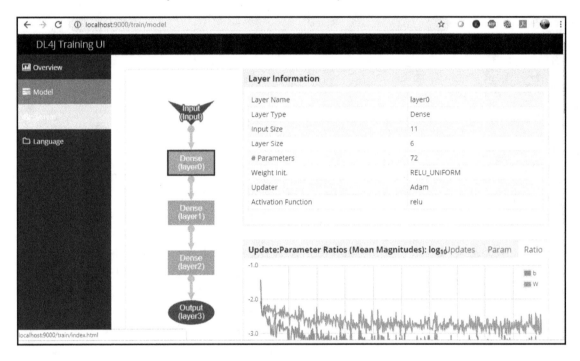

For analysis of memory consumption and JVM, we can navigate to the **System** tab on the left sidebar:

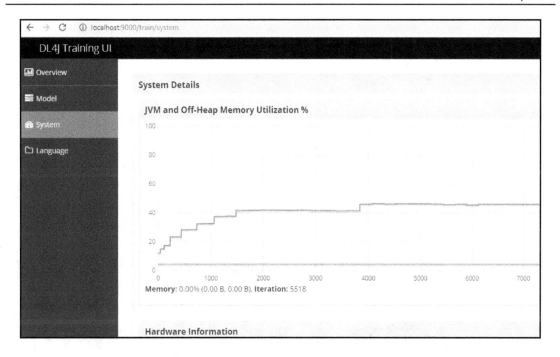

We can also review the hardware/software metrics in detail at the same place:

This is very useful for benchmarking as well. As we can see, the memory consumption of the neural network is clearly marked and the JVM/off-heap memory consumption is mentioned in the UI to analyze how well the benchmarking is done.

After step 8, evaluation results will be displayed on console:

```
[main] INFO org.deeplearning4j.optimize.listeners.ScoreIterationListener - Score at iteration 99900 is 0.37973061203956604


==================Evaluation Metrics==================
 # of classes:    2
 Accuracy:        0.8575
 Precision:       0.8059
 Recall:          0.6900
 F1 Score:        0.5320
Precision, recall & F1: reported for positive class (class 1 - "1") only


==================Confusion Matrix==================
    0    1
  ----------
 1553   57 | 0 = 0
  228  162 | 1 = 1

Confusion matrix format: Actual (rowClass) predicted as (columnClass) N times
==================================================
```

In the above screenshot, the console shows various evaluation metrics by which the model is evaluated. We cannot rely on a specific metrics in all the cases; hence, it is good to evaluate the model against multiple metrics.

Our model is showing an accuracy level of 85.75% at the moment. We have four different performance metrics, named accuracy, precision, recall, and F1 score. As you can see in the preceding screenshot, recall metrics are not so good, which means our model still has false negative cases. The F1 score is also significant here, since our dataset has an uneven proportion of output classes. We will not discuss these metrics in detail, since they are outside the scope of this book. Just remember that all these metrics are important for consideration, rather than just relying on accuracy alone. Of course, the evaluation trade-offs vary depending upon the problem. The current code has already been optimized. Hence, you will find almost stable accuracy from the evaluation metrics. For a well-trained network model, these performance metrics will have values close to 1.

It is important to check how stable our evaluation metrics are. If we notice unstable evaluation metrics for unseen data, then we need to reconsider changes in the network configuration.

Activation functions on the output layer have influence on the stability of the outputs. Hence, a good understanding on output requirements will definitely save you a lot of time choosing an appropriate output function (loss function). We need to ensure stable predictive power from our neural network.

There's more...

Learning rate is one of the factors that decides the efficiency of the neural network. A high learning rate will diverge from the actual output, while a low learning rate will result in slow learning due to slow convergence. Neural network efficiency also depends on the weights that we assign to the neurons in every layer. Hence, a uniform distribution of weights during the early stages of training might help.

The most commonly followed approach is to introduce dropouts to the layers. This forces the neural network to ignore some of the neurons during the training process. This will effectively prevent the neural network from memorizing the prediction process. How do we find out if a network has memorized the results? Well, we just need to expose the network to new data. If your accuracy metrics become worse after that, then you've got a case of overfitting.

Another possibility for increasing the efficiency of the neural network (and thus reducing overfitting) is to try for L1/L2 regularization in the network layers. When we add L1/L2 regularization to network layers, it will add an extra penalty term to the error function. L1 penalizes with the sum of the absolute value of the weights in the neurons, while L2 penalizes using the sum of squares of the weights. L2 regularization will give much better predictions when the output variable is a function of all input features. However, L1 regularization is preferred when the dataset has outliers and if not all the attributes are contributing to predicting the output variable. In most cases, the major reason for overfitting is the issue of memorization. Also, if we drop too many neurons, it will eventually underfit the data. This means we lose more useful data than we need to.

Note that the trade-off can vary depending on the different kinds of problems. Accuracy alone cannot ensure a good model performance every time. It is good to measure precision if we cannot afford the cost of a false positive prediction (such as in spam email detection). It is good to measure recall if we cannot afford the cost of a false negative prediction (such as in fraudulent transaction detection). The F1 score is optimal if there's an uneven distribution of the classes in the dataset. ROC curves are good to measure when there are approximately equal numbers of observations for each output class.

Once the evaluations are stable, we can check on the means to optimize the efficiency of the neural network. There are multiple methods to choose from. We can perform several training sessions to try to find out the optimal number of hidden layers, epochs, dropouts, and activation functions.

The following screenshot points to various hyper parameters that can influence neural network efficiency:

Note that `dropOut(0.9)` means we ignore 10% of neurons during training.

Other attributes/methods in the screenshot are the following:

- `weightInit()` : This is to specify how the weights are assigned neurons at each layer.
- `updater()`: This is to specify the gradient updater configuration. `Adam` is a gradient update algorithm.

In `Chapter 12`, *Benchmarking and Neural Network Optimization*, we will walk through an example of hyperparameter optimization to automatically find the optimal parameters for you. It simply performs multiple training sessions on our behalf to find the optimal values by a single program execution. You may refer to `Chapter 12`, *Benchmarking and Neural Network Optimization*, if you're interested in applying benchmarks to the application.

Deploying the neural network model and using it as an API

After the training instance, we should be able to persist the model and then reuse its capabilities as an API. API access to the customer churn model will enable an external application to predict the customer retention. We will use Spring Boot, along with Thymeleaf, for the UI demonstration. We will deploy and run the application locally for the demonstration. In this recipe, we will create an API for a customer churn example.

Getting ready

As a prerequisite for API creation, you need to run the main example source code:
https://github.com/PacktPublishing/Java-Deep-Learning-Cookbook/blob/master/03_
Building_Deep_Neural_Networks_for_Binary_classification/sourceCode/cookbookapp/
src/main/java/com/javadeeplearningcookbook/examples/
CustomerRetentionPredictionExample.java

DL4J has a utility class called `ModelSerializer` to save and restore models. We have used `ModelSerializer` to persist the model to disk, as follows:

```
File file = new File("model.zip");
ModelSerializer.writeModel(multiLayerNetwork,file,true);
ModelSerializer.addNormalizerToModel(file,dataNormalization);
```

For more information, refer to:

https://github.com/PacktPublishing/Java-Deep-Learning-Cookbook/blob/master/03_
Building_Deep_Neural_Networks_for_Binary_classification/sourceCode/cookbookapp/
src/main/java/com/javadeeplearningcookbook/examples/
CustomerRetentionPredictionExample.java#L124.

Also, note that we need to persist the normalizer preprocessor along with the model. Then we can reuse the same to normalize user inputs on the go. In the previously mentioned code, we persisted the normalizer by calling `addNormalizerToModel()` from `ModelSerializer`.

You also need to be aware of the following input attributes to the `addNormalizerToModel()` method:

- `multiLayerNetwork`: The model that the neural network was trained on
- `dataNormalization`: The normalizer that we used for our training

Please refer to the following example for a concrete API implementation:
`https://github.com/PacktPublishing/Java-Deep-Learning-Cookbook/blob/master/03_Building_Deep_Neural_Networks_for_Binary_classification/sourceCode/cookbookapp/src/main/java/com/javadeeplearningcookbook/api/CustomerRetentionPredictionApi.java`

In our API example, we restore the model file (model that was persisted before) to generate predictions.

How to do it...

1. Create a method to generate a schema for the user input:

```
private static Schema generateSchema(){
 Schema schema = new Schema.Builder()
 .addColumnString("RowNumber")
 .addColumnInteger("CustomerId")
 .addColumnString("Surname")
 .addColumnInteger("CreditScore")
 .addColumnCategorical("Geography",
Arrays.asList("France","Germany","Spain"))
 .addColumnCategorical("Gender", Arrays.asList("Male","Female"))
 .addColumnsInteger("Age", "Tenure")
 .addColumnDouble("Balance")
 .addColumnsInteger("NumOfProducts","HasCrCard","IsActiveMember")
 .addColumnDouble("EstimatedSalary")
 .build();
 return schema;
 }
```

2. Create a `TransformProcess` from the schema:

```
private static RecordReader applyTransform(RecordReader
recordReader, Schema schema){
 final TransformProcess transformProcess = new
TransformProcess.Builder(schema)
 .removeColumns("RowNumber","CustomerId","Surname")
 .categoricalToInteger("Gender")
 .categoricalToOneHot("Geography")
 .removeColumns("Geography[France]")
 .build();
 final TransformProcessRecordReader transformProcessRecordReader =
new TransformProcessRecordReader(recordReader,transformProcess);
 return transformProcessRecordReader;
 }
```

3. Load the data into a record reader instance:

```
private static RecordReader generateReader(File file) throws
IOException, InterruptedException {
  final RecordReader recordReader = new CSVRecordReader(1,',');
  recordReader.initialize(new FileSplit(file));
  final RecordReader
transformProcessRecordReader=applyTransform(recordReader,generateSc
hema());
```

4. Restore the model using `ModelSerializer`:

```
File modelFile = new File(modelFilePath);
 MultiLayerNetwork network =
ModelSerializer.restoreMultiLayerNetwork(modelFile);
 NormalizerStandardize normalizerStandardize =
ModelSerializer.restoreNormalizerFromFile(modelFile);
```

5. Create an iterator to traverse through the entire set of input records:

```
DataSetIterator dataSetIterator = new
RecordReaderDataSetIterator.Builder(recordReader,1).build();
 normalizerStandardize.fit(dataSetIterator);
 dataSetIterator.setPreProcessor(normalizerStandardize);
```

6. Design an API function to generate output from user input:

```
public static INDArray generateOutput(File inputFile, String
modelFilePath) throws IOException, InterruptedException {
 File modelFile = new File(modelFilePath);
 MultiLayerNetwork network =
ModelSerializer.restoreMultiLayerNetwork(modelFile);
   RecordReader recordReader = generateReader(inputFile);
 NormalizerStandardize normalizerStandardize =
ModelSerializer.restoreNormalizerFromFile(modelFile);
 DataSetIterator dataSetIterator = new
RecordReaderDataSetIterator.Builder(recordReader,1).build();
 normalizerStandardize.fit(dataSetIterator);
 dataSetIterator.setPreProcessor(normalizerStandardize);
 return network.output(dataSetIterator);
 }
```

For a further example, see: `https://github.com/PacktPublishing/Java-Deep-Learning-Cookbook/blob/master/03_Building_Deep_Neural_Networks_for_Binary_classification/sourceCode/cookbookapp/src/main/java/com/javadeeplearningcookbook/api/CustomerRetentionPredictionApi.java`

7. Build a shaded JAR of your DL4J API project by running the Maven command:

```
mvn clean install
```

8. Run the Spring Boot project included in the source directory. Import the Maven project to your IDE: https://github.com/PacktPublishing/Java-Deep-Learning-Cookbook/tree/master/03_Building_Deep_Neural_Networks_for_Binary_classification/sourceCode/spring-dl4j.

Add the following VM options in under run configurations:

```
-DmodelFilePath={PATH-TO-MODEL-FILE}
```

PATH-TO-MODEL-FILE is the location where you stored the actual model file. It can be on your local disk or in a cloud as well.

Then, run the SpringDl4jApplication.java file:

9. Test your Spring Boot app at http://localhost:8080/:

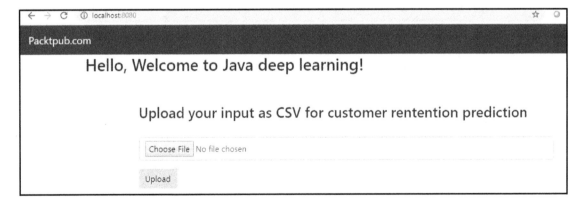

10. Verify the functionality by uploading an input CSV file.

Use a sample CSV file to upload into the web application: `https://github.com/PacktPublishing/Java-Deep-Learning-Cookbook/blob/master/03_Building_Deep_Neural_Networks_for_Binary_classification/sourceCode/cookbookapp/src/main/resources/test.csv`.

The prediction results will be displayed as shown here:

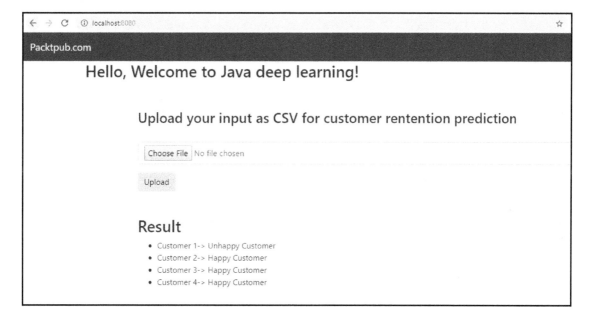

How it works...

We need to create an API to take the inputs from end users and generate the output. The end user will upload a CSV file with the inputs, and API returns the prediction output back to the user.

In step 1, we added schema for the input data. User input should follow the schema structure in which we trained the model except that the `Exited` label is not added because that is the expected task for the trained model. In step 2, we have created `TransformProcess` from `Schema` that was created in step 1.

In step 3, we used `TransformProcess` from step 2 to create a record reader instance. This is to load the data from the dataset.

We expect the end users to upload batches of inputs to generate outcomes. So, an iterator needs to be created as per step 5 to traverse through the entire set of input records. We set the preprocessor for the iterator using the pretrained model from step 4. Also, we used a `batchSize` value of 1. If you have more input samples, you can specify a reasonable batch size.

In step 6, we used a file path named `modelFilePath` to represent the model file location. We pass this as a command-line argument from the Spring application. Thereby you can configure your own custom path where the model file is persisted. After step 7, a shaded JAR with all DL4J dependencies will be created and saved in the local Maven repository. You can also view the JAR file in the project target repository.

Dependencies of customer retention API are added to the `pom.xml` file of the Spring Boot project, as shown here:

```
<dependency>
    <groupId>com.javadeeplearningcookbook.app</groupId>
    <artifactId>cookbookapp</artifactId>
    <version>1.0-SNAPSHOT</version>
</dependency>
```

Once you have created a shaded JAR for the API by following step 7, the Spring Boot project will be able to fetch the dependencies from your local repository. So, you need to build the API project first before importing the Spring Boot project. Also, make sure to add the model file path as a VM argument, as mentioned in step 8.

In a nutshell, these are the steps required to run the use case:

1. Import and build the Customer Churn API project: `https://github.com/PacktPublishing/Java-Deep-Learning-Cookbook/blob/master/03_Building_Deep_Neural_Networks_for_Binary_classification/sourceCode/cookbookapp/`.

2. Run the main example to train the model and persist the model file: `https://github.com/PacktPublishing/Java-Deep-Learning-Cookbook/blob/master/03_Building_Deep_Neural_Networks_for_Binary_classification/sourceCode/cookbookapp/src/main/java/com/javadeeplearningcookbook/examples/CustomerRetentionPredictionExample.java`.

3. Build the customer churn API project: `https://github.com/PacktPublishing/
Java-Deep-Learning-Cookbook/blob/master/03_Building_Deep_Neural_
Networks_for_Binary_classification/sourceCode/cookbookapp/`.

4. Run the Spring Boot project by running the Starter here (with the earlier
mentioned VM arguments): `https://github.com/PacktPublishing/Java-Deep-
Learning-Cookbook/blob/master/03_Building_Deep_Neural_Networks_for_
Binary_classification/sourceCode/spring-dl4j/src/main/java/com/
springdl4j/springdl4j/SpringDl4jApplication.java`.

4

Building Convolutional Neural Networks

In this chapter, we are going to develop a **convolutional neural network** (**CNN**) for an image classification example using DL4J. We will develop the components of our application step by step while we progress through the recipes. The chapter assumes that you have read Chapter 1, *Introduction to Deep Learning in Java*, and Chapter 2, *Data Extraction, Transformation, and Loading*, and that you have set up DL4J on your computer, as mentioned in Chapter 1, *Introduction to Deep Learning in Java*. Let's go ahead and discuss the specific changes required for this chapter.

For demonstration purposes, we will have classifications for four different species. CNNs convert complex images into an abstract format that can be used for prediction. Hence, a CNN would be an optimal choice for this image classification problem.

CNNs are just like any other deep neural network that abstracts the decision process and gives us an interface to transform input to output. The only difference is that they support other types of layers and different orderings of layers. Unlike other forms of input, such as text or CSV, images are complex. Considering the fact that each pixel is a source of information, training will become resource intensive and time consuming for large numbers of high-resolution images.

In this chapter, we will cover the following recipes:

- Extracting images from disk
- Creating image variations for training data
- Image preprocessing and the design of input layers
- Constructing hidden layers for a CNN
- Constructing output layers for output classification
- Training images and evaluating CNN output
- Creating an API endpoint for the image classifier

Technical requirements

Implementation of the use case discussed in this chapter can be found here: `https://github.com/PacktPublishing/Java-Deep-Learning-Cookbook/tree/master/04_Building_Convolutional_Neural_Networks/sourceCode`.

After cloning our GitHub repository, navigate to the following directory: `Java-Deep-Learning-Cookbook/04_Building_Convolutional_Neural_Networks/sourceCode`. Then, import the `cookbookapp` project as a Maven project by importing `pom.xml`.

You will also find a basic Spring project, `spring-dl4j`, which can be imported as a Maven project as well.

We will be using the dog breeds classification dataset from Oxford for this chapter.

The principal dataset can be downloaded from the following link: `https://www.kaggle.com/zippyz/cats-and-dogs-breeds-classification-oxford-dataset`.

To run this chapter's source code, download the dataset (four labels only) from here: `https://github.com/PacktPublishing/Java-Deep-Learning-Cookbook/raw/master/04_Building%20Convolutional%20Neural%20Networks/dataset.zip` (it can be found in the `Java-Deep-Learning-Cookbook/04_Building Convolutional Neural Networks/` directory).

Extract the compressed dataset file. Images are kept in different directories. Each directory represents a label/category. For demonstration purposes, we have used four labels. However, you are allowed to experiment with more images from different categories in order to run our example from GitHub.

Note that our example is optimized for four species. Experimentation with a larger number of labels requires further network configuration optimization.

To leverage the capabilities of the OpenCV library in your CNN, add the following Maven dependency:

```
<dependency>
 <groupId>org.bytedeco.javacpp-presets</groupId>
 <artifactId>opencv-platform</artifactId>
 <version>4.0.1-1.4.4</version>
</dependency>
```

We will be using the Google Cloud SDK to deploy the application in the cloud. For instructions in this regard, refer to `https://github.com/GoogleCloudPlatform/app-maven-plugin`. For Gradle instructions, refer to `https://github.com/GoogleCloudPlatform/app-gradle-plugin`.

Extracting images from disk

For classification based on *N* labels, there are *N* subdirectories created in the parent directory. The parent directory path is mentioned for image extraction. Subdirectory names will be regarded as labels. In this recipe, we will extract images from disk using DataVec.

How to do it...

1. Use `FileSplit` to define the range of files to load into the neural network:

```
FileSplit fileSplit = new FileSplit(parentDir,
NativeImageLoader.ALLOWED_FORMATS,new Random(42));
 int numLabels =
fileSplit.getRootDir().listFiles(File::isDirectory).length;
```

2. Use `ParentPathLabelGenerator` and `BalancedPathFilter` to sample the labeled dataset and split it into train/test sets:

```
ParentPathLabelGenerator parentPathLabelGenerator = new
ParentPathLabelGenerator();
 BalancedPathFilter balancedPathFilter = new BalancedPathFilter(new
Random(42),NativeImageLoader.ALLOWED_FORMATS,parentPathLabelGenerat
or);
 InputSplit[] inputSplits =
fileSplit.sample(balancedPathFilter,trainSetRatio,testSetRatio);
```

How it works...

In step 1, we used `FileSplit` to filter the images based on the file type (PNG, JPEG, TIFF, and so on).

We also passed in a random number generator based on a single seed. This seed value is an integer (`42` in our example). `FileSplit` will be able to generate a list of file paths in random order (random order of files) by making use of a random seed. This will introduce more randomness to the probabilistic decision and thereby increase the model's performance (accuracy metrics).

If you have a ready-made dataset with an unknown number of labels, it is crucial to calculate `numLabels`. Hence, we used `FileSplit` to calculate them programmatically:

```
int numLabels = fileSplit.getRootDir().listFiles(File::isDirectory).length;
```

In step 2, we used `ParentPathLabelGenerator` to generate the label for files based on the directory path. Also, `BalancedPathFilter` is used to randomize the order of paths in an array. Randomization will help overcome overfitting issues. `BalancedPathFilter` also ensures the same number of paths for each label and helps to obtain optimal batches for training.

With `testSetRatio` as `20`, 20 percent of the dataset will be used as the test set for the model evaluation. After step 2, the array elements in `inputSplits` will represent the train/test datasets:

- `inputSplits[0]` will represent the train dataset.
- `inputSplits[1]` will represent the test dataset.

- `NativeImageLoader.ALLOWED_FORMATS` uses `JavaCV` to load images. Allowed image formats are `.bmp`, `.gif`, `.jpg`, `.jpeg`, `.jp2`, `.pbm`, `.pgm`, `.ppm`, `.pnm`, `.png`, `.tif`, `.tiff`, `.exr`, and `.webp`.
- `BalancedPathFilter` randomizes the order of file paths in an array and removes them randomly to have the same number of paths for each label. It will also form the paths on the output based on their labels, so as to obtain easily optimal batches for training. So, it is more than just random sampling.
- `fileSplit.sample()` samples the file paths based on the path filter mentioned.

It will further split the results into an array of `InputSplit` objects. Each object will refer to the train/test set, and its size is proportional to the weights mentioned.

Creating image variations for training data

We create image variations and further train our network model on top of them to increase the generalization power of the CNN. It is crucial to train our CNN with as many image variations as possible so as to increase the accuracy. We basically obtain more samples of the same image by flipping or rotating them. In this recipe, we will transform and create samples of images using a concrete implementation of `ImageTransform` in DL4J.

How to do it...

1. Use `FlipImageTransform` to flip the images horizontally or vertically (randomly or not randomly):

```
ImageTransform flipTransform = new FlipImageTransform(new
Random(seed));
```

2. Use `WarpImageTransform` to warp the perspective of images deterministically or randomly:

```
ImageTransform warpTransform = new WarpImageTransform(new
Random(seed),delta);
```

3. Use `RotateImageTransform` to rotate the images deterministically or randomly:

```
ImageTransform rotateTransform = new RotateImageTransform(new
Random(seed), angle);
```

4. Use `PipelineImageTransform` to add image transformations to the pipeline:

```
List<Pair<ImageTransform,Double>> pipeline = Arrays.asList(
 new Pair<>(flipTransform, flipImageTransformRatio),
 new Pair<>(warpTransform , warpImageTransformRatio)
 );
ImageTransform transform = new PipelineImageTransform(pipeline);
```

How it works...

In step 1, if we don't need a random flip but a specified mode of flip (deterministic), then we can do the following:

```
int flipMode = 0;
ImageTransform flipTransform = new FlipImageTransform(flipMode);
```

`flipMode` is the deterministic flip mode.

- `flipMode = 0`: Flips around the x axis
- `flipMode > 0`: Flips around the y axis
- `flipMode < 0`: Flips around both axes

In step 2, we passed in two attributes: `Random(seed)` and `delta`. `delta` is the magnitude in which an image is warped. Check the following image sample for the demonstration of image warping:

(Image source: https://commons.wikimedia.org/wiki/File:Image_warping_example.jpg
License: CC BY-SA 3.0)

`WarpImageTransform(new Random(seed),delta)` internally calls the following constructor:

```
public WarpImageTransform(java.util.Random random,
  float dx1,
  float dy1,
  float dx2,
  float dy2,
  float dx3,
  float dy3,
  float dx4,
  float dy4
```

It will assume `dx1=dy1=dx2=dy2=dx3=dy3=dx4=dy4=delta`.

Here are the parameter descriptions:

- `dx1`: Maximum warping in x for the top-left corner (pixels)
- `dy1`: Maximum warping in y for the top-left corner (pixels)
- `dx2`: Maximum warping in x for the top-right corner (pixels)
- `dy2`: Maximum warping in y for the top-right corner (pixels)
- `dx3`: Maximum warping in x for the bottom-right corner (pixels)
- `dy3`: Maximum warping in y for the bottom-right corner (pixels)
- `dx4`: Maximum warping in x for the bottom-left corner (pixels)
- `dy4`: Maximum warping in y for the bottom-left corner (pixels)

The value of delta will be auto adjusted as per the normalized width/height while creating `ImageRecordReader`. This means that the given value of delta will be treated relative to the normalized width/height specified while creating `ImageRecordReader`. So, let's say we perform 10 pixels of warping across the *x/y* axis in an image with a size of 100 x 100. If the image is normalized to a size of 30 x 30, then 3 pixels of warping will happen across the *x/y* axis. You need to experiment with different values for `delta` since there's no constant/min/max `delta` value that can solve all types of image classification problems.

In step 3, we used `RotateImageTransform` to perform rotational image transformations by rotating the image samples on the angle mentioned.

In step 4, we added multiple image transformations with the help of `PipelineImageTransform` into a pipeline to load them sequentially or randomly for training purposes. We have created a pipeline with the `List<Pair<ImageTransform,Double>>` type. The `Double` value in `Pair` is the *probability* that the particular element (`ImageTransform`) in the pipeline is executed.

Image transformations will help CNN to learn image patterns better. Training on top of transformed images will further avoid the chances of overfitting.

There's more...

`WarpImageTransform` under the hood makes an internal call to the JavaCPP method, `warpPerspective()`, with the given properties, `interMode`, `borderMode`, and `borderValue`. JavaCPP is an API that parses native C/C++ files and generates Java interfaces to act as a wrapper. We added the JavaCPP dependency for OpenCV in `pom.xml` earlier. This will enable us to exploit OpenCV libraries for image transformation.

Image preprocessing and the design of input layers

Normalization is a crucial preprocessing step for a CNN, just like for any feed forward networks. Image data is complex. Each image has several pixels of information. Also, each pixel is a source of information. We need to normalize this pixel value so that the neural network will not overfit/underfit while training. Convolution/subsampling layers also need to be specified while designing input layers for CNN. In this recipe, we will normalize and then design input layers for the CNN.

How to do it...

1. Create `ImagePreProcessingScaler` for image normalization:

    ```
    DataNormalization scaler = new ImagePreProcessingScaler(0,1);
    ```

2. Create a neural network configuration and add default hyperparameters:

    ```
    MultiLayerConfiguration.Builder builder = new
    NeuralNetConfiguration.Builder().weightInit(WeightInit.DISTRIBUTION
    )
      .dist(new NormalDistribution(0.0, 0.01))
      .activation(Activation.RELU)
      .updater(new Nesterovs(new StepSchedule(ScheduleType.ITERATION,
    1e-2, 0.1, 100000), 0.9))
      .biasUpdater(new Nesterovs(new
    ```

```
StepSchedule(ScheduleType.ITERATION, 2e-2, 0.1, 100000), 0.9))
.gradientNormalization(GradientNormalization.RenormalizeL2PerLayer)
// normalize to prevent vanishing or exploding gradients
.l2(l2RegularizationParam)
.list();
```

3. Create convolution layers for a CNN using `ConvolutionLayer`:

```
builder.layer(new ConvolutionLayer.Builder(11,11)
.nIn(channels)
.nOut(96)
.stride(1,1)
.activation(Activation.RELU)
.build());
```

4. Configure subsampling layers using `SubsamplingLayer`:

```
builder.layer(new SubsamplingLayer.Builder(PoolingType.MAX)
.kernelSize(kernelSize,kernelSize)
.build());
```

5. Normalize activation between layers using `LocalResponseNormalization`:

```
builder.layer(1, new
LocalResponseNormalization.Builder().name("lrn1").build());
```

How it works...

In step 1, `ImagePreProcessingScaler` normalizes the pixels in a specified range of values (0, 1) . We will use this normalizer once we create iterators for the data.

In step 2, we have added hyperparameters such as an L2 regularization coefficient, a gradient normalization strategy, a gradient update algorithm, and an activation function globally (applicable for all layers).

In step 3, `ConvolutionLayer` requires you to mention the kernel dimensions (11*11 for the previous code). A kernel acts as a feature detector in the context of a CNN:

- `stride`: Directs the space between each sample in an operation on a pixel grid.
- `channels`: The number of input neurons. We mention the number of color channels here (RGB: 3).
- `OutGoingConnectionCount`: The number of output neurons.

In step 4, `SubsamplingLayer` is a downsampling layer to reduce the amount of data to be transmitted or stored, and, at the same time, keep the significant features intact. Max pooling is the most commonly used sampling method. `ConvolutionLayer` is always followed by `SubsamplingLayer`.

Efficiency is a challenging task in the case of a CNN. It requires a lot of images, along with transformations, to train better. In step 4, `LocalResponseNormalization` improves the generalization power of a CNN. It performs a normalization operation right before performing ReLU activation

We add this as a separate layer placed between a convolution layer and a subsampling layer:

- `ConvolutionLayer` is similar to a feed forward layer, but for performing two-dimensional convolution on images.
- `SubsamplingLayer` is required for pooling/downsampling in CNNs.
- `ConvolutionLayer` and `SubsamplingLayer` together form the input layers for a CNN and extract abstract features from images and pass them to the hidden layers for further processing.

Constructing hidden layers for a CNN

The input layers of a CNN produce abstract images and pass them to hidden layers. The abstract image features are passed from input layers to the hidden layers. If there are multiple hidden layers in your CNN, then each of them will have unique responsibilities for the prediction. For example, one of them can detect lights and dark in the image, and the following layer can detect edges/shapes with the help of the preceding hidden layer. The next layer can then discern more complex objects from the edges/recipes from the preceding hidden layer, and so on.

In this recipe, we will design hidden layers for our image classification problem.

How to do it...

1. Build hidden layers using `DenseLayer`:

```
new DenseLayer.Builder()
 .nOut(nOut)
 .dist(new NormalDistribution(0.001, 0.005))
 .activation(Activation.RELU)
 .build();
```

2. Add `AddDenseLayer` to the layer structure by calling `layer()`:

```
builder.layer(new DenseLayer.Builder()
 .nOut(500)
 .dist(new NormalDistribution(0.001, 0.005))
 .activation(Activation.RELU)
 .build());
```

How it works...

In step 1, hidden layers are created using `DenseLayer`, which are preceded by convolution/subsampling layers.

In step 2, note that we didn't mention the number of input neurons in hidden layers, since it would be same as the preceding layer's (`SubSamplingLayer`) outgoing neurons.

Constructing output layers for output classification

We need to perform image classification using logistic regression (`SOFTMAX`), resulting in probabilities of occurrence for each of the image labels. Logistic regression is a predictive analysis algorithm and, hence, more suitable for prediction problems. In this recipe, we will design output layers for the image classification problem.

How to do it...

1. Design the output layer using `OutputLayer`:

```
builder.layer(new
OutputLayer.Builder(LossFunctions.LossFunction.NEGATIVELOGLIKELIHOO
D)
  .nOut(numLabels)
  .activation(Activation.SOFTMAX)
  .build());
```

2. Set the input type using `setInputType()`:

```
builder.setInputType(InputType.convolutional(30,30,3));
```

How it works...

In step 1, `nOut()` expects the number of image labels that we calculated using `FileSplit` in an earlier recipe.

In step 2, we have used `setInputType()` to set the convolutional input type. This will trigger computation/settings of the input neurons and add preprocessors (`LocalResponseNormalization`) to handle data flow from the convolutional/subsampling layers to the dense layers.

The `InputType` class is used to track and define the types of activations. This is most useful for automatically adding preprocessors between layers, and automatically setting `nIn` (number of input neurons) values. That's how we skipped specifying `nIn` values earlier when configuring the model. The convolutional input type is four-dimensional in shape `[miniBatchSize, channels, height, width]`.

Training images and evaluating CNN output

We have layer configurations in place. Now, we need to train the CNN to make it suitable for predictions. In a CNN, filter values will be adjusted during the training process. The network will learn by itself how to choose proper filters (feature maps) to produce the best results. We will also see that the efficiency and performance of the CNN becomes a challenging task because of the complexity involved in computation. In this recipe, we will train and evaluate our CNN model.

How to do it...

1. Load and initialize the training data using `ImageRecordReader`:

```
ImageRecordReader imageRecordReader = new
ImageRecordReader(imageHeight,imageWidth,channels,parentPathLabelGe
nerator);
 imageRecordReader.initialize(trainData,null);
```

2. Create a dataset iterator using `RecordReaderDataSetIterator`:

```
DataSetIterator dataSetIterator = new
RecordReaderDataSetIterator(imageRecordReader,batchSize,1,numLabels
);
```

3. Add the normalizer to the dataset iterator:

```
DataNormalization scaler = new ImagePreProcessingScaler(0,1);
 scaler.fit(dataSetIterator);
 dataSetIterator.setPreProcessor(scaler);
```

4. Train the model by calling `fit()`:

```
MultiLayerConfiguration config = builder.build();
 MultiLayerNetwork model = new MultiLayerNetwork(config);
 model.init();
 model.setListeners(new ScoreIterationListener(100));
 model.fit(dataSetIterator,epochs);
```

5. Train the model again with image transformations:

```
imageRecordReader.initialize(trainData,transform);
 dataSetIterator = new
RecordReaderDataSetIterator(imageRecordReader,batchSize,1,numLabels
);
 scaler.fit(dataSetIterator);
 dataSetIterator.setPreProcessor(scaler);
 model.fit(dataSetIterator,epochs);
```

6. Evaluate the model and observe the results:

```
Evaluation evaluation = model.evaluate(dataSetIterator);
 System.out.println(evaluation.stats());
```

The evaluation metrics will appear as follows:

```
=======================Evaluation Metrics=======================
# of classes:     4
Accuracy:         0.3462
Precision:        0.3625
Recall:           0.3487
F1 Score:         0.3418
Precision, recall & F1: macro-averaged (equally weighted avg. of 4 classes)


=======================Confusion Matrix=======================
 0 1 2 3
---------
 7 2 3 8 | 0 = American Bull Dog
 3 7 7 2 | 1 = Basset Hound
 2 5 310 | 2 = Beagle
 0 7 210 | 3 = Boxer

Confusion matrix format: Actual (rowClass) predicted as (columnClass) N times
=====================================================]
```

7. Add support for the GPU-accelerated environment by adding the following dependencies:

```xml
<dependency>
  <groupId>org.nd4j</groupId>
  <artifactId>nd4j-cuda-9.1-platform</artifactId>
  <version>1.0.0-beta3</version>
</dependency>

<dependency>
  <groupId>org.deeplearning4j</groupId>
  <artifactId>deeplearning4j-cuda-9.1</artifactId>
  <version>1.0.0-beta3</version>
</dependency>
```

How it works...

In step 1, the parameters included are as follows:

- `parentPathLabelGenerator`—created during the data extraction stage (see the *Extracting images from disk* recipe in this chapter).
- `channels`—The number of color channels (default = 3 for RGB).

- `ImageRecordReader(imageHeight, imageWidth, channels, parentPathLabelGenerator)`—resize the actual image to the specified size (`imageHeight, imageWidth`) to reduce the data loading effort.
- The null attribute in the `initialize()` method is to indicate that we are not training transformed images.

In step 3, we use `ImagePreProcessingScaler` for min-max normalization. Note that we need to use both `fit()` and `setPreProcessor()` to apply normalization to the data.

For GPU-accelerated environments, we can use `PerformanceListener` instead of `ScoreIterationListener` in step 4 to optimize the training process further. `PerformanceListener` tracks the time spent on training per iteration, while `ScoreIterationListener` reports the score of the network every *N* iterations during training. Make sure that GPU dependencies are added as per step 7.

In step 5, we have trained the model again with the image transformations that were created earlier. Make sure to apply normalization to the transformed images as well.

There's more...

Our CNN has an accuracy of around 50%. We trained our neural network using 396 images across 4 categories. For an i7 processor with 8 GB of RAM, it will take 15-30 minutes to complete the training. This can vary depending on the applications that are running parallel to the training instance. Training time can also change depending on the quality of the hardware. You will observe better evaluation metrics if you train with more images. More data will contribute toward better predictions. And, of course, it demands extended training time.

Another important aspect is to experiment with the number of hidden layers and subsampling/convolution layers to give you the optimal results. Too many layers could result in overfitting, hence, you really have to experiment by adding a different number of layers to your network configuration. Do not add large values for `stride`, or overly small dimensions for the images. That may cause excessive downsampling and will result in feature loss.

We can also try different values for the weights or how weights are distributed across neurons and test different gradient normalization strategies, applying L2 regularization and dropouts. There is no rule of thumb to choose a constant value for L1/L2 regularization or for dropouts. However, the L2 regularization constant takes a smaller value as it forces the weights to decay toward zero. Neural networks can safely accommodate dropout of 10-20 percent, beyond which it can actually cause underfitting. There is no constant value that will apply in every instance, as it varies from case to case:

```
MultiLayerConfiguration config;
config = new NeuralNetConfiguration.Builder()
    .weightInit(WeightInit.DISTRIBUTION)
    .dist(new NormalDistribution( mean 0.0,  std 0.01))
    .activation(Activation.RELU)
    .updater(new Nesterovs(new StepSchedule(ScheduleType.ITERATION,  initialValue: 1e-2,  decayRate 0.1,  step 100000),  momentum 0.9
    .biasUpdater(new Nesterovs(new StepSchedule(ScheduleType.ITERATION,  initialValue: 2e-2,  decayRate 0.1,  step 100000),  momentum
    .gradientNormalization(GradientNormalization.RenormalizeL2PerLayer) // normalize to prevent vanishing or exploding gradients
    .l2(5 * 1e-4)
    // .weightInit(WeightInit.XAVIER)
    // .updater(new Nesterovs(0.008D,0.9D))
    .list()
    .layer(new ConvolutionLayer.Builder( .kernelSize 11,11)
        .nIn(channels)
        .nOut(96)
        .stride(1,1)
        .activation(Activation.RELU)
        .build())
    .layer( ind 1, new LocalResponseNormalization.Builder().name("lrn1").build())
    .layer(new SubsamplingLayer.Builder(PoolingType.MAX)
        .kernelSize(3,3)
        .build())
```

A GPU-accelerated environment will help decrease the training time. DL4J supports CUDA, and it can be accelerated further using cuDNN. Most two-dimensional CNN layers (such as `ConvolutionLayer` and `SubsamplingLayer`) support cuDNN.

The NVIDIA **CUDA Deep Neural Network** (**cuDNN**) library is a GPU-accelerated library of primitives for deep learning networks. You can read more about cuDNN here: `https://developer.nvidia.com/cudnn`.

Creating an API endpoint for the image classifier

We want to leverage the image classifier as an API to use them in external applications. An API can be accessed externally, and prediction results can be obtained without setting up anything. In this recipe, we will create an API endpoint for the image classifier.

How to do it...

1. Persist the model using `ModelSerializer`:

```
File file = new File("cnntrainedmodel.zip");
ModelSerializer.writeModel(model,file,true);
ModelSerializer.addNormalizerToModel(file,scaler);
```

2. Restore the trained model using `ModelSerializer` to perform predictions:

```
MultiLayerNetwork network =
ModelSerializer.restoreMultiLayerNetwork(modelFile);
NormalizerStandardize normalizerStandardize =
ModelSerializer.restoreNormalizerFromFile(modelFile);
```

3. Design an API method that accepts inputs from users and returns results. An example API method would look like the following:

```
public static INDArray generateOutput(File file) throws
IOException, InterruptedException {
  final File modelFile = new File("cnnmodel.zip");
  final MultiLayerNetwork model =
ModelSerializer.restoreMultiLayerNetwork(modelFile);
  final RecordReader imageRecordReader = generateReader(file);
  final NormalizerStandardize normalizerStandardize =
ModelSerializer.restoreNormalizerFromFile(modelFile);
  final DataSetIterator dataSetIterator = new
RecordReaderDataSetIterator.Builder(imageRecordReader,1).build();
  normalizerStandardize.fit(dataSetIterator);
  dataSetIterator.setPreProcessor(normalizerStandardize);
  return model.output(dataSetIterator);
  }
```

4. Create a URI mapping to service client requests, as shown in the following example:

```
@GetMapping("/")
 public String main(final Model model){
 model.addAttribute("message", "Welcome to Java deep learning!");
 return "welcome";
 }

@PostMapping("/")
 public String fileUpload(final Model model, final
@RequestParam("uploadFile")MultipartFile multipartFile) throws
IOException, InterruptedException {
 final List<String> results =
```

```
cookBookService.generateStringOutput(multipartFile);
 model.addAttribute("message", "Welcome to Java deep learning!");
 model.addAttribute("results",results);
 return "welcome";
 }
```

5. Build a `cookbookapp-cnn` project and add the API dependency to your Spring project:

```
<dependency>
 <groupId>com.javadeeplearningcookbook.app</groupId>
 <artifactId>cookbookapp-cnn</artifactId>
 <version>1.0-SNAPSHOT</version>
 </dependency>
```

6. Create the `generateStringOutput()` method in the service layer to serve API content:

```
@Override
 public List<String> generateStringOutput(MultipartFile
multipartFile) throws IOException, InterruptedException {
 //TODO: MultiPartFile to File conversion (multipartFile ->
convFile)
 INDArray indArray = ImageClassifierAPI.generateOutput(convFile);

 for(int i=0; i<indArray.rows();i++){
         for(int j=0;j<indArray.columns();j++){
                 DecimalFormat df2 = new DecimalFormat("#.####");
results.add(df2.format(indArray.getDouble(i,j)*100)+"%");
                 //Later add them from list to the model display on
UI.
             }
         }
  convFile.deleteOnExit();
   return results;
 }
```

7. Download and install the Google Cloud SDK: https://cloud.google.com/sdk/.

8. Install the Cloud SDK `app-engine-java` component by running the following command on the Google Cloud console:

```
gcloud components install app-engine-java
```

9. Log in and configure Cloud SDK using the following command:

```
gcloud init
```

10. Add the following dependency for Maven App Engine in `pom.xml`:

```
<plugin>
 <groupId>com.google.cloud.tools</groupId>
 <artifactId>appengine-maven-plugin</artifactId>
 <version>2.1.0</version>
 </plugin>
```

11. Create an `app.yaml` file in your project as per the Google Cloud documentation: `https://cloud.google.com/appengine/docs/flexible/java/configuring-your-app-with-app-yaml`.

12. Navigate to Google App Engine and click on the **Create Application** button:

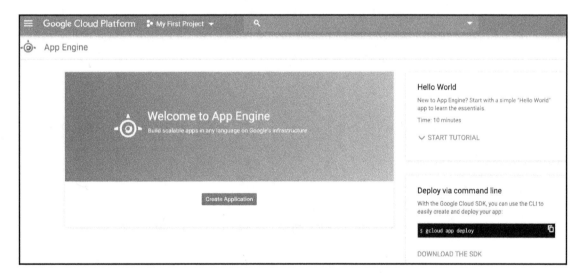

13. Pick a region and click on **Create app**:

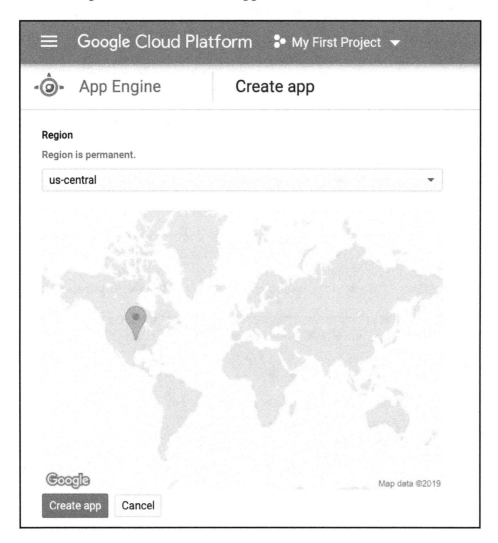

14. Select **Java** and click the **Next** button:

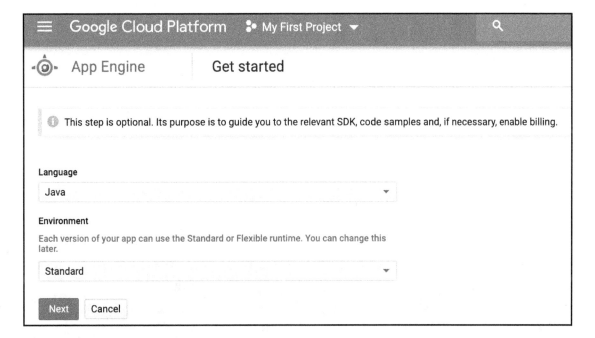

Now, your app engine has been created at Google Cloud.

15. Build the spring boot application using Maven:

```
mvn clean install
```

16. Deploy the application using the following command:

```
mvn appengine:deploy
```

How it works...

In step 1 and step 2, we have persisted the model to reuse the model capabilities in API.

In step 3, an API method is created to accept user inputs and return the results from the image classifier.

In step 4, the URI mappings will accept client requests (GET/POST). A GET request will serve the home page at the very beginning. A POST request will serve the end user request for image classification.

In step 5, we added an API dependency to the `pom.xml` file. For demonstration purposes, we build the API JAR file and the JAR file is stored in the local Maven repository. For production, you need to submit your API (JAR file) in a private repository so that Maven can fetch it from there.

In step 6, we are calling the ImageClassifier API at our Spring Boot application service layer to retrieve the results and return them to the controller class.

In the previous chapter, we deployed the application locally for demonstration purposes. In this chapter, we have deployed the application in Google Cloud. Steps 7 to 16 are dedicated to deployment in Google Cloud.

We have used Google App Engine, although we can set up the same thing in more customized ways using Google Compute Engine or Dataproc. Dataproc is designed to deploy your application in a Spark distributed environment.

Once deployment is successful, you should see something like the following:

```
5a2c5095ccal: waiting
1e73997959b4: Layer already exists
269898bd648c: Layer already exists
8466a968f110: Layer already exists
8261521a4d83: Layer already exists
ac0f931ff2d8: Layer already exists
fe63816dcc7d: Layer already exists
5a2c5095ccal: Layer already exists
ffa07944dec4: Pushed
latest: digest: sha256:ebff8273190d731a6d447f41fb19e104695e297f35b51c87c9a2585b50e29d9f size: 1998
DONE
--------------------------------------------------------------------------------
Updating service [default]...
................................................................................
.....done.
Updating service [default]...
waiting for operation [apps/practical-theme-183616/operations/e1c0129d-13ae-4d0a-a095-f7a0cd81a871] to complete...
...............done.
done.
Deployed service [default] to [https            -            .appspot.com]
```

When you hit the URL (which starts with `https://xx.appspot.com`), you should be able to see the web page (the same as in the previous chapter) where end users can upload images for image classification.

5
Implementing Natural Language Processing

In this chapter, we will discuss word vectors (Word2Vec) and paragraph vectors (Doc2Vec) in DL4J. We will develop a complete running example step by step, covering all the stages, such as ETL, model configuration, training, and evaluation. Word2Vec and Doc2Vec are **natural language processing** (**NLP**) implementations in DL4J. It is worth mentioning a little about the bag-of-words algorithm before we talk about Word2Vec.

Bag-of-words is an algorithm that counts the instances of words in documents. This will allow us to perform document classification. Bag of words and Word2Vec are just two different types of text classification. **Word2Vec** can use a bag of words extracted from a document to create vectors. In addition to these text classification methods, **term frequency–inverse document frequency** (**TF-IDF**) can be used to judge the topic/context of the document. In the case of TF-IDF, a score will be calculated for all the words, and word counts will be replaced with this score. TF-IDF is a simple scoring scheme, but word embeddings may be a better choice, as the semantic similarity can be captured by word embedding. Also, if your dataset is small and the context is domain-specific, then bag of words may be a better choice than Word2Vec.

Word2Vec is a two-layer neural network that processes text. It converts the text corpus to vectors.

Note that Word2Vec is not a **deep neural network** (**DNN**). It transforms text data into a numerical format that a DNN can understand, making customization possible.

We can even combine Word2Vec with DNNs to serve this purpose. It doesn't train the input words through reconstruction; instead, it trains words using the neighboring words in the corpus.

Doc2Vec (paragraph vectors) associates documents with labels, and is an extension of Word2Vec. Word2Vec tries to correlate words with words, while Doc2Vec (paragraph vectors) correlates words with labels. Once we represent documents in vector formats, we can then use these formats as an input to a supervised learning algorithm to map these vectors to labels.

In this chapter, we will cover the following recipes:

- Reading and loading text data
- Tokenizing data and training the model
- Evaluating the model
- Generating plots from the model
- Saving and reloading the model
- Importing Google News vectors
- Troubleshooting and tuning Word2Vec models
- Using Word2Vec for sentence classification using CNNs
- Using Doc2Vec for document classification

Technical requirements

The examples discussed in this chapter can be found at `https://github.com/PacktPublishing/Java-Deep-Learning-Cookbook/tree/master/05_Implementing_NLP/sourceCode/cookbookapp/src/main/java/com/javadeeplearningcookbook/examples`.

After cloning our GitHub repository, navigate to the directory called `Java-Deep-Learning-Cookbook/05_Implementing_NLP/sourceCode`. Then, import the `cookbookapp` project as a Maven project by importing `pom.xml`.

To get started with NLP in DL4J, add the following Maven dependency in `pom.xml`:

```
<dependency>
 <groupId>org.deeplearning4j</groupId>
 <artifactId>deeplearning4j-nlp</artifactId>
 <version>1.0.0-beta3</version>
 </dependency>
```

Data requirements

The project directory has a `resource` folder with the required data for the `LineIterator` examples:

For `CnnWord2VecSentenceClassificationExample` or `GoogleNewsVectorExampleYou`, you can download datasets from the following URLs:

- **Google News vector**:
  https://deeplearning4jblob.blob.core.windows.net/resources/wordvectors
  /GoogleNews-vectors-negative300.bin.gz
- **IMDB review data**: http://ai.stanford.edu/~amaas/data/sentiment/
  aclImdb_v1.tar.gz

Note that IMDB review data needs to be extracted twice in order to get the actual dataset folder.

For the **t-Distributed Stochastic Neighbor Embedding** (**t-SNE**) visualization example, the required data (`words.txt`) can be located in the project root directory itself.

Reading and loading text data

We need to load raw sentences in text format and iterate them using an underlined iterator that serves the purpose. A text corpus can also be subjected to preprocessing, such as lowercase conversion. Stop words can be mentioned while configuring the Word2Vec model. In this recipe, we will extract and load text data from various data-input scenarios.

Getting ready

Select an iterator approach from step 1 to step 5 depending on what kind of data you're looking for and how you want to load it.

How to do it...

1. Create a sentence iterator using `BasicLineIterator`:

```
File file = new File("raw_sentences.txt");
SentenceIterator iterator = new BasicLineIterator(file);
```

For an example, go to `https://github.com/PacktPublishing/Java-Deep-Learning-Cookbook/blob/master/05_Implementing_NLP/sourceCode/cookbookapp/src/main/java/com/javadeeplearningcookbook/examples/BasicLineIteratorExample.java`.

2. Create a sentence iterator using `LineSentenceIterator`:

```
File file = new File("raw_sentences.txt");
SentenceIterator iterator = new LineSentenceIterator(file);
```

For an example, go to `https://github.com/PacktPublishing/Java-Deep-Learning-Cookbook/blob/master/05_Implementing_NLP/sourceCode/cookbookapp/src/main/java/com/javadeeplearningcookbook/examples/LineSentenceIteratorExample.java`.

3. Create a sentence iterator using `CollectionSentenceIterator`:

```
List<String> sentences= Arrays.asList("sample text", "sample text",
"sample text");
SentenceIterator iter = new CollectionSentenceIterator(sentences);
```

For an example, go to `https://github.com/PacktPublishing/Java-Deep-Learning-Cookbook/blob/master/05_Implementing_NLP/sourceCode/cookbookapp/src/main/java/com/javadeeplearningcookbook/examples/CollectionSentenceIteratorExample.java`.

4. Create a sentence iterator using `FileSentenceIterator`:

```
SentenceIterator iter = new FileSentenceIterator(new
File("/home/downloads/sentences.txt"));
```

For an example, go to `https://github.com/PacktPublishing/Java-Deep-Learning-Cookbook/blob/master/05_Implementing_NLP/sourceCode/cookbookapp/src/main/java/com/javadeeplearningcookbook/examples/FileSentenceIteratorExample.java`.

5. Create a sentence iterator using `UimaSentenceIterator`.

Add the following Maven dependency:

```
<dependency>
 <groupId>org.deeplearning4j</groupId>
 <artifactId>deeplearning4j-nlp-uima</artifactId>
 <version>1.0.0-beta3</version>
</dependency>
```

Then use the iterator, as shown here:

```
SentenceIterator iterator =
UimaSentenceIterator.create("path/to/your/text/documents");
```

You can also use it like this:

```
SentenceIterator iter =
UimaSentenceIterator.create("path/to/your/text/documents");
```

For an example, go to `https://github.com/PacktPublishing/Java-Deep-Learning-Cookbook/blob/master/05_Implementing_NLP/sourceCode/cookbookapp/src/main/java/com/javadeeplearningcookbook/examples/UimaSentenceIteratorExample.java`.

6. Apply the preprocessor to the text corpus:

```
iterator.setPreProcessor(new SentencePreProcessor() {
 @Override
 public String preProcess(String sentence) {
 return sentence.toLowerCase();
 }
});
```

For an example, go to `https://github.com/PacktPublishing/Java-Deep-Learning-Cookbook/blob/master/05_Implementing_NLP/sourceCode/cookbookapp/src/main/java/com/javadeeplearningcookbook/examples/SentenceDataPreProcessor.java`.

How it works...

In step 1, we used `BasicLineIterator`, which is a basic, single-line sentence iterator without any customization involved.

In step 2, we used `LineSentenceIterator` to iterate through multi-sentence text data. Each line is considered a sentence here. We can use them for multiple lines of text.

In step 3, `CollectionSentenceIterator` will accept a list of strings as text input where each string represents a sentence (document). This can be a list of tweets or articles.

In step 4, `FileSentenceIterator` processes sentences in a file/directory. Sentences will be processed line by line from each file.

For anything complex, we recommend that you use `UimaSentenceIterator`, which is a proper machine learning level pipeline. It iterates over a set of files and segments the sentences. The `UimaSentenceIterator` pipeline can perform tokenization, lemmatization, and part-of-speech tagging. The behavior can be customized based on the analysis engines that are passed on. This iterator is the best fit for complex data, such as data returned from the Twitter API. An analysis engine is a text-processing pipeline.

 You need to use the `reset()` method if you want to begin the iterator traversal from the beginning after traversing once.

We can normalize the data and remove anomalies by defining a preprocessor on the data iterator. Hence, we defined a normalizer (preprocessor) in step 5.

There's more...

We can also create a sentence iterator using `UimaSentenceIterator` by passing an analysis engine, as shown in the following code:

```
SentenceIterator iterator = new
UimaSentenceIterator(path,AnalysisEngineFactory.createEngine(
AnalysisEngineFactory.createEngineDescription(TokenizerAnnotator.getDescrip
tion(), SentenceAnnotator.getDescription())));
```

The concept of an analysis engine is borrowed from UIMA's text-processing pipeline. DL4J has standard analysis engines available for common tasks that enable further text customization and decide how sentences are defined. Analysis engines are thread safe compared to OpenNLP text-processing pipelines. ClearTK-based pipelines are also used to handle common text-processing tasks in DL4J.

See also

- **UIMA**: http://uima.apache.org/
- **OpenNLP**: http://opennlp.apache.org/

Tokenizing data and training the model

We need to perform tokenization in order to build the Word2Vec models. The context of a sentence (document) is determined by the words in it. Word2Vec models require words rather than sentences (documents) to feed in, so we need to break the sentence into atomic units and create a token each time a white space is hit. DL4J has a tokenizer factory that is responsible for creating the tokenizer. The `TokenizerFactory` generates a tokenizer for the given string. In this recipe, we will tokenize the text data and train the Word2Vec model on top of them.

How to do it...

1. Create a tokenizer factory and set the token preprocessor:

```
TokenizerFactory tokenFactory = new DefaultTokenizerFactory();
tokenFactory.setTokenPreProcessor(new CommonPreprocessor());
```

2. Add the tokenizer factory to the Word2Vec model configuration:

```
Word2Vec model = new Word2Vec.Builder()
 .minWordFrequency(wordFrequency)
 .layerSize(numFeatures)
 .seed(seed)
 .epochs(numEpochs)
 .windowSize(windowSize)
 .iterate(iterator)
 .tokenizerFactory(tokenFactory)
 .build();
```

3. Train the Word2Vec model:

```
model.fit();
```

How it works...

In step 1, we used `DefaultTokenizerFactory()` to create the tokenizer factory to tokenize the words. This is the default tokenizer for Word2Vec and it is based on a string tokenizer, or stream tokenizer. We also used `CommonPreprocessor` as the token preprocessor. A preprocessor will remove anomalies from the text corpus. The `CommonPreprocessor` is a token preprocessor implementation that removes punctuation marks and converts the text to lowercase. It uses the `toLowerCase(String)` method and its behavior depends on the default locale.

Here are the configurations that we made in step 2:

- `minWordFrequency()`: This is the minimum number of times in which a word must exist in the text corpora. In our example, if a word appears fewer than five times, then it is not learned. Words should occur multiple times in text corpora in order for the model to learn useful features about them. In very large text corpora, it's reasonable to raise the minimum value of word occurrences.
- `layerSize()`: This defines the number of features in a word vector. This is equivalent to the number of dimensions in the feature space. Words represented by 100 features become points in a 100-dimensional space.
- `iterate()`: This specifies the batch on which the training is taking place. We can pass in an iterator to convert to word vectors. In our case, we passed in a sentence iterator.
- `epochs()`: This specifies the number of iterations over the training corpus as a whole.
- `windowSize()`: This defines the context window size.

There's more...

The following are the other tokenizer factory implementations available in DL4J Word2Vec to generate tokenizers for the given input:

- `NGramTokenizerFactory`: This is the tokenizer factory that creates a tokenizer based on the *n*-gram model. N-grams are a combination of contiguous words or letters of length *n* that are present in the text corpus.

- `PosUimaTokenizerFactory`: This creates a tokenizer that filters part of the speech tags.
- `UimaTokenizerFactory`: This creates a tokenizer that uses the UIMA analysis engine for tokenization. The analysis engine performs an inspection of unstructured information, makes a discovery, and represents semantic content. Unstructured information is included, but is not restricted to text documents.

Here are the inbuilt token preprocessors (not including `CommonPreprocessor`) available in DL4J:

- `EndingPreProcessor`: This is a preprocessor that gets rid of word endings in the text corpus—for example, it removes *s*, *ed*, *.*, *ly*, and *ing* from the text.
- `LowCasePreProcessor`: This is a preprocessor that converts text to lowercase format.
- `StemmingPreprocessor`: This tokenizer preprocessor implements basic cleaning inherited from `CommonPreprocessor` and performs English porter stemming on tokens.
- `CustomStemmingPreprocessor`: This is the stemming preprocessor that is compatible with different stemming processors defined as lucene/tartarus `SnowballProgram`, such as `RussianStemmer`, `DutchStemmer`, and `FrenchStemmer`. This means that it is suitable for multilanguage stemming.
- `EmbeddedStemmingPreprocessor`: This tokenizer preprocessor uses a given preprocessor and performs English porter stemming on tokens on top of it.

We can also implement our own token preprocessor—for example, a preprocessor to remove all stop words from the tokens.

Evaluating the model

We need to check the feature vector quality during the evaluation process. This will give us an idea of the quality of the Word2Vec model that was generated. In this recipe, we will follow two different approaches to evaluate the Word2Vec model.

How to do it...

1. Find similar words to a given word:

```
Collection<String> words = model.wordsNearest("season",10);
```

You will see an *n* output similar to the following:

```
week
game
team
year
world
night
time
country
last
group
```

2. Find the cosine similarity of the given two words:

```
double cosSimilarity = model.similarity("season","program");
System.out.println(cosSimilarity);
```

For the preceding example, the cosine similarity is calculated as follows:

```
0.2720930874347687
```

How it works...

In step 1, we found the top *n* similar words (similar in context) to a given word by calling `wordsNearest()`, providing both the input and count `n`. The `n` count is the number of words that we want to list.

In step 2, we tried to find the similarity of two given words. To do this, we actually calculated the **cosine similarity** between the two given words. The cosine similarity is one of the useful metrics that we can use to find the similarity between words/documents. We converted input words into vectors using our trained model.

There's more...

Cosine similarity is the similarity between two nonzero vectors measured by the cosine of the angle between them. This metric measures the orientation instead of the magnitude because cosine similarity calculates the angle between document vectors instead of the word count. If the angle is zero, then the cosine value reaches 1, indicating that they are very similar. If the cosine similarity is near zero, then this indicates that there's less similarity between documents, and the document vectors will be orthogonal (perpendicular) to each other. Also, the documents that are dissimilar to each other will yield a negative cosine similarity. For such documents, cosine similarity can go up to -1, indicating an angle of 1,800 between document vectors.

Generating plots from the model

We have mentioned that we have been using a layer size of `100` while training the Word2Vec model. This means that there can be 100 features and, eventually, a 100-dimensional feature space. It is impossible to plot a 100-dimensional space, and therefore we rely on t-SNE to perform dimensionality reduction. In this recipe, we will generate 2D plots from the Word2Vec model.

Getting ready

For this recipe, refer to the t-SNE visualization example found at: `//github.com/PacktPublishing/Java-Deep-Learning-Cookbook/blob/master/05_Implementing_NLP/sourceCode/cookbookapp/src/main/java/com/javadeeplearningcookbook/examples/TSNEVisualizationExample.java`.

The example generates t-SNE plots in a CSV file.

How to do it...

1. Add the following snippet (at the beginning of the source code) to set the data type for the current JVM runtime:

```
Nd4j.setDataType(DataBuffer.Type.DOUBLE);
```

2. Write word vectors into a file:

```
WordVectorSerializer.writeWordVectors(model.lookupTable(),new
File("words.txt"));
```

3. Separate the weights of the unique words into their own list using
`WordVectorSerializer`:

```
Pair<InMemoryLookupTable,VocabCache> vectors =
WordVectorSerializer.loadTxt(new File("words.txt"));
VocabCache cache = vectors.getSecond();
INDArray weights = vectors.getFirst().getSyn0();
```

4. Create a list to add all unique words:

```
List<String> cacheList = new ArrayList<>();
for(int i=0;i<cache.numWords();i++){
cacheList.add(cache.wordAtIndex(i));
}
```

5. Build a dual-tree t-SNE model for dimensionality reduction using
`BarnesHutTsne`:

```
BarnesHutTsne tsne = new BarnesHutTsne.Builder()
 .setMaxIter(100)
 .theta(0.5)
 .normalize(false)
 .learningRate(500)
 .useAdaGrad(false)
 .build();
```

6. Establish the t-SNE values and save them to a file:

```
tsne.fit(weights);
tsne.saveAsFile(cacheList,"tsne-standard-coords.csv");
```

How it works...

In step 2, word vectors from the trained model are saved to your local machine for further processing.

In step 3, we extracted data from all the unique word vectors by using `WordVectorSerializer`. Basically, this will load an in-memory VocabCache from the mentioned input words. But it doesn't load whole vocab/lookup tables into the memory, so it is capable of processing large vocabularies served over the network.

A `VocabCache` manages the storage of information required for the Word2Vec lookup table. We need to pass the labels to the t-SNE model, and labels are nothing but the words represented by word vectors.

In step 4, we created a list to add all unique words.

The `BarnesHutTsne` phrase is the DL4J implementation class for the dual-tree t-SNE model. The Barnes–Hut algorithm takes a dual-tree approximation strategy. It is recommended that you reduce the dimension by up to 50 using another method, such as **principal component analysis (PCA)** or similar.

In step 5, we used `BarnesHutTsne` to design a t-SNE model for the purpose. This model contained the following components:

- `theta()`: This is the Barnes–Hut trade-off parameter.
- `useAdaGrad()`: This is the legacy AdaGrad implementation for use in NLP applications.

Once the t-SNE model is designed, we can fit it with weights loaded from words. We can then save the feature plots to an Excel file, as demonstrated in step 6.

The feature coordinates will look like the following:

10313.24	-3208.58	i
9226.621	-20785.3	it
-1897.82	-14958.3	
-16017.7	205.2945	do
-16463.6	-12740.4	to
-12282.4	-1568.77	nt
-18311.8	-13064.7	?
-8450.18	18511.09	the
-10171.5	-26072.3	that
-12794.7	-15793.5	'
-2573.43	17713.4	he
7983.138	-14088.4	you
14693.47	21993.78	we
-14406	7192.472	what
-10893.4	-16106.2	they
124.8612	26304.67	said
-9002.77	15979.93	not
15987.31	5136.879	but
-14423.8	6216.467	and
940.4331	11966.52	go
8750.142	880.8116	know
3906.896	13513.67	a
14468.13	-14220.9	wa
14668.22	4229.939	did
3289.117	18491.64	are
18241.01	-15675.7	have
3186.297	58044.83	thi
1430.845	-2961.4	there
-17356.3	-8191.13	be

tsne-standard-coords

We can plot these coordinates using gnuplot or any other third-party libraries. DL4J also supports JFrame-based visualizations.

Saving and reloading the model

Model persistence is a key topic, especially while operating with different platforms. We can also reuse the model for further training (transfer learning) or performing tasks.

In this recipe, we will persist (save and reload) the Word2Vec models.

How to do it...

1. Save the Word2Vec model using `WordVectorSerializer`:

   ```
   WordVectorSerializer.writeWord2VecModel(model, "model.zip");
   ```

2. Reload the Word2Vec model using `WordVectorSerializer`:

   ```
   Word2Vec word2Vec =
   WordVectorSerializer.readWord2VecModel("model.zip");
   ```

How it works...

In step 1, the `writeWord2VecModel()` method saves the Word2Vec model into a compressed ZIP file and sends it to the output stream. It saves the full model, including `Syn0` and `Syn1`. The `Syn0` is the array that holds raw word vectors and is a projection layer that can convert one-hot encoding of a word into a dense embedding vector of the right dimension. The `Syn1` array represents the model's internal hidden weights to process the input/output.

In step 2, the `readWord2VecModel()` method loads the models that are in the following format:

- Binary model, either compressed or not compressed
- Popular CSV/Word2Vec text format
- DL4J compressed format

 Note that only weights will be loaded by this method.

Importing Google News vectors

Google provides a large, pretrained Word2Vec model with around 3 million 300-dimension English word vectors. It is large enough, and pretrained to display promising results. We will use Google vectors as our input word vectors for the evaluation. You will need at least 8 GB of RAM to run this example. In this recipe, we will import the Google News vectors and then perform an evaluation.

How to do it...

1. Import the Google News vectors:

```
File file = new File("GoogleNews-vectors-negative300.bin.gz");
Word2Vec model = WordVectorSerializer.readWord2VecModel(file);
```

2. Run an evaluation on the Google News vectors:

```
model.wordsNearest("season",10))
```

How it works...

In step 1, the `readWord2VecModel()` method is used to load the pretrained Google News vector that was saved in compressed file format.

In step 2, the `wordsNearest()` method is used to find the nearest words to the given word based on positive/negative scores.

After performing step 2, we should see the following results:

```
GoogleNewsVectorExample
[main] INFO org.nd4j.nativeblas.Nd4jBlas - Number of threads used for BLAS: 4
[main] INFO org.nd4j.linalg.api.ops.executioner.DefaultOpExecutioner - Backend used: [CPU]; OS: [Windows 10]
[main] INFO org.nd4j.linalg.api.ops.executioner.DefaultOpExecutioner - Cores: [8]; Memory: [5.2GB];
[main] INFO org.nd4j.linalg.api.ops.executioner.DefaultOpExecutioner - Blas vendor: [MKL]
[main] INFO org.deeplearning4j.models.embeddings.loader.WordVectorSerializer - Projected memory use for model: [3.35 GB]
[[seasons, sesaon, seson, seaosn, seaon, preseason, sesason, postseason, theseason, midseason]]  ◄─────

Process finished with exit code 0
```

You can try this technique using your own inputs to see different results.

There's more...

The Google News vector's compressed model file is sized at 1.6 GB. It can take a while to load and evaluate the model. You might observe an `OutOfMemoryError` error if you're running the code for the first time:

```
Exception in thread "main" java.lang.OutOfMemoryError: Cannot allocate new FloatPointer(900000000): totalBytes = 78125K, physicalBytes = 223M
    at org.bytedeco.javacpp.FloatPointer.<init>(FloatPointer.java:76)
    at org.nd4j.linalg.api.buffer.BaseDataBuffer.<init>(BaseDataBuffer.java:610)
    at org.nd4j.linalg.api.buffer.FloatBuffer.<init>(FloatBuffer.java:54)
    at org.nd4j.linalg.api.buffer.factory.DefaultDataBufferFactory.createFloat(DefaultDataBufferFactory.java:256)
    at org.nd4j.linalg.factory.Nd4j.createBuffer(Nd4j.java:1500)
    at org.nd4j.linalg.factory.Nd4j.createBuffer(Nd4j.java:1474)
    at org.nd4j.linalg.api.ndarray.BaseNDArray.<init>(BaseNDArray.java:272)
    at org.nd4j.linalg.cpu.nativecpu.NDArray.<init>(NDArray.java:143)
    at org.nd4j.linalg.cpu.nativecpu.CpuNDArrayFactory.create(CpuNDArrayFactory.java:172)
    at org.nd4j.linalg.factory.Nd4j.create(Nd4j.java:4374)
    at org.nd4j.linalg.factory.Nd4j.create(Nd4j.java:4324)
    at org.nd4j.linalg.factory.Nd4j.create(Nd4j.java:3789)
    at org.deeplearning4j.models.embeddings.loader.WordVectorSerializer.readBinaryModel(WordVectorSerializer.java:177)
    at org.deeplearning4j.models.embeddings.loader.WordVectorSerializer.readWord2VecModel(WordVectorSerializer.java:2400)
    at org.deeplearning4j.models.embeddings.loader.WordVectorSerializer.readWord2VecModel(WordVectorSerializer.java:2198)
    at com.javadeeplearningcookbook.examples.GoogleNewsVectorExample.main(GoogleNewsVectorExample.java:13)
```

We now need to adjust the **VM options** to accommodate more memory for the application. You can adjust the **VM options** in IntelliJ IDE, as shown in the following screenshot. You just need to make sure that you assign enough memory value and restart the application:

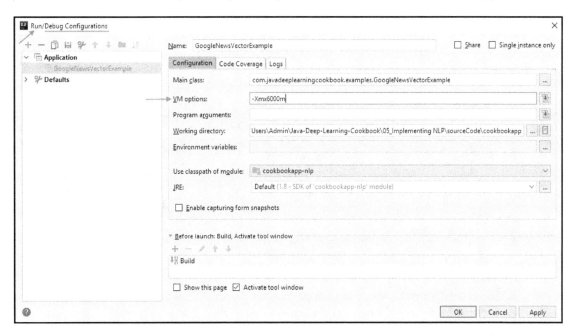

Troubleshooting and tuning Word2Vec models

Word2Vec models can be tuned further to produce better results. Runtime errors can happen in situations where there is high memory demand and less resource availability. We need to troubleshoot them to understand why they are happening and take preventative measures. In this recipe, we will troubleshoot Word2Vec models and tune them.

How to do it...

1. Monitor `OutOfMemoryError` in the application console/logs to check whether the heap space needs to be increased.
2. Check your IDE console for out-of-memory errors. If there are out-of-memory errors, then add VM options to your IDE to increase the Java memory heap.
3. Monitor `StackOverflowError` while running Word2Vec models. Watch out for the following error:

```
java.lang.StackOverflowError: null

at java.lang.ref.Reference.<init>(Reference.java:254) ~[na:1.8.0_11]

at java.lang.ref.WeakReference.<init>(WeakReference.java:69) ~[na:1.8.0_11]

at java.io.ObjectStreamClass$WeakClassKey.<init>(ObjectStreamClass.java:2306) [na:1.8

at java.io.ObjectStreamClass.lookup(ObjectStreamClass.java:322) ~[na:1.8.0_11]

at java.io.ObjectOutputStream.writeObject0(ObjectOutputStream.java:1134) ~[na:1.8.0_1

at java.io.ObjectOutputStream.defaultWriteFields(ObjectOutputStream.java:1548) ~[na:1
```

This error can happen because of unwanted temporary files in a project.

4. Perform hyperparameter tuning for Word2Vec models. You might need to perform multiple training sessions with different values for the hyperparameters, such as `layeSize`, `windowSize`, and so on.
5. Derive the memory consumption at the code level. Calculate the memory consumption based on the data types used in the code and how much data is being consumed by them.

How it works...

Out-of-memory errors are an indication that VM options need to be adjusted. How you adjust these parameters will depend on the RAM capacity of the hardware. For step 1, if you're using an IDE such as IntelliJ, you can provide the VM options using VM attributes such as -Xmx, -Xms, and so on. VM options can also be used from the command line.

For example, to increase the maximum memory consumption to 8 GB, you will need to add the -Xmx8G VM argument to your IDE.

To mitigate StackOverflowError mentioned in step 2, we need to delete the temporary files created under the project directory where our Java program is executed. These temporary files should look like the following:

```
ehcache_auto_created2810726831714447871diskstore

ehcache_auto_created47277876699919058795diskstore

ehcache_auto_created3883187579728988119diskstore

ehcache_auto_created91012296116340514478diskstore
```

With regard to step 3, if you observe that your Word2Vec model doesn't hold all the words from the raw text data, then you might be interested in increasing the layer size of the Word2Vec model. This layerSize is nothing but the output vector dimension or the feature space dimension. For example, we had layerSize of 100 in our code. This means that we can increase it to a larger value, say 200, as a workaround:

```
Word2Vec model = new Word2Vec.Builder()
  .iterate(iterator)
  .tokenizerFactory(tokenizerFactory)
  .minWordFrequency(5)
  .layerSize(200)
  .seed(42)
  .windowSize(5)
  .build();
```

If you have a GPU-powered machine, you can use this to accelerate the Word2Vec training time. Just make sure that the dependencies for the DL4J and ND4J backend are added as usual. If the results still don't look right, then make sure there are no normalization issues.

 Tasks such as wordsNearest() use normalized weights by default, and others require weights without normalization applied.

With regard to step 4, we can use the conventional approach. The weights matrix has the most memory consumption in Word2Vec. It is calculated as follows:

*NumberOfWords * NumberOfDimensions * 2 * DataType memory footprint*

For example, if our Word2Vec model with 100,000 words uses `long` as the data type, and 100 dimensions, the memory footprint will be 100,000 * 100 * 2 * 8 (long data type size) = 160 MB RAM, just for the weights matrix.

Note that DL4J UI will only provide a high-level overview of memory consumption.

See also

- Refer to the official DL4J documentation at `https://deeplearning4j.org/docs/latest/deeplearning4j-config-memory` to learn more about memory management

Using Word2Vec for sentence classification using CNNs

Neural networks require numerical inputs to perform their operations as expected. For text inputs, we cannot directly feed text data into a neural network. Since Word2Vec converts text data to vectors, it is possible to exploit Word2Vec so that we can use it with neural networks. We will use a pretrained Google News vector model as a reference and train a CNN network on top of it. At the end of this process, we will develop an IMDB review classifier to classify reviews as positive or negative. As per the paper found at `https://arxiv.org/abs/1408.5882`, combining a pretrained Word2Vec model with a CNN will give us better results.

We will employ custom CNN architecture along with the pretrained word vector model as suggested by Yoon Kim in his 2014 publication, `https://arxiv.org/abs/1408.5882`. The architecture is slightly more advanced than standard CNN models. We will also be using two huge datasets, and so the application might require a fair amount of RAM and performance benchmarks to ensure a reliable training duration and no `OutOfMemory` errors.

In this recipe, we will perform sentence classification using both Word2Vec and a CNN.

Getting ready

Use the example found at `https://github.com/PacktPublishing/Java-Deep-Learning-Cookbook/blob/master/05_Implementing_NLP/sourceCode/cookbookapp/src/main/java/com/javadeeplearningcookbook/examples/CnnWord2VecSentenceClassificationExample.java` for reference.

You should also make sure that you add more Java heap space through changing the VM options—for example, if you have 8 GB of RAM, then you may set `-Xmx2G` `-Xmx6G` as VM arguments.

We will extract the IMDB data to start with in step 1. The file structure will look like the following:

test	4/20/2019 11:27 AM	File folder	
train	4/20/2019 11:27 AM	File folder	
imdb.vocab	4/12/2011 10:44 PM	VOCAB File	827 KB
imdbEr	6/12/2011 4:24 AM	Text Document	882 KB
README	6/26/2011 5:48 AM	File	4 KB

If we further navigate to the dataset directories, you will see them labeled as follows:

Name	Date modified	Type	Size
neg	4/20/2019 11:34 AM	File folder	
pos	4/20/2019 11:36 AM	File folder	
unsup	4/20/2019 11:45 AM	File folder	
labeledBow.feat	4/12/2011 10:47 PM	FEAT File	20,529 KB
unsupBow.feat	4/12/2011 10:52 PM	FEAT File	40,380 KB
urls_neg	4/12/2011 3:18 PM	Text Document	599 KB
urls_pos	4/12/2011 3:18 PM	Text Document	599 KB
urls_unsup	4/12/2011 3:17 PM	Text Document	2,393 KB

How to do it...

1. Load the word vector model using `WordVectorSerializer`:

```
WordVectors wordVectors = WordVectorSerializer.loadStaticModel(new
File(WORD_VECTORS_PATH));
```

2. Create a sentence provider using `FileLabeledSentenceProvider`:

```
Map<String,List<File>> reviewFilesMap = new HashMap<>();
reviewFilesMap.put("Positive",
Arrays.asList(filePositive.listFiles()));
reviewFilesMap.put("Negative",
Arrays.asList(fileNegative.listFiles()));
LabeledSentenceProvider sentenceProvider = new
FileLabeledSentenceProvider(reviewFilesMap, rndSeed);
```

3. Create train iterators or test iterators using `CnnSentenceDataSetIterator` to load the IMDB review data:

```
CnnSentenceDataSetIterator iterator = new
CnnSentenceDataSetIterator.Builder(CnnSentenceDataSetIterator.Forma
t.CNN2D)
  .sentenceProvider(sentenceProvider)
  .wordVectors(wordVectors) //we mention word vectors here
  .minibatchSize(minibatchSize)
  .maxSentenceLength(maxSentenceLength) //words with length greater
than this will be ignored.
  .useNormalizedWordVectors(false)
  .build();
```

4. Create a `ComputationGraph` configuration by adding default hyperparameters:

```
ComputationGraphConfiguration.GraphBuilder builder = new
NeuralNetConfiguration.Builder()
  .weightInit(WeightInit.RELU)
  .activation(Activation.LEAKYRELU)
  .updater(new Adam(0.01))
  .convolutionMode(ConvolutionMode.Same) //This is important so we
can 'stack' the results later
  .l2(0.0001).graphBuilder();
```

5. Configure layers for `ComputationGraph` using the `addLayer()` method:

```
builder.addLayer("cnn3", new ConvolutionLayer.Builder()
.kernelSize(3,vectorSize) //vectorSize=300 for google vectors
.stride(1,vectorSize)
.nOut(100)
.build(), "input");
builder.addLayer("cnn4", new ConvolutionLayer.Builder()
.kernelSize(4,vectorSize)
.stride(1,vectorSize)
.nOut(100)
.build(), "input");
builder.addLayer("cnn5", new ConvolutionLayer.Builder()
.kernelSize(5,vectorSize)
.stride(1,vectorSize)
.nOut(100)
.build(), "input");
```

6. Set the convolution mode to stack the results later:

```
builder.addVertex("merge", new MergeVertex(), "cnn3", "cnn4",
"cnn5")
```

7. Create a `ComputationGraph` model and initialize it:

```
ComputationGraphConfiguration config = builder.build();
 ComputationGraph net = new ComputationGraph(config);
  net.init();
```

8. Perform the training using the `fit()` method:

```
for (int i = 0; i < numEpochs; i++) {
 net.fit(trainIterator);
 }
```

9. Evaluate the results:

```
Evaluation evaluation = net.evaluate(testIter);
System.out.println(evaluation.stats());
```

10. Retrieve predictions for the IMDB reviews data:

```
INDArray features =
((CnnSentenceDataSetIterator)testIterator).loadSingleSentence(conte
nts);
 INDArray predictions = net.outputSingle(features);
 List<String> labels = testIterator.getLabels();
 System.out.println("\n\nPredictions for first negative review:");
```

```
for( int i=0; i<labels.size(); i++ ){
System.out.println("P(" + labels.get(i) + ") = " +
predictions.getDouble(i));
 }
```

How it works...

In step 1, we used `loadStaticModel()` to load the model from the given path; however, you can also use `readWord2VecModel()`. Unlike `readWord2VecModel()`, `loadStaticModel()` utilizes host memory.

In step 2, `FileLabeledSentenceProvider` is used as a data source to load the sentences/documents from the files. We created `CnnSentenceDataSetIterator` using the same. `CnnSentenceDataSetIterator` handles the conversion of sentences to training data for CNNs, where each word is encoded using the word vector from the specified word vector model. Sentences and labels are provided by a `LabeledSentenceProvider` interface. Different implementations of `LabeledSentenceProvider` provide different ways of loading the sentence/documents with labels.

In step 3, we created `CnnSentenceDataSetIterator` to create train/test dataset iterators. The parameters we configured here are as follows:

- `sentenceProvider()`: Adds a sentence provider (data source) to `CnnSentenceDataSetIterator`
- `wordVectors()`: Adds a word vector reference to the dataset iterator—for example, the Google News vectors
- `useNormalizedWordVectors()`: Sets whether normalized word vectors can be used

In step 5, we created layers for a `ComputationGraph` model.

The `ComputationGraph` configuration is a configuration object for neural networks with an arbitrary connection structure. It is analogous to multilayer configuration, but allows considerably greater flexibility for the network architecture.

We also created multiple convolution layers stacked together with multiple filter widths and feature maps.

In step 6, `MergeVertex` performs in-depth concatenation on activation of these three convolution layers.

Once all steps up to step 8 are completed, we should see the following evaluation metrics:

```
CnnWord2VecSentenceClassificationExample
    [main] INFO org.deeplearning4j.optimize.listeners.ScoreIterationListener - Score at iteration 200 is 0.4343756264415397
    [main] INFO org.deeplearning4j.optimize.listeners.ScoreIterationListener - Score at iteration 300 is 0.6078348196314656
    [main] INFO org.deeplearning4j.optimize.listeners.ScoreIterationListener - Score at iteration 400 is 0.7803642512349673
    [main] INFO org.deeplearning4j.optimize.listeners.ScoreIterationListener - Score at iteration 500 is 0.7455179831259787
    [main] INFO org.deeplearning4j.optimize.listeners.ScoreIterationListener - Score at iteration 600 is 0.7572661556249657
    [main] INFO org.deeplearning4j.optimize.listeners.ScoreIterationListener - Score at iteration 700 is 0.8266019944546046
Epoch 0 complete. Starting evaluation:


========================Evaluation Metrics========================
 # of classes:    2
 Accuracy:        0.8528
 Precision:       0.8543
 Recall:          0.8528
 F1 Score:        0.8478
Precision, recall & F1: reported for positive class (class 1 - "Positive") only


========================Confusion Matrix========================
     0     1
  ---------------
 11070  1430 | 0 = Negative
  2251 10249 | 1 = Positive

Confusion matrix format: Actual (rowClass) predicted as (columnClass) N times
==================================================================
```

In step 10, `contents` refers to the content from a single-sentence document in string format.

For negative review content, we would see the following result after step 9:

```
Predictions for first negative review:
P(Negative) = 0.778581440448761
P(Positive) = 0.22141852974891663
```

This means that the document has a 77.8% probability of having a negative sentiment.

There's more...

Initializing word vectors with those retrieved from pretrained unsupervised models is a known method for increasing performance. If you can recall what we have done in this recipe, you will remember that we used pretrained Google News vectors for the same purpose. For a CNN, when applied to text instead of images, we will be dealing with one-dimensional array vectors that represent the text. We perform the same steps, such as convolution and max pooling with feature maps, as discussed in Chapter 4, *Building Convolutional Neural Networks*. The only difference is that instead of image pixels, we use vectors that represent text. CNN architectures have subsequently shown great results against NLP tasks. The paper found at https://www.aclweb.org/anthology/D14-1181 will contain further insights on this.

The network architecture of a computation graph is a directed acyclic graph, where each vertex in the graph is a graph vertex. A graph vertex can be a layer or a vertex that defines a random forward/backward pass functionality. Computation graphs can have a random number of inputs and outputs. We needed to stack multiple convolution layers, which was not possible in the case of a normal CNN architecture.

ComputaionGraph has an option to set the configuration known as convolutionMode. convolutionMode determines the network configuration and how the convolution operations should be performed for convolutional and subsampling layers (for a given input size). Network configurations such as stride/padding/kernelSize are applicable for a given convolution mode. We are setting the convolution mode using convolutionMode because we want to stack the results of all three convolution layers as one and generate the prediction.

The output sizes for convolutional and subsampling layers are calculated in each dimension as follows:

$$outputSize = (inputSize - kernelSize + 2*padding) / stride + 1$$

If outputSize is not an integer, an exception will be thrown during the network initialization or forward pass. We have discussed MergeVertex, which was used to combine the activations of two or more layers. We used MergeVertex to perform the same operation with our convolution layers. The merge will depend on the type of inputs—for example, if we wanted to merge two convolution layers with a sample size (batchSize) of 100, and depth of depth1 and depth2 respectively, then merge will stack the results where the following applies:

$$depth = depth1 + depth2$$

Using Doc2Vec for document classification

Word2Vec correlates words with words, while the purpose of Doc2Vec (also known as paragraph vectors) is to correlate labels with words. We will discuss Doc2Vec in this recipe. Documents are labeled in such a way that the subdirectories under the document's root represent document labels. For example, all finance-related data should be placed under the `finance` subdirectory. In this recipe, we will perform document classification using Doc2Vec.

How to do it...

1. Extract and load the data using `FileLabelAwareIterator`:

```
LabelAwareIterator labelAwareIterator = new
FileLabelAwareIterator.Builder()
 .addSourceFolder(new
ClassPathResource("label").getFile()).build();
```

2. Create a tokenizer using `TokenizerFactory`:

```
TokenizerFactory tokenizerFactory = new DefaultTokenizerFactory();
tokenizerFactory.setTokenPreProcessor(new CommonPreprocessor());
```

3. Create a `ParagraphVector` model definition:

```
ParagraphVectors paragraphVectors = new ParagraphVectors.Builder()
 .learningRate(learningRate)
 .minLearningRate(minLearningRate)
 .batchSize(batchSize)
 .epochs(epochs)
 .iterate(labelAwareIterator)
 .trainWordVectors(true)
 .tokenizerFactory(tokenizerFactory)
 .build();
```

4. Train `ParagraphVectors` by calling the `fit()` method:

```
paragraphVectors.fit();
```

5. Assign labels to unlabeled data and evaluate the results:

```
ClassPathResource unClassifiedResource = new
ClassPathResource("unlabeled");
 FileLabelAwareIterator unClassifiedIterator = new
FileLabelAwareIterator.Builder()
```

```
.addSourceFolder(unClassifiedResource.getFile())
.build();
```

6. Store the weight lookup table:

```
InMemoryLookupTable<VocabWord> lookupTable =
(InMemoryLookupTable<VocabWord>)paragraphVectors.getLookupTable();
```

7. Predict labels for every unclassified document, as shown in the following pseudocode:

```
while (unClassifiedIterator.hasNextDocument()) {
//Calculate the domain vector of each document.
//Calculate the cosine similarity of the domain vector with all
//the given labels
 //Display the results
 }
```

8. Create the tokens from the document and use the iterator to retrieve the document instance:

```
LabelledDocument labelledDocument =
unClassifiedIterator.nextDocument();
 List<String> documentAsTokens =
tokenizerFactory.create(labelledDocument.getContent()).getTokens();
```

9. Use the lookup table to get the vocabulary information (VocabCache):

```
VocabCache vocabCache = lookupTable.getVocab();
```

10. Count all the instances where the words are matched in VocabCache:

```
AtomicInteger cnt = new AtomicInteger(0);
 for (String word: documentAsTokens) {
 if (vocabCache.containsWord(word)){
 cnt.incrementAndGet();
 }
 }
 INDArray allWords = Nd4j.create(cnt.get(),
lookupTable.layerSize());
```

11. Store word vectors of the matching words in the vocab:

```
cnt.set(0);
 for (String word: documentAsTokens) {
 if (vocabCache.containsWord(word))
 allWords.putRow(cnt.getAndIncrement(), lookupTable.vector(word));
 }
```

12. Calculate the domain vector by calculating the mean of the word embeddings:

```
INDArray documentVector = allWords.mean(0);
```

13. Check the cosine similarity of the document vector with labeled word vectors:

```
List<String> labels =
labelAwareIterator.getLabelsSource().getLabels();
 List<Pair<String, Double>> result = new ArrayList<>();
 for (String label: labels) {
 INDArray vecLabel = lookupTable.vector(label);
 if (vecLabel == null){
 throw new IllegalStateException("Label '"+ label+"' has no known
vector!");
 }
 double sim = Transforms.cosineSim(documentVector, vecLabel);
 result.add(new Pair<String, Double>(label, sim));
 }
```

14. Display the results:

```
for (Pair<String, Double> score: result) {
log.info(" " + score.getFirst() + ": " + score.getSecond());
}
```

How it works...

In step 1, we created a dataset iterator using `FileLabelAwareIterator`.

The `FileLabelAwareIterator` is a simple filesystem-based `LabelAwareIterator` interface. It assumes that you have one or more folders organized in the following way:

- **First-level subfolder**: Label name
- **Second-level subfolder**: The documents for that label

Look at the following screenshot for an example of this data structure:

In step 3, we created `ParagraphVector` by adding all required hyperparameters. The purpose of paragraph vectors is to associate arbitrary documents with labels. Paragraph vectors are an extension to Word2Vec that learn to correlate labels and words, while Word2Vec correlates words with other words. We need to define labels for the paragraph vectors to work.

For more information on what we did in step 5, refer to the following directory structure (under the `unlabeled` directory in the project):

The directory names can be random and no specific labels are required. Our task is to find the proper labels (document classifications) for these documents. Word embeddings are stored in the lookup table. For any given word, a word vector of numbers will be returned.

Word embeddings are stored in the lookup table. For any given word, a word vector will be returned from the lookup table.

In step 6, we created `InMemoryLookupTable` from paragraph vectors. `InMemoryLookupTable` is the default word lookup table in DL4J. Basically, the lookup table operates as the hidden layer and the word/document vectors refer to the output.

Step 8 to step 12 are solely used for the calculation of the domain vector of each document.

In step 8, we created tokens for the document using the tokenizer that was created in step 2. In step 9, we used the lookup table that was created in step 6 to obtain `VocabCache`. `VocabCache` stores the information needed to operate the lookup table. We can look up words in the lookup table using `VocabCache`.

In step 11, we store the word vectors along with the occurrence of a particular word in an INDArray.

In step 12, we calculated the mean of this INDArray to get the document vector.

The mean across the zero dimension means that it is calculated across all dimensions.

In step 13, the cosine similarity is calculated by calling the `cosineSim()` method provided by ND4J. We use cosine similarity to calculate the similarity of document vectors. ND4J provides a functional interface to calculate the cosine similarity of two domain vectors. `vecLabel` represents the document vector for the labels from classified documents. Then, we compared `vecLabel` with our unlabeled document vector, `documentVector`.

After step 14, you should see an output similar to the following:

```
ParagraphVectorExample
[main] INFO org.deeplearning4j.models.sequencevectors.SequenceVectors - Epoch [3] finished; Elements processed so far: [22770];  Sequences processed: [30]
[main] INFO org.deeplearning4j.models.sequencevectors.SequenceVectors - Epoch [4] finished; Elements processed so far: [30360];  Sequences processed: [30]
[main] INFO org.deeplearning4j.models.sequencevectors.SequenceVectors - Epoch [5] finished; Elements processed so far: [37950];  Sequences processed: [30]
[main] INFO org.deeplearning4j.models.sequencevectors.SequenceVectors - Time spent on training: 15694 ms
[main] INFO com.javadeeplearningcookbook.examples.ParagraphVectorExample -         finance: 0.6973586121994019
[main] INFO com.javadeeplearningcookbook.examples.ParagraphVectorExample -         health: -0.5593153834342957
[main] INFO com.javadeeplearningcookbook.examples.ParagraphVectorExample -         science: -0.07580675184726715
[main] INFO com.javadeeplearningcookbook.examples.ParagraphVectorExample -         finance: -0.6245677471160889
[main] INFO com.javadeeplearningcookbook.examples.ParagraphVectorExample -         health: 0.5324505567550659
[main] INFO com.javadeeplearningcookbook.examples.ParagraphVectorExample -         science: 0.3302365243434906

Process finished with exit code 0
```

We can choose the label that has the higher cosine similarity value. From the preceding screenshots, we can infer that the first document is more likely finance-related content with a 69.7% probability. The second document is more likely health-related content with a 53.2% probability.

Constructing an LSTM Network for Time Series

6

In this chapter, we will discuss how to construct a **long short-term memory (LSTM)** neural network to solve a medical time series problem. We will be using data from 4,000 **intensive care unit (ICU)** patients. Our goal is to predict the mortality of patients using a given set of generic and sequential features. We have six generic features, such as age, gender, and weight. Also, we have 37 sequential features, such as cholesterol level, temperature, pH, and glucose level. Each patient has multiple measurements recorded against these sequential features. The number of measurements taken from each patient differs. Furthermore, the time between measurements also differs among patients.

LSTM is well-suited to this type of problem due to the sequential nature of the data. We could also solve it using a regular **recurrent neural network (RNN)**, but the purpose of LSTM is to avoid vanishing and exploding gradients. LSTM is capable of capturing long-term dependencies because of its cell state.

In this chapter, we will cover the following recipes:

- Extracting and reading clinical data
- Loading and transforming data
- Constructing input layers for a network
- Constructing output layers for a network
- Training time series data
- Evaluating the LSTM network's efficiency

Technical requirements

A concrete implementation of the use case discussed in this chapter can be found here: `https://github.com/PacktPublishing/Java-Deep-Learning-Cookbook/blob/master/06_Constructing_LSTM_Network_for_time_series/sourceCode/cookbookapp-lstm-time-series/src/main/java/LstmTimeSeriesExample.java`.

After cloning the GitHub repository, navigate to the `Java-Deep-Learning-Cookbook/06_Constructing_LSTM_Network_for_time_series/sourceCode` directory. Then, import the `cookbookapp-lstm-time-series` project as a Maven project by importing `pom.xml`.

Download the clinical time series data from here: `https://skymindacademy.blob.core.windows.net/physionet2012/physionet2012.tar.gz`. The dataset is from the PhysioNet Cardiology Challenge 2012.

Unzip the package after the download. You should see the following directory structure:

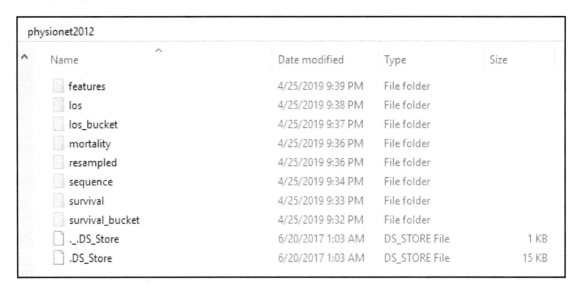

The features are contained in a directory called `sequence` and the labels are contained in a directory called `mortality`. Ignore the other directories for now. You need to update file paths to features/labels in the source code to run the example.

Extracting and reading clinical data

ETL (short for **Extract, Transform, and Load**) is the most important step in any deep learning problem. We're focusing on data extraction in this recipe, where we will discuss how to extract and process clinical time series data. We have learned about regular data types, such as normal CSV/text data and images, in previous chapters. Now, let's discuss how to deal with time series data. We will use clinical time series data to predict the mortality of patients.

How to do it...

1. Create an instance of `NumberedFileInputSplit` to club all feature files together:

   ```
   new NumberedFileInputSplit(FEATURE_DIR+"/%d.csv",0,3199);
   ```

2. Create an instance of `NumberedFileInputSplit` to club all label files together:

   ```
   new NumberedFileInputSplit(LABEL_DIR+"/%d.csv",0,3199);
   ```

3. Create record readers for features/labels:

   ```
   SequenceRecordReader trainFeaturesReader = new
   CSVSequenceRecordReader(1, ",");
    trainFeaturesReader.initialize(new
   NumberedFileInputSplit(FEATURE_DIR+"/%d.csv",0,3199));
    SequenceRecordReader trainLabelsReader = new
   CSVSequenceRecordReader();
    trainLabelsReader.initialize(new
   NumberedFileInputSplit(LABEL_DIR+"/%d.csv",0,3199));
   ```

How it works...

Time series data is three-dimensional. Each sample is represented by its own file. Feature values in columns are measured on different time steps denoted by rows. For instance, in step 1, we saw the following snapshot, where time series data is displayed:

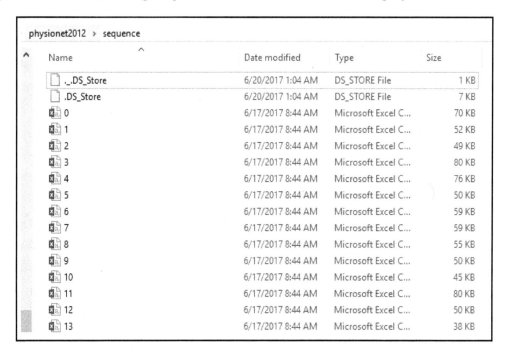

physionet2012 > sequence			
Name	Date modified	Type	Size
._.DS_Store	6/20/2017 1:04 AM	DS_STORE File	1 KB
.DS_Store	6/20/2017 1:04 AM	DS_STORE File	7 KB
0	6/17/2017 8:44 AM	Microsoft Excel C...	70 KB
1	6/17/2017 8:44 AM	Microsoft Excel C...	52 KB
2	6/17/2017 8:44 AM	Microsoft Excel C...	49 KB
3	6/17/2017 8:44 AM	Microsoft Excel C...	80 KB
4	6/17/2017 8:44 AM	Microsoft Excel C...	76 KB
5	6/17/2017 8:44 AM	Microsoft Excel C...	50 KB
6	6/17/2017 8:44 AM	Microsoft Excel C...	59 KB
7	6/17/2017 8:44 AM	Microsoft Excel C...	59 KB
8	6/17/2017 8:44 AM	Microsoft Excel C...	55 KB
9	6/17/2017 8:44 AM	Microsoft Excel C...	50 KB
10	6/17/2017 8:44 AM	Microsoft Excel C...	45 KB
11	6/17/2017 8:44 AM	Microsoft Excel C...	80 KB
12	6/17/2017 8:44 AM	Microsoft Excel C...	50 KB
13	6/17/2017 8:44 AM	Microsoft Excel C...	38 KB

Each file represents a different sequence. When you open the file, you will see the observations (features) recorded on different time steps, as shown here:

Time	Elapsed	ALP	ALPMissi	ALT	ALTMissin	AST	ASTMissi	Age	AgeMissi	Albumin	Albumin	BUN	BUNMissi	Bilirubin	Bilirubin
0	0	0.078056	1	0.006392	1	0.006452	1	0.914286	0	0.517241	1	0.140351	1	0.023055	1
0.25	0.25	0.078056	1	0.006392	1	0.006452	1	0.914286	0	0.517241	1	0.140351	1	0.023055	1
0.75	0.5	0.078056	1	0.006392	1	0.006452	1	0.914286	0	0.517241	1	0.140351	1	0.023055	1
1.25	0.5	0.078056	1	0.006392	1	0.006452	1	0.914286	0	0.517241	1	0.140351	1	0.023055	1
1.75	0.5	0.078056	1	0.006392	1	0.006452	1	0.914286	0	0.517241	1	0.140351	0	0.023055	1
2.25	0.5	0.078056	1	0.006392	1	0.006452	1	0.914286	0	0.517241	1	0.140351	1	0.023055	1
3	0.75	0.078056	1	0.006392	1	0.006452	1	0.914286	0	0.517241	1	0.140351	1	0.023055	1
3.25	0.25	0.078056	1	0.006392	1	0.006452	1	0.914286	0	0.517241	1	0.140351	1	0.023055	1
4.75	1.5	0.078056	1	0.006392	1	0.006452	1	0.914286	0	0.517241	1	0.140351	1	0.023055	1
5.25	0.5	0.078056	1	0.006392	1	0.006452	1	0.914286	0	0.517241	1	0.140351	1	0.023055	1
5.433333	0.183333	0.078056	1	0.006392	1	0.006452	1	0.914286	0	0.517241	1	0.131579	0	0.023055	1
5.75	0.316667	0.078056	1	0.006392	1	0.006452	1	0.914286	0	0.517241	1	0.131579	1	0.023055	1
6.25	0.5	0.078056	1	0.006392	1	0.006452	1	0.914286	0	0.517241	1	0.131579	1	0.023055	1
8.466667	2.216667	0.078056	1	0.006392	1	0.006452	1	0.914286	0	0.517241	1	0.131579	1	0.023055	1
10	1.533333	0.078056	1	0.006392	1	0.006452	1	0.914286	0	0.517241	1	0.131579	1	0.023055	1
10.08333	0.083333	0.078056	1	0.006392	1	0.006452	1	0.914286	0	0.517241	1	0.131579	1	0.023055	1

The labels are contained in a single CSV file, which contains a value of 0, indicating death, or a value of 1, indicating survival. For example, for the features in 1.csv, the output labels are in 1.csv under the mortality directory. Note that we have a total of 4,000 samples. We divide the entire dataset into train/test sets so that our training data has 3,200 examples and the testing data has 800 examples.

In step 3, we used NumberedFileInputSplit to read and club all the files (features/labels) with a numbered format.

CSVSequenceRecordReader is to read sequences of data in CSV format, where each sequence is defined in its own file.

As you can see in the preceding screenshots, the first row is just meant for feature labels and needs to be bypassed.

Hence, we have created the following CSV sequence reader:

```
SequenceRecordReader trainFeaturesReader = new CSVSequenceRecordReader(1,
",");
```

Loading and transforming data

After the data extraction phase, we need to transform the data before loading it into a neural network. During data transformation, it is very important to ensure that any non-numeric fields in the dataset are transformed into numeric fields. The role of data transformation doesn't end there. We can also remove any noise in the data and adjust the values. In this recipe, we load the data into a dataset iterator and transform the data as required.

We extracted the time series data into record reader instances in the previous recipe. Now, let's create train/test iterators from them. We will also analyze the data and transform it if needed.

Getting ready

Before we proceed, refer to the dataset in the following screenshot to understand how every sequence of the data looks:

Time	Elapsed	ALP	ALPMissi	ALT	ALTMissin	AST	ASTMissi	Age	AgeMissi	Albumin	Albumin	BUN	BUNMissi	Bilirubin	Bilirubin
0	0	0.078056	1	0.006392	1	0.006452	1	0.914286	0	0.517241	1	0.140351	1	0.023055	1
0.25	0.25	0.078056	1	0.006392	1	0.006452	1	0.914286	0	0.517241	1	0.140351	1	0.023055	1
0.75	0.5	0.078056	1	0.006392	1	0.006452	1	0.914286	0	0.517241	1	0.140351	1	0.023055	1
1.25	0.5	0.078056	1	0.006392	1	0.006452	1	0.914286	0	0.517241	1	0.140351	1	0.023055	1
1.75	0.5	0.078056	1	0.006392	1	0.006452	1	0.914286	0	0.517241	1	0.140351	0	0.023055	1
2.25	0.5	0.078056	1	0.006392	1	0.006452	1	0.914286	0	0.517241	1	0.140351	1	0.023055	1
3	0.75	0.078056	1	0.006392	1	0.006452	1	0.914286	0	0.517241	1	0.140351	1	0.023055	1
3.25	0.25	0.078056	1	0.006392	1	0.006452	1	0.914286	0	0.517241	1	0.140351	1	0.023055	1
4.75	1.5	0.078056	1	0.006392	1	0.006452	1	0.914286	0	0.517241	1	0.140351	1	0.023055	1
5.25	0.5	0.078056	1	0.006392	1	0.006452	1	0.914286	0	0.517241	1	0.140351	1	0.023055	1
5.433333	0.183333	0.078056	1	0.006392	1	0.006452	1	0.914286	0	0.517241	1	0.131579	0	0.023055	1
5.75	0.316667	0.078056	1	0.006392	1	0.006452	1	0.914286	0	0.517241	1	0.131579	1	0.023055	1
6.25	0.5	0.078056	1	0.006392	1	0.006452	1	0.914286	0	0.517241	1	0.131579	1	0.023055	1
8.466667	2.216667	0.078056	1	0.006392	1	0.006452	1	0.914286	0	0.517241	1	0.131579	1	0.023055	1
10	1.533333	0.078056	1	0.006392	1	0.006452	1	0.914286	0	0.517241	1	0.131579	1	0.023055	1
10.08333	0.083333	0.078056	1	0.006392	1	0.006452	1	0.914286	0	0.517241	1	0.131579	1	0.023055	1

Firstly, we need to check for the existence of any non-numeric features in the data. We need to load the data into the neural network for training, and it should be in a format that the neural network can understand. We have a sequenced dataset and it appears that non-numeric values are not present. All 37 features are numeric. If you look at the range of feature data, it is close to a normalized format.

How to do it...

1. Create the training iterator using `SequenceRecordReaderDataSetIterator`:

```
DataSetIterator trainDataSetIterator = new
SequenceRecordReaderDataSetIterator(trainFeaturesReader,trainLabels
Reader,batchSize,numberOfLabels,false,
SequenceRecordReaderDataSetIterator.AlignmentMode.ALIGN_END);
```

2. Create the test iterator using `SequenceRecordReaderDataSetIterator`:

```
DataSetIterator testDataSetIterator = new
SequenceRecordReaderDataSetIterator(testFeaturesReader,testLabelsRe
ader,batchSize,numberOfLabels,false,
SequenceRecordReaderDataSetIterator.AlignmentMode.ALIGN_END);
```

How it works...

In steps 1 and 2, we used `AlignmentMode` while creating the iterators for the training and test datasets. The `AlignmentMode` deals with input/labels of varying lengths (for example, one-to-many and many-to-one situations). Here are some types of alignment modes:

- `ALIGN_END`: This is intended to align labels or input at the last time step. Basically, it adds zero padding at the end of either the input or the labels.
- `ALIGN_START`: This is intended to align labels or input at the first time step. Basically, it adds zero padding at the end of the input or the labels.
- `EQUAL_LENGTH`: This assumes that the input time series and label are of the same length, and all examples are the same length.
- `SequenceRecordReaderDataSetIterator`: This helps to generate a time series dataset from the record reader passed in. The record reader should be based on sequence data and is optimal for time series data. Check out the attributes passed to the constructor:

```
DataSetIterator testDataSetIterator = new
SequenceRecordReaderDataSetIterator(testFeaturesReader,testLabelsRe
ader,batchSize,numberOfLabels,false,
SequenceRecordReaderDataSetIterator.AlignmentMode.ALIGN_END);
```

`testFeaturesReader` and `testLabelsReader` are record reader objects for input data (features) and labels (for evaluation), respectively. The Boolean attribute (`false`) refers to whether we have regression samples. Since we are talking about time series classification, this is going to be false. For regression data, this has to be set to `true`.

Constructing input layers for the network

LSTM layers will have gated cells that are capable of capturing long-term dependencies, unlike regular RNN. Let's discuss how we can add a special LSTM layer in our network configuration. We can use a multilayer network or computation graph to create the model.

In this recipe, we will discuss how to create input layers for our LSTM neural network. In the following example, we will construct a computation graph and add custom layers to it.

How to do it...

1. Configure the neural network using `ComputationGraph`, as shown here:

```
ComputationGraphConfiguration.GraphBuilder builder = new
NeuralNetConfiguration.Builder()
  .seed(RANDOM_SEED)
.optimizationAlgo(OptimizationAlgorithm.STOCHASTIC_GRADIENT_DESCENT
)
  .weightInit(WeightInit.XAVIER)
  .updater(new Adam())
  .dropOut(0.9)
  .graphBuilder()
  .addInputs("trainFeatures");
```

2. Configure the LSTM layer:

```
new LSTM.Builder()
  .nIn(INPUTS)
  .nOut(LSTM_LAYER_SIZE)
  .forgetGateBiasInit(1)
  .activation(Activation.TANH)
  .build(),"trainFeatures");
```

3. Add the LSTM layer to the `ComputationGraph` configuration:

```
builder.addLayer("L1", new LSTM.Builder()
  .nIn(86)
  .nOut(200)
  .forgetGateBiasInit(1)
  .activation(Activation.TANH)
  .build(),"trainFeatures");
```

How it works...

In step 1, we defined a graph vertex input as the following after calling the
`graphBuilder()` method:

```
builder.addInputs("trainFeatures");
```

By calling `graphBuilder()`, we are actually constructing a graph builder to create a
computation graph configuration.

Once the LSTM layers are added into the `ComputationGraph` configuration in step 3, they will act as input layers in the `ComputationGraph` configuration. We pass the previously mentioned graph vertex input (`trainFeatures`) to our LSTM layer, as follows:

```
builder.addLayer("L1", new LSTM.Builder()
      .nIn(INPUTS)
      .nOut(LSTM_LAYER_SIZE)
      .forgetGateBiasInit(1)
      .activation(Activation.TANH)
      .build(),"trainFeatures");
```

The last attribute, `trainFeatures`, refers to the graph vertex input. Here, we're specifying that the `L1` layer is the input layer.

The main purpose of the LSTM neural network is to capture the long-term dependencies in the data. The derivatives of a `tanh` function can sustain for a long range before reaching the zero value. Hence, we use `Activation.TANH` as the activation function for the LSTM layer.

The `forgetGateBiasInit()` set forgets gate bias initialization. Values in the range of `1` to `5` could potentially help with learning or long-term dependencies.

We use the `Builder` strategy to define the LSTM layers along with the required attributes, such as `nIn` and `nOut`. These are input/output neurons, as we saw in Chapters 3, *Building Deep Neural Networks for Binary Classification*, and Chapter 4, *Building Convolutional Neural Networks*. We add LSTM layers using the `addLayer` method.

Constructing output layers for the network

The output layer design is the last step in configuring the neural network layer. Our aim is to implement a time series prediction model. We need to develop a time series classifier to predict patient mortality. The output layer design should reflect this purpose. In this recipe, we will discuss how to construct the output layer for our use case.

How to do it...

1. Design the output layer using `RnnOutputLayer`:

```
new RnnOutputLayer.Builder(LossFunctions.LossFunction.MCXENT)
  .activation(Activation.SOFTMAX)
  .nIn(LSTM_LAYER_SIZE).nOut(labelCount).build()
```

2. Use the `addLayer()` method to add an output layer to the network configuration:

```
builder.addLayer("predictMortality", new
RnnOutputLayer.Builder(LossFunctions.LossFunction.MCXENT)
 .activation(Activation.SOFTMAX)
 .nIn(LSTM_LAYER_SIZE).nOut(labelCount).build(),"L1");
```

How it works...

While constructing the output layer, make note of the `nOut` value of the preceding LSTM input layer. This will be taken as `nIn` for the output layer. `nIn` should be the same as `nOut` of the preceding LSTM input layer.

In steps 1 and step 2, we are essentially creating an LSTM neural network, an extended version of a regular RNN. We used gated cells to have some sort of internal memory to hold long-term dependencies. For a predictive model to make predictions (patient mortality), we need to have probability produced by the output layer. In step 2, we see that `SOFTMAX` is used at the output layer of a neural network. This activation function is very helpful for computing the probability for the specific label. `MCXENT` is the ND4J implementation for the negative loss likelihood error function. Since we use the negative loss likelihood loss function, it will push the results when the probability value is found to be high for a label on a particular iteration.

`RnnOutputLayer` is more like an extended version of regular output layers found in feed-forward networks. We can also use `RnnOutputLayer` for one-dimensional CNN layers. There is also another output layer, named `RnnLossLayer`, where the input and output activations are the same. In the case of `RnnLossLayer`, we have three dimensions with the `[miniBatchSize,nIn,timeSeriesLength]` and `[miniBatchSize,nOut,timeSeri esLength]` shape, respectively.

Note that we'll have to specify the input layer that is to be connected to the output layer. Take a look at this code again:

```
builder.addLayer("predictMortality", new
RnnOutputLayer.Builder(LossFunctions.LossFunction.MCXENT)
 .activation(Activation.SOFTMAX)
 .nIn(LSTM_LAYER_SIZE).nOut(labelCount).build(),"L1")
```

We mentioned that the `L1` layer is the input layer to the output layer.

Training time series data

So far, we have constructed network layers and parameters to define the model configuration. Now it's time to train the model and see the results. We can then check whether any of the previously-defined model configuration can be altered to obtain optimal results. Be sure to run the training instance multiple times before making any conclusions from the very first training session. We need to observe a consistent output to ensure stable performance.

In this recipe, we train our LSTM neural network against the loaded time series data.

How to do it...

1. Create the `ComputationGraph` model from the previously-created model configuration:

```
ComputationGraphConfiguration configuration = builder.build();
    ComputationGraph model = new ComputationGraph(configuration);
```

2. Load the iterator and train the model using the `fit()` method:

```
for(int i=0;i<epochs;i++){
   model.fit(trainDataSetIterator);
 }
```

You can use the following approach as well:

```
model.fit(trainDataSetIterator,epochs);
```

We can then avoid using a `for` loop by directly specifying the `epochs` parameter in the `fit()` method.

How it works...

In step 2, we pass both the dataset iterator and epoch count to start the training session. We use a very large time series dataset, hence a large epoch value will result in more training time. Also, a large epoch may not always guarantee good results, and may end up overfitting. So, we need to run the training experiment multiple times to arrive at an optimal value for epochs and other important hyperparameters. An optimal value would be the bound where you observe the maximum performance for the neural network.

Effectively, we are optimizing our training process using memory-gated cells in layers. As we discussed earlier, in the *Constructing input layers for the network* recipe, LSTMs are good for holding long-term dependencies in datasets.

Evaluating the LSTM network's efficiency

After each training iteration, the network's efficiency is measured by evaluating the model against a set of evaluation metrics. We optimize the model further on upcoming training iterations based on the evaluation metrics. We use the test dataset for evaluation. Note that we are performing binary classification for the given use case. We predict the chances of that patient surviving. For classification problems, we can plot a **Receiver Operating Characteristics (ROC)** curve and calculate the **Area Under The Curve (AUC)** score to evaluate the model's performance. The AUC score ranges from 0 to 1. An AUC score of 0 represents 100% failed predictions and 1 represents 100% successful predictions.

How to do it...

1. Use ROC for the model evaluation:

```
ROC evaluation = new ROC(thresholdSteps);
```

2. Generate output from features in the test data:

```
DataSet batch = testDataSetIterator.next();
 INDArray[] output = model.output(batch.getFeatures());
```

3. Use the ROC evaluation instance to perform the evaluation by calling evalTimeseries():

```
INDArray actuals = batch.getLabels();
   INDArray predictions = output[0]
     evaluation.evalTimeSeries(actuals, predictions);
```

4. Display the AUC score (evaluation metrics) by calling calculateAUC():

```
System.out.println(evaluation.calculateAUC());
```

How it works...

In step 3, `actuals` are the actual output for the test input, and `predictions` are the observed output for the test input.

The evaluation metrics are based on the difference between `actuals` and `predictions`. We used ROC evaluation metrics to find this difference. An ROC evaluation is ideal for binary classification problems with datasets that have a uniform distribution of the output classes. Predicting patient mortality is just another binary classification puzzle.

`thresholdSteps` in the parameterized constructor of `ROC` is the number of threshold steps to be used for the ROC calculation. When we decrease the threshold, we get more positive values. It increases the sensitivity and means that the neural network will be less confident in uniquely classifying an item under a class.

In step 4, we printed the ROC evaluation metrics by calling `calculateAUC()`:

```
evaluation.calculateAUC();
```

The `calculateAUC()` method will calculate the area under the ROC curve plotted from the test data. If you print the results, you should see a probability value between `0` and `1`. We can also call the `stats()` method to display the whole ROC evaluation metrics, as shown here:

```
72          ROC evaluation = new ROC( thresholdSteps: 100);
73          while (testDataSetIterator.hasNext()) {
74              DataSet batch = testDataSetIterator.next();
75              INDArray[] output = model.output(batch.getFeatures());
76              evaluation.evalTimeSeries(batch.getLabels(), output[0]);
77          }
78
79          System.out.println(evaluation.calculateAUC());
80          System.out.println(evaluation.stats());
81      }
82  }
83
```

```
LstmTimeSeriesExample   main()

LstmTimeSeriesExample
/Library/Java/JavaVirtualMachines/jdk1.8.0_121.jdk/Contents/Home/bin/java ...
objc[1222]: Class JavaLaunchHelper is implemented in both /Library/Java/JavaVirtualMachines/jdk1.8.0_121.jdk/Contents/Home/bin/java (0x1027f74c0)
[main] INFO org.nd4j.linalg.factory.Nd4jBackend - Loaded [CpuBackend] backend
[main] INFO org.nd4j.nativeblas.NativeOpsHolder - Number of threads used for NativeOps: 6
[main] INFO org.nd4j.nativeblas.Nd4jBlas - Number of threads used for BLAS: 6
[main] INFO org.nd4j.linalg.api.ops.executioner.DefaultOpExecutioner - Backend used: [CPU]; OS: [Mac OS X]
[main] INFO org.nd4j.linalg.api.ops.executioner.DefaultOpExecutioner - Cores: [12]; Memory: [3.6GB];
[main] INFO org.nd4j.linalg.api.ops.executioner.DefaultOpExecutioner - Blas vendor: [MKL]
[main] INFO org.deeplearning4j.nn.graph.ComputationGraph - Starting ComputationGraph with WorkspaceModes set to [training: ENABLED; inference:
0.7654207465579799
AUC (Area under ROC Curve):           0.7654207465579799
AUPRC (Area under Precision/Recall Curve): 0.346697424222832
[Note: Thresholded AUC/AUPRC calculation used with 100 steps]; accuracy may reduced compared to exact mode]

Process finished with exit code 0
```

The stats() method will display the AUC score along with the **AUPRC** (short for **Area Under Precision/Recall Curve**) metrics. AUPRC is another performance metric where the curve represents the trade-off between precision and recall values. For a model with a good AUPRC score, positive samples can be found with fewer false positive results.

7
Constructing an LSTM Neural Network for Sequence Classification

In the previous chapter, we discussed classifying time series data for multi-variate features. In this chapter, we will create a **long short-term memory** (**LSTM**) neural network to classify univariate time series data. Our neural network will learn how to classify a univariate time series. We will have **UCI** (short for **University of California Irvine**) synthetic control data on top of which the neural network will be trained. There will be 600 sequences of data, with every sequence separated by a new line to make our job easier. Every sequence will have values recorded at 60 time steps. Since it is a univariate time series, we will only have columns in CSV files for every example recorded. Every sequence is an example recorded. We will split these sequences of data into train/test sets to perform training and evaluation respectively. The possible categories of class/labels are as follows:

- Normal
- Cyclic
- Increasing trend
- Decreasing trend
- Upward shift
- Downward shift

In this chapter, we will cover the following recipes:

- Extracting time series data
- Loading training data
- Normalizing training data

- Constructing input layers for the network
- Constructing output layers for the network
- Evaluating the LSTM network for classified output

Let's begin.

Technical requirements

This chapter's implementation code can be found at `https://github.com/PacktPublishing/Java-Deep-Learning-Cookbook/blob/master/07_Constructing_LSTM_Neural_network_for_sequence_classification/sourceCode/cookbookapp/src/main/java/UciSequenceClassificationExample.java`.

After cloning our GitHub repository, navigate to the `Java-Deep-Learning-Cookbook/07_Constructing_LSTM_Neural_network_for_sequence_classification/sourceCode` directory. Then import the `cookbookapp` project as a Maven project by importing `pom.xml`.

Download the data from this UCI website: `https://archive.ics.uci.edu/ml/machine-learning-databases/synthetic_control-mld/synthetic_control.data`.

We need to create directories to store the train and test data. Refer to the following directory structure:

We need to create two separate folders for the train and test datasets and then create subdirectories for `features` and `labels` respectively:

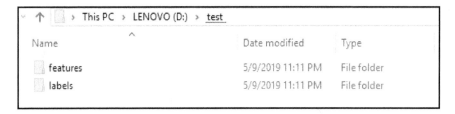

This folder structure is a prerequisite for the aforementioned data extraction. We separate features and labels while performing the extraction.

Note that, throughout this cookbook, we are using the DL4J version 1.0.0-beta 3, except in this chapter. You might come across the following error while executing the code that we discuss in this chapter:

```
Exception in thread "main" java.lang.IllegalStateException: C (result)
array is not F order or is a view. Nd4j.gemm requires the result array to
be F order and not a view. C (result) array: [Rank: 2,Offset: 0 Order: f
Shape: [10,1], stride: [1,10]]
```

At the time of writing, a new version of DL4J has been released that resolves the issue. Hence, we will use version 1.0.0-beta 4 to run the examples in this chapter.

Extracting time series data

We are using another time series use case, but this time we are targeting time series univariate sequence classification. ETL needs to be discussed before we configure the LSTM neural network. Data extraction is the first phase in the ETL process. This recipe covers data extraction for this use case.

How to do it...

1. Categorize the sequence data programmatically:

```
// convert URI to string
final String data = IOUtils.toString(new URL(url),"utf-8");
// Get sequences from the raw data
final String[] sequences = data.split("\n");
final List<Pair<String,Integer>> contentAndLabels = new
ArrayList<>();
int lineCount = 0;
for(String sequence : sequences) {
// Record each time step in new line
sequence = sequence.replaceAll(" +","\n");
// Labels: first 100 examples (lines) are label 0, second 100
examples are label 1, and so on
contentAndLabels.add(new Pair<>(sequence, lineCount++ / 100));
}
```

2. Store the features/labels in their corresponding directories by following the numbered format:

```
for(Pair<String,Integer> sequencePair : contentAndLabels) {
if(trainCount<450) {
featureFile = new File(trainfeatureDir+trainCount+".csv");
labelFile = new File(trainlabelDir+trainCount+".csv");
trainCount++;
} else {
featureFile = new File(testfeatureDir+testCount+".csv");
labelFile = new File(testlabelDir+testCount+".csv");
testCount++;
}
}
```

3. Use `FileUtils` to write the data into files:

```
FileUtils.writeStringToFile(featureFile,sequencePair.getFirst(),"ut
f-8");
FileUtils.writeStringToFile(labelFile,sequencePair.getSecond().toSt
ring(),"utf-8");
```

How it works...

When we open the synthetic control data after the download, it will look like the following:

```
28.7812 34.4632 31.3381 31.2834 28.9207 33.7596 25.3969 27.7849 35.2479 27.1159 32.8717
29.2171 36.0253 32.337  34.5249 32.8717 34.1173 26.5235 27.6623 26.3693 25.7744 29.27
30.7326 29.5054 33.0292 25.04   28.9167 24.3437 26.1203 34.9424 25.0293 26.6311 35.6541
28.4353 29.1495 28.1584 26.1927 33.3182 30.9772 27.0443 35.5344 26.2353 28.9964 32.0036
31.0558 34.2553 28.0721 28.9402 35.4973 29.747  31.4333 24.5556 33.7431 25.0466 34.9318
34.9879 32.4721 33.3759 25.4652 25.8717
24.8923 25.741  27.5532 32.8217 27.8789 31.5926 31.4861 35.5469 27.9516 31.6595 27.5415
31.1887 27.4867 31.391  27.811  24.488  27.5918 35.6273 35.4102 31.4167 30.7447 24.1311
35.1422 30.4719 31.9874 33.6615 25.5511 30.4686 33.6472 25.0701 34.0765 32.5981 28.3038
26.1471 26.9414 31.5203 33.1089 24.1491 28.5157 25.7906 35.9519 26.5301 24.8578 25.9562
32.8357 28.5322 26.3458 30.6213 28.9861 29.4047 32.5577 31.0205 26.6418 28.4331 33.6564
26.4244 28.4661 34.2484 32.1005 26.691
31.3987 30.6316 26.3983 24.2905 27.8613 28.5491 24.9717 32.4358 25.2239 27.3068 31.8387
27.2587 28.2572 26.5819 24.0455 35.0625 31.5717 32.5614 31.0308 34.1202 26.9337 31.4781
35.0173 32.3851 24.3323 30.2001 31.2452 26.6814 31.5137 28.8778 27.3086 24.246  26.9631
25.2919 31.6114 24.7131 27.4809 24.2075 26.8059 35.1253 32.6293 31.0561 26.3583 28.0861
31.4391 27.3057 29.6082 35.9725 34.1444 27.1717 33.6318 26.5966 25.5387 32.5434 25.5772
29.9897 31.351  33.9002 29.5446 29.343
```

A single sequence is marked in the preceding screenshot. There are 600 sequences in total, and each sequence is separated by a new line. In our example, we can split the dataset in such a way that 450 sequences will be used for training and the remaining 150 sequences will be used for evaluation. We are trying to categorize a given sequence against six known classes.

Note that this is a univariate time series. The data that is recorded in a single sequence is spread across different time steps. We create separate files for every single sequence. A single data unit (observation) is separated by a space within the file. We will replace spaces with new line characters so that measurements for every time step in a single sequence will appear on a new line. The first 100 sequences represent category 1, and the next 100 sequences represent category 2, and so on. Since we have univariate time series data, there is only one column in the CSV files. So, one single feature is recorded over multiple time steps.

In step 1, the `contentAndLabels` list will have sequence-to-label mappings. Each sequence represents a label. The sequence and label together form a pair.

Now we can have two different approaches to splitting data for training/testing purposes:

- Randomly shuffle the data and take 450 sequences for training and the remaining 150 sequences for evaluation/testing purposes.
- Split the train/test data in such a way that the categories are equally distributed across the dataset. For example, we can have 420 sequences of train data with 70 samples for each of the six categories.

We use randomization as a measure to increase the generalization power of the neural network. Every sequence-to-label pair was written to a separate CSV file following the numbered file naming convention.

In step 2, we mention that there are 450 samples for training, and the remaining 150 are for evaluation.

In step 3, we use `FileUtils` from the Apache Commons library to write the data to a file. The final code will look like the following:

```
for(Pair<String,Integer> sequencePair : contentAndLabels) {
    if(trainCount<traintestSplit) {
        featureFile = new File(trainfeatureDir+trainCount+".csv");
        labelFile = new File(trainlabelDir+trainCount+".csv");
        trainCount++;
    } else {
        featureFile = new File(testfeatureDir+testCount+".csv");
        labelFile = new File(testlabelDir+testCount+".csv");
```

```
        testCount++;
    }
FileUtils.writeStringToFile(featureFile,sequencePair.getFirst(),"utf-8");
FileUtils.writeStringToFile(labelFile,sequencePair.getSecond().toString(),"
utf-8");
    }
```

We fetch the sequence data and add it to the `features` directory, and each sequence will be represented by a separate CSV file. Similarly, we add the respective labels to a separate CSV file.

`1.csv` in the `label` directory will be the respective label for the `1.csv` feature in the `feature` directory.

Loading training data

Data transformation is, as usual, the second phase after data extraction. The time series data we're discussing doesn't have any non-numeric fields or noise (it had already been cleaned). So we can focus on constructing the iterators from the data and loading them directly into the neural network. In this recipe, we will load univariate time series data for neural network training. We have extracted the synthetic control data and stored it in a suitable format so the neural network can process it effortlessly. Every sequence is captured over 60 time steps. In this recipe, we will load the time series data into an appropriate dataset iterator, which can be fed to the neural network for further processing.

How to do it...

1. Create a `SequenceRecordReader` instance to extract and load features from the time series data:

   ```
   SequenceRecordReader trainFeaturesSequenceReader = new
   CSVSequenceRecordReader();
    trainFeaturesSequenceReader.initialize(new
   NumberedFileInputSplit(new
   File(trainfeatureDir).getAbsolutePath()+"/%d.csv",0,449));
   ```

2. Create a `SequenceRecordReader` instance to extract and load labels from the time series data:

   ```
   SequenceRecordReader trainLabelsSequenceReader = new
   CSVSequenceRecordReader();
    trainLabelsSequenceReader.initialize(new
   ```

```
NumberedFileInputSplit(new
File(trainlabelDir).getAbsolutePath()+"/%d.csv",0,449));
```

3. Create sequence readers for testing and evaluation:

```
SequenceRecordReader testFeaturesSequenceReader = new
CSVSequenceRecordReader();
 testFeaturesSequenceReader.initialize(new
NumberedFileInputSplit(new
File(testfeatureDir).getAbsolutePath()+"/%d.csv",0,149));
 SequenceRecordReader testLabelsSequenceReader = new
CSVSequenceRecordReader();
 testLabelsSequenceReader.initialize(new NumberedFileInputSplit(new
File(testlabelDir).getAbsolutePath()+"/%d.csv",0,149));|
```

4. Use `SequenceRecordReaderDataSetIterator` to feed the data into our neural network:

```
DataSetIterator trainIterator = new
SequenceRecordReaderDataSetIterator(trainFeaturesSequenceReader,tra
inLabelsSequenceReader,batchSize,numOfClasses);

DataSetIterator testIterator = new
SequenceRecordReaderDataSetIterator(testFeaturesSequenceReader,test
LabelsSequenceReader,batchSize,numOfClasses);
```

5. Rewrite the train/test iterator (with `AlignmentMode`) to support time series of varying lengths:

```
DataSetIterator trainIterator = new
SequenceRecordReaderDataSetIterator(trainFeaturesSequenceReader,tra
inLabelsSequenceReader,batchSize,numOfClasses,false,
SequenceRecordReaderDataSetIterator.AlignmentMode.ALIGN_END);
```

How it works...

We have used `NumberedFileInputSplit` in step 1. It is necessary to use `NumberedFileInputSplit` to load data from multiple files that follow a numbered file naming convention. Refer to step 1 in this recipe:

```
SequenceRecordReader trainFeaturesSequenceReader = new
CSVSequenceRecordReader();
 trainFeaturesSequenceReader.initialize(new NumberedFileInputSplit(new
File(trainfeatureDir).getAbsolutePath()+"/%d.csv",0,449));
```

We stored files as a sequence of numbered files in the previous recipe. There are 450 files, and each one of them represents a sequence. Note that we have stored 150 files for testing as demonstrated in step 3.

In step 5, `numOfClasses` specifies the number of categories against which the neural network is trying to make a prediction. In our example, it is 6. We mentioned `AlignmentMode.ALIGN_END` while creating the iterator. The alignment mode deals with input/labels of varying lengths. For example, our time series data has 60 time steps, and there's only one label at the end of the 60th time step. That's the reason why we use `AlignmentMode.ALIGN_END` in the iterator definition, as follows:

```
DataSetIterator trainIterator = new
SequenceRecordReaderDataSetIterator(trainFeaturesSequenceReader,trainLabels
SequenceReader,batchSize,numOfClasses,false,
SequenceRecordReaderDataSetIterator.AlignmentMode.ALIGN_END);
```

We can also have time series data that produces labels at every time step. These cases refer to many-to-many input/label connections.

In step 4, we started with the regular way of creating iterators, as follows:

```
DataSetIterator trainIterator = new
SequenceRecordReaderDataSetIterator(trainFeaturesSequenceReader,trainLabels
SequenceReader,batchSize,numOfClasses);

DataSetIterator testIterator = new
SequenceRecordReaderDataSetIterator(testFeaturesSequenceReader,testLabelsSe
quenceReader,batchSize,numOfClasses);
```

Note that this is not the only way to create sequence reader iterators. There are multiple implementations available in DataVec to support different configurations. We can also align the input/label at the last time step of the sample. For this purpose, we added `AlignmentMode.ALIGN_END` into the iterator definition. If there are varying time steps, shorter time series will be padded to the length of the longest time series. So, if there are samples that have fewer than 60 time steps recorded for a sequence, then zero values will be padded to the time series data.

Normalizing training data

Data transformation alone may not improve the neural network's efficiency. The existence of large and small ranges of values within the same dataset can lead to overfitting (the model captures noise rather than signals). To avoid these situations, we normalize the dataset, and there are multiple DL4J implementations to do this. The normalization process converts and fits the raw time series data into a definite value range, for example, *(0, 1)*. This will help the neural network process the data with less computational effort. We also discussed normalization in previous chapters, showing that it will reduce favoritism toward any specific label in the dataset while training a neural network.

How to do it...

1. Create a standard normalizer and fit the data:

```
DataNormalization normalization = new NormalizerStandardize();
 normalization.fit(trainIterator);
```

2. Call the `setPreprocessor()` method to normalize the data on the fly:

```
trainIterator.setPreProcessor(normalization);
 testIterator.setPreProcessor(normalization);
```

How it works...

In step 1, we used `NormalizerStandardize` to normalize the dataset. `NormalizerStandardize` normalizes the data (features) so they have a mean of *0* and a standard deviation of *1*. In other words, all the values in the dataset will be normalized within the range of *(0, 1)*:

```
DataNormalization normalization = new NormalizerStandardize();
 normalization.fit(trainIterator);
```

This is a standard normalizer in DL4J, although there are other normalizer implementations available in DL4J. Also, note that we don't need to call `fit()` on test data because we use the scaling parameters learned during training to scale the test data.

We need to call the `setPreprocessor()` method as we demonstrated in step 2 for both train/test iterators. Once we have set the normalizer using `setPreprocessor()`, the data returned by the iterator will be auto-normalized using the specified normalizer. Hence it is important to call `setPreprocessor()` along with the `fit()` method.

Constructing input layers for the network

Layer configuration is an important step in neural network configuration. We need to create input layers to receive the univariate time series data that was loaded from disk. In this recipe, we will construct an input layer for our use case. We will also add an LSTM layer as a hidden layer for the neural network. We can use either a computation graph or a regular multilayer network to build the network configuration. In most cases, a regular multilayer network is more than enough; however, we are using a computation graph for our use case. In this recipe, we will configure input layers for the network.

How to do it...

1. Configure the neural network with default configurations:

```
NeuralNetConfiguration.Builder neuralNetConfigBuilder = new
NeuralNetConfiguration.Builder();
 neuralNetConfigBuilder.seed(123);
 neuralNetConfigBuilder.weightInit(WeightInit.XAVIER);
 neuralNetConfigBuilder.updater(new Nadam());
neuralNetConfigBuilder.gradientNormalization(GradientNormalization.
ClipElementWiseAbsoluteValue);
 neuralNetConfigBuilder.gradientNormalizationThreshold(0.5);
```

2. Specify the input layer labels by calling `addInputs()`:

```
ComputationGraphConfiguration.GraphBuilder compGraphBuilder =
neuralNetConfigBuilder.graphBuilder();
 compGraphBuilder.addInputs("trainFeatures");
```

3. Add an LSTM layer using the `addLayer()` method:

```
compGraphBuilder.addLayer("L1", new
LSTM.Builder().activation(Activation.TANH).nIn(1).nOut(10).build(),
"trainFeatures");
```

How it works...

In step 1, we specify the default `seed` values, the initial default weights (`weightInit`), the weight `updater`, and so on. We set the gradient normalization strategy to `ClipElementWiseAbsoluteValue`. We have also set the gradient threshold to `0.5` as an input to the `gradientNormalization` strategy.

The neural network calculates the gradients across neurons at each layer. We normalized the input data earlier in the *Normalizing training data* recipe, using a normalizer. It makes sense to mention that we need to normalize the gradient values to achieve data preparation goals. As we can see in step 1, we have used `ClipElementWiseAbsoluteValue` gradient normalization. It works in such a way that the absolute value of the gradient cannot be greater than the threshold. For example, if the gradient threshold value is 3, then the value range would be [-3, 3]. Any gradient values that are less than -5 would be treated as -3 and any gradient values that are higher than 3 would be treated as 3. Gradient values in the range [-3, 3] will be unmodified. We have mentioned the gradient normalization strategy as well as the threshold in the network configuration, as shown here:

```
neuralNetConfigBuilder.gradientNormalization(GradientNormalization.ClipElem
entWiseAbsoluteValue);
  neuralNetConfigBuilder.gradientNormalizationThreshold(thresholdValue);
```

In step 3, the `trainFeatures` label is referred to the input layer label. The inputs are basically the graph vertex objects returned by the `graphBuilder()` method. The specified LSTM layer name (`L1` in our example) in step 2 will be used while configuring the output layer. If there's a mismatch, our program will throw an error during execution saying that the layers are configured in such a way that they are disconnected. We will discuss this in more depth in the next recipe, when we design output layers for the neural network. Note that we have yet to add output layers in the configuration.

Constructing output layers for the network

The very next step after the input/hidden layer design is the output layer design. As we mentioned in earlier chapters, the output layer should reflect the output you want to receive from the neural network. You may need a classifier or a regression model depending on the use case. Accordingly, the output layer has to be configured. The activation function and error function need to be justified for their use in the output layer configuration. This recipe assumes that the neural network configuration has been completed up to the input layer definition. This is going to be the last step in network configuration.

How to do it...

1. Use `setOutputs()` to set the output labels:

```
compGraphBuilder.setOutputs("predictSequence");
```

2. Construct an output layer using the `addLayer()` method and `RnnOutputLayer`:

```
compGraphBuilder.addLayer("predictSequence", new
RnnOutputLayer.Builder(LossFunctions.LossFunction.MCXENT)
.activation(Activation.SOFTMAX).nIn(10).nOut(numOfClasses).build(),
"L1");
```

How it works...

In step 1, we have added a `predictSequence` label for the output layer. Note that we mentioned the input layer reference when defining the output layer. In step 2, we specified it as `L1`, which is the LSTM input layer created in the previous recipe. We need to mention this to avoid any errors during execution due to disconnection between the LSTM layer and the output layer. Also, the output layer definition should have the same layer name we specified in the `setOutput()` method.

In step 2, we have used `RnnOutputLayer` to construct the output layer. This DL4J output layer implementation is used for use cases that involve recurrent neural networks. It is functionally the same as `OutputLayer` in multi-layer perceptrons, but output and label reshaping are automatically handled.

Evaluating the LSTM network for classified output

Now that we have configured the neural network, the next step is to start the training instance, followed by evaluation. The evaluation phase is very important for the training instance. The neural network will try to optimize the gradients for optimal results. An optimal neural network will have good and stable evaluation metrics. So it is important to evaluate the neural network to direct the training process toward the desired results. We will use the test dataset to evaluate the neural network.

In the previous chapter, we explored a use case for time series binary classification. Now we have six labels against which to predict. We have discussed various ways to enhance the network's efficiency. We follow the same approach in the next recipe to evaluate the neural network for optimal results.

How to do it...

1. Initialize the `ComputationGraph` model configuration using the `init()` method:

```
ComputationGraphConfiguration configuration =
compGraphBuilder.build();
   ComputationGraph model = new ComputationGraph(configuration);
 model.init();
```

2. Set a score listener to monitor the training process:

```
model.setListeners(new ScoreIterationListener(20), new
EvaluativeListener(testIterator, 1, InvocationType.EPOCH_END));
```

3. Start the training instance by calling the `fit()` method:

```
model.fit(trainIterator,numOfEpochs);
```

4. Call `evaluate()` to calculate the evaluation metrics:

```
Evaluation evaluation = model.evaluate(testIterator);
 System.out.println(evaluation.stats());
```

How it works...

In step 1, we used a computation graph when configuring the neural network's structure. Computation graphs are the best choice for recurrent neural networks. We get an evaluation score of approximately 78% with a multi-layer network and a whopping 94% while using a computation graph. We get better results with `ComputationGraph` than the regular multi-layer perceptron. `ComputationGraph` is meant for complex network structures and can be customized to accommodate different types of layers in various orders. `InvocationType.EPOCH_END` is used (score iteration) in step 1 to call the score iterator at the end of a test iteration.

Note that we're calling the score iterator for every test iteration, and not for the training set iteration. Proper listeners need to be set by calling `setListeners()` before your training event starts to log the scores for every test iteration, as shown here:

```
model.setListeners(new ScoreIterationListener(20), new
EvaluativeListener(testIterator, 1, InvocationType.EPOCH_END));
```

In step 4, the model was evaluated by calling `evaluate()`:

```
Evaluation evaluation = model.evaluate(testIterator);
```

We passed the test dataset to the `evaluate()` method in the form of an iterator that was created earlier in the *Loading the training data* recipe.

Also, we use the `stats()` method to display the results. For a computation graph with 100 epochs, we get the following evaluation metrics:

```
UciSequenceClassificationExample

=======================Evaluation Metrics========================
 # of classes:    6
 Accuracy:        0.9400
 Precision:       0.9415
 Recall:          0.9430
 F1 Score:        0.9394
Precision, recall & F1: macro-averaged (equally weighted avg. of 6 classes)


=======================Confusion Matrix========================
   0  1  2  3  4  5
 ---------------------
  26  0  0  0  0  0 | 0 = 0
   0 28  0  0  0  1 | 1 = 1
   0  0 21  0  1  0 | 2 = 2
   0  0  0 19  0  2 | 3 = 3
   0  0  5  0 25  0 | 4 = 4
   0  0  0  0  0 22 | 5 = 5

Confusion matrix format: Actual (rowClass) predicted as (columnClass) N times
==============================================================


Process finished with exit code 0
```

Now, the following are the experiments you can perform to optimize the results even better.

We used 100 epochs in our example. Reduce the epochs from 100 or increase this setting to a specific value. Note the direction that gives better results. Stop when the results are optimal. We can evaluate the results once in every epoch to understand the direction in which we can proceed. Check out the following training instance logs:

The accuracy declines after the previous epoch in the preceding example. Accordingly, you can decide on the optimal number of epochs. The neural network will simply memorize the results if we go for large epochs, and this leads to overfitting.

Instead of randomizing the data at first, you can ensure that the six categories are uniformly distributed across the training set. For example, we can have 420 samples for training and 180 samples for testing. Then, each category will be represented by 70 samples. We can now perform randomization followed by iterator creation. Note that we had 450 samples for training in our example. In this case, the distribution of labels/categories isn't unique and we are totally relying on the randomization of data in this case.

Performing Anomaly Detection on Unsupervised Data

8

In this chapter, we will perform anomaly detection with the **Modified National Institute of Standards and Technology** (**MNIST**) dataset using a simple autoencoder without any pretraining. We will identify the outliers in the given MNIST data. Outlier digits can be considered as most untypical or not normal digits. We will encode the MNIST data and then decode it back in the output layer. Then, we will calculate the reconstruction error for the MNIST data.

The MNIST sample that closely resembles a digit value will have low reconstruction error. We will then sort them based on the reconstruction errors and then display the best samples and the worst samples (outliers) using the JFrame window. The autoencoder is constructed using a feed-forward network. Note that we are not performing any pretraining. We can process feature inputs in an autoencoder and we won't require MNIST labels at any stage.

In this chapter, we will cover the following recipes:

- Extracting and preparing MNIST data
- Constructing dense layers for input
- Constructing output layers
- Training with MNIST images
- Evaluating and sorting the results based on the anomaly score
- Saving the resultant model

Let's begin.

Technical requirements

The code for this chapter can be found here: `https://github.com/PacktPublishing/Java-Deep-Learning-Cookbook/blob/master/08_Performing_Anomaly_detection_on_unsupervised%20data/sourceCode/cookbook-app/src/main/java/MnistAnomalyDetectionExample.java`.

The JFrame-specific implementation can be found here:
`https://github.com/PacktPublishing/Java-Deep-Learning-Cookbook/blob/master/08_Performing_Anomaly_detection_on_unsupervised%20data/sourceCode/cookbook-app/src/main/java/MnistAnomalyDetectionExample.java#L134`.

After cloning our GitHub repository, navigate to the `Java-Deep-Learning-Cookbook/08_Performing_Anomaly_detection_on_unsupervised data/sourceCode` directory. Then, import the `cookbook-app` project as a Maven project by importing `pom.xml`.

Note that we use the MNIST dataset from here: `http://yann.lecun.com/exdb/mnist/`.

However, we don't have to download the dataset for this chapter: DL4J has a custom implementation that allows us to fetch MNIST data automatically. We will be using this in this chapter.

Extracting and preparing MNIST data

Unlike supervised image classification use cases, we will perform an anomaly detection task on the MNIST dataset. On top of that, we are using an unsupervised model, which means that we will not be using any type of label to perform the training process. To start the ETL process, we will extract this unsupervised MNIST data and prepare it so that it is usable for neural network training.

How to do it...

1. Create iterators for the MNIST data using `MnistDataSetIterator`:

```
DataSetIterator iter = new
MnistDataSetIterator(miniBatchSize,numOfExamples,binarize);
```

2. Use `SplitTestAndTrain` to split the base iterator into train/test iterators:

```
DataSet ds = iter.next();
 SplitTestAndTrain split = ds.splitTestAndTrain(numHoldOut, new
Random(12345));
```

3. Create lists to store the feature sets from the train/test iterators:

```
List<INDArray> featuresTrain = new ArrayList<>();
 List<INDArray> featuresTest = new ArrayList<>();
 List<INDArray> labelsTest = new ArrayList<>();
```

4. Populate the values into the feature/label lists that were previously created:

```
featuresTrain.add(split.getTrain().getFeatures());
 DataSet dsTest = split.getTest();
 featuresTest.add(dsTest.getFeatures());
 INDArray indexes = Nd4j.argMax(dsTest.getLabels(),1);
 labelsTest.add(indexes);
```

5. Call `argmax()` for every iterator instance to convert the labels to one dimensional data if it's multidimensional:

```
while(iter.hasNext()){
 DataSet ds = iter.next();
 SplitTestAndTrain split = ds.splitTestAndTrain(80, new
Random(12345)); // 80/20 split (from miniBatch = 100)
 featuresTrain.add(split.getTrain().getFeatures());
 DataSet dsTest = split.getTest();
 featuresTest.add(dsTest.getFeatures());
 INDArray indexes = Nd4j.argMax(dsTest.getLabels(),1);
 labelsTest.add(indexes);
 }
```

How it works...

In step 1, we have used `MnistDataSetIterator` to extract and load MNIST data in one place. DL4J comes with this specialized iterator to load MNIST data without having to worry about downloading the data on your own. You might notice that MNIST data on the official website follows the `ubyte` format. This is certainly not the desired format, and we need to extract all the images separately to load them properly on the neural network.

Therefore, it is very convenient to have an MNIST iterator implementation such as `MnistDataSetIterator` in DL4J. It simplifies the typical task of handling MNIST data in the `ubyte` format. MNIST data has a total of 60,000 training digits, 10,000 test digits, and 10 labels. Digit images have a dimension of 28 x 28, the shape of the data is in a flattened format: [minibatch, 784]. `MnistDataSetIterator` internally uses the `MnistDataFetcher` and `MnistManager` classes to fetch the MNIST data and load them into the proper format. In step 1, `binarize: true` or `false` indicates whether to binarize the MNIST data.

Note that in step 2, `numHoldOut` indicates the number of samples to be held for training. If `miniBatchSize` is `100` and `numHoldOut` is `80`, then the remaining 20 samples are meant for testing and evaluation. We can use `DataSetIteratorSplitter` instead of `SplitTestAndTrain` for splitting of data, as mentioned in step 2.

In step 3, we created lists to maintain the features and labels with respect to training and testing. We need them for the training and evaluation stages, respectively. We also created a list to store labels from the test set to map the outliers with labels during the test and evaluation phases. These lists are populated once in every occurrence of a batch. For example, in the case of `featuresTrain` or `featuresTest`, a batch of features (after data splitting) is represented by an `INDArray` item. We have also used an `argMax()` function from ND4J. This converts the labels array into a one-dimensional array. MNIST labels from `0` to `9` effectively need just one-dimensional space for representation.

In the following code, `1` denotes the dimension:

```
Nd4j.argMax(dsTest.getLabels(),1);
```

Also, note that we use the labels for mapping outliers to labels and not for training.

Constructing dense layers for input

The core of the neural network design is the layer architecture. For autoencoders, we need to design dense layers that do encoding at the front and decoding at the other end. Basically, we are reconstructing the inputs in this way. Accordingly, we need to make our layer design.

Let's start configuring our autoencoder using the default settings and then proceed further by defining the necessary input layers for our autoencoder. Remember that the number of incoming connections to the neural network will be equal to the number of outgoing connections from the neural network.

How to do it...

1. Use `MultiLayerConfiguration` to construct the autoencoder network:

```
NeuralNetConfiguration.Builder configBuilder = new
NeuralNetConfiguration.Builder();
 configBuilder.seed(12345);
 configBuilder.weightInit(WeightInit.XAVIER);
 configBuilder.updater(new AdaGrad(0.05));
 configBuilder.activation(Activation.RELU);
 configBuilder.l2(l2RegCoefficient);
 NeuralNetConfiguration.ListBuilder builder = configBuilder.list();
```

2. Create input layers using `DenseLayer`:

```
builder.layer(new DenseLayer.Builder().nIn(784).nOut(250).build());
 builder.layer(new DenseLayer.Builder().nIn(250).nOut(10).build());
```

How it works...

In step 1, while configuring generic neural network parameters, we set the default learning rate as shown here:

```
configBuilder.updater(new AdaGrad(learningRate));
```

The `Adagrad` optimizer is based on how frequently a parameter gets updated during training. `Adagrad` is based on a vectorized learning rate. The learning rate will be small when there are many updates received. This is crucial for high-dimensional problems. Hence, this optimizer can be a good fit for our autoencoder use case.

We are performing dimensionality reduction at the input layers in an autoencoder architecture. This is also known as encoding the data. We want to ensure that the same set of features are decoded from the encoded data. We calculate reconstruction errors to measure how close we are compared to the real feature set before encoding. In step 2, we are trying to encode the data from a higher dimension (784) to a lower dimension (10).

Constructing output layers

As a final step, we need to decode the data back from the encoded state. Are we able to reconstruct the input just the way it is? If yes, then it's all good. Otherwise, we need to calculate an associated reconstruction error. Remember that the incoming connections to the output layer should be the same as the outgoing connections from the preceding layer.

How to do it...

1. Create an output layer using `OutputLayer`:

```
OutputLayer outputLayer = new
OutputLayer.Builder().nIn(250).nOut(784)
  .lossFunction(LossFunctions.LossFunction.MSE)
  .build();
```

2. Add `OutputLayer` to the layer definitions:

```
builder.layer(new OutputLayer.Builder().nIn(250).nOut(784)
  .lossFunction(LossFunctions.LossFunction.MSE)
  .build());
```

How it works...

We have mentioned the **mean square error** (**MSE**) as the error function associated with the output layer. `lossFunction`, which is used in autoencoder architecture, is MSE in most cases. MSE is optimal in calculating how close the reconstructed input is to the original input. ND4J has an implementation for MSE, which is `LossFunction.MSE`.

In the output layer, we get the reconstructed input in their original dimensions. We will then use an error function to calculate the reconstruction error. In step 1, we're constructing an output layer that calculates the reconstruction error for anomaly detection. It is important to keep the incoming and outgoing connections the same at the input and output layers, respectively. Once the output layer definition is created, we need to add it to a stack of layer configurations that is maintained to create the neural network configuration. In step 2, we added the output layer to the previously maintained neural network configuration builder. In order to follow an intuitive approach, we have created configuration builders first, unlike the straightforward approach here: `https://github. com/PacktPublishing/Java-Deep-Learning-Cookbook/blob/master/08_Performing_ Anomaly_detection_on_unsupervised%20data/sourceCode/cookbook-app/src/main/java/ MnistAnomalyDetectionExample.java`.

You can obtain a configuration instance by calling the `build()` method on the `Builder` instance.

Training with MNIST images

Once the layers are constructed and the neural network is formed, we can initiate the training session. During the training session, we reconstruct the input multiple times and evaluate the reconstruction error. In previous recipes, we completed the autoencoder network configuration by defining the input and output layers as required. Note that we are going to train the network with its own input features, not the labels. Since we use an autoencoder for anomaly detection, we encode the data and then decode it back to measure the reconstruction error. Based on that, we list the most probable anomalies in MNIST data.

How to do it...

1. Choose the correct training approach. Here is what is expected to happen during the training instance:

   ```
   Input -> Encoded Input -> Decode -> Output
   ```

   So, we need to train output against input (output ~ input, in an ideal case).

2. Train every feature set using the `fit()` method:

   ```
   int nEpochs = 30;
   for( int epoch=0; epoch<nEpochs; epoch++ ){
   for(INDArray data : featuresTrain){
   net.fit(data,data);
   }
   }
   ```

How it works...

The `fit()` method accepts both features and labels as attributes for the first and second attributes, respectively. We reconstruct the MNIST features against themselves. In other words, we are trying to recreate the features once they are encoded and check how much they vary from actual features. We measure the reconstruction error during training and bother only about the feature values. So, the output is validated against the input and resembles how an autoencoder functions. So, step 1 is crucial for the evaluation stage as well.

Refer to this block of code:

```
for(INDArray data : featuresTrain){
 net.fit(data,data);
}
```

That's the reason why we train the autoencoder against its own features (inputs) as we call `fit()` in this way: `net.fit(data,data)` in step 2.

Evaluating and sorting the results based on the anomaly score

We need to calculate the reconstruction error for all the feature sets. Based on that, we will find the outlier data for all the MNIST digits (0 to 9). Finally, we will display the outlier data in the JFrame window. We also need feature values from a test set for the evaluation. We also need label values from the test set, not for evaluation, but for mapping anomalies with labels. Then, we can plot outlier data against each label. The labels are only used for plotting outlier data in JFrame against respective labels. In this recipe, we evaluate the trained autoencoder model for MNIST anomaly detection, and then sort the results and display them.

How to do it...

1. Compose a map that relates each MNIST digit to a list of (score, feature) pairs:

```
Map<Integer,List<Pair<Double,INDArray>>> listsByDigit = new
HashMap<>();
```

2. Iterate through each and every test feature, calculate the reconstruction error, make a score-feature pair for the purpose of displaying the sample with a low reconstruction error:

```
for( int i=0; i<featuresTest.size(); i++ ){
 INDArray testData = featuresTest.get(i);
 INDArray labels = labelsTest.get(i);
 for( int j=0; j<testData.rows(); j++){
 INDArray example = testData.getRow(j, true);
 int digit = (int)labels.getDouble(j);
 double score = net.score(new DataSet(example,example));
 // Add (score, example) pair to the appropriate list
 List digitAllPairs = listsByDigit.get(digit);
```

```
digitAllPairs.add(new Pair<>(score, example));
}
}
```

3. Create a custom comparator to sort the map:

```
Comparator<Pair<Double, INDArray>> sortComparator = new
Comparator<Pair<Double, INDArray>>() {
@Override
public int compare(Pair<Double, INDArray> o1, Pair<Double,
INDArray> o2) {
return Double.compare(o1.getLeft(),o2.getLeft());
}
};
```

4. Sort the map using `Collections.sort()`:

```
for(List<Pair<Double, INDArray>> digitAllPairs :
listsByDigit.values()){
 Collections.sort(digitAllPairs, sortComparator);
}
```

5. Collect the best/worst data to display in a JFrame window for visualization:

```
List<INDArray> best = new ArrayList<>(50);
 List<INDArray> worst = new ArrayList<>(50);
 for( int i=0; i<10; i++ ){
 List<Pair<Double,INDArray>> list = listsByDigit.get(i);
 for( int j=0; j<5; j++ ){
 best.add(list.get(j).getRight());
 worst.add(list.get(list.size()-j-1).getRight());
 }
 }
```

6. Use a custom JFrame implementation for visualization, such as `MNISTVisualizer`, to visualize the results:

```
//Visualize the best and worst digits
 MNISTVisualizer bestVisualizer = new
MNISTVisualizer(imageScale,best,"Best (Low Rec. Error)");
 bestVisualizer.visualize();
 MNISTVisualizer worstVisualizer = new
MNISTVisualizer(imageScale,worst,"Worst (High Rec. Error)");
 worstVisualizer.visualize();
```

How it works...

Using step 1 and step 2, for every MNIST digit, we maintain a list of (score, feature) pairs. We composed a map that relates each MNIST digit to this list of pairs. In the end, we just have to sort it to find the best/worst cases.

Also, we used the `score()` function to calculate the reconstruction error:

```
double score = net.score(new DataSet(example,example));
```

During the evaluation, we reconstruct the test features and measure how much it differs from actual feature values. A high reconstruction error indicates the presence of a high percentage of outliers.

After step 4, we should see JFrame visualization for reconstruction errors, as shown here:

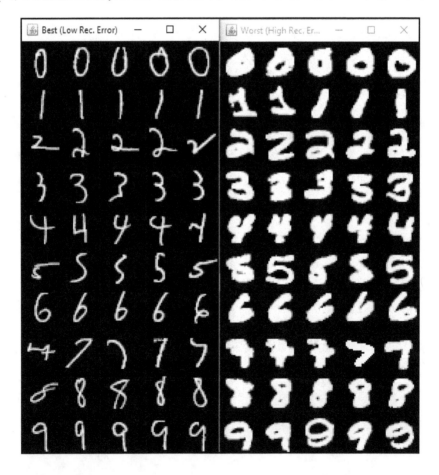

Visualization is JFrame dependent. Basically, what we do is take the *N* best/worst pairs from the previously created map in step 1. We make a list of best/worst data and pass it to our JFrame visualization logic to display the outlier in the JFrame window. The JFrame window on the right side represents the outlier data. We are leaving the JFrame implementation aside as it is beyond the scope for this book. For the complete JFrame implementation, refer to GitHub source mentioned in the *Technical requirements* section.

Saving the resultant model

Model persistence is very important as it enables the reuse of neural network models without having to train more than once. Once the autoencoder is trained to perform outlier detection, we can save the model to the disk for later use. We explained the `ModelSerializer` class in a previous chapter. We use this to save the autoencoder model.

How to do it...

1. Use `ModelSerializer` to persist the model:

```
File modelFile = new File("model.zip");
    ModelSerializer.writeModel(multiLayerNetwork,file, saveUpdater);
```

2. Add a normalizer to the persisted model:

```
ModelSerializer.addNormalizerToModel(modelFile,dataNormalization);
```

How it works...

We officially target the DL4J version 1.0.0-beta 3 in this chapter. We used `ModelSerializer` to save the models to disk. If you use the new version, 1.0.0-beta 4, there is another recommended way to save the model by using the `save()` method offered by `MultiLayerNetwork`:

```
File locationToSave = new File("MyMultiLayerNetwork.zip");
    model.save(locationToSave, saveUpdater);
```

Use `saveUpdater = true` if you want to train the network in the future.

There's more...

To restore the network model, call the `restoreMultiLayerNetwork()` method:

```
ModelSerializer.restoreMultiLayerNetwork(new File("model.zip"));
```

Additionally, if you use the latest version, 1.0.0-beta 4, you can use the `load()` method offered by `MultiLayerNetwork`:

```
MultiLayerNetwork restored = MultiLayerNetwork.load(locationToSave,
saveUpdater);
```

Using RL4J for Reinforcement Learning

9

Reinforcement learning is a goal-oriented machine learning algorithm that trains an agent to make a sequence of decisions. In the case of deep learning models, we train them on existing data and apply the learning on new or unseen data. Reinforcement learning exhibits dynamic learning by adjusting its own actions based on continuous feedback in order to maximize the reward. We can introduce deep learning into a reinforcement learning system, which is known as deep reinforcement learning.

RL4J is a reinforcement learning framework integrated with DL4J. RL4J supports two reinforcement algorithms: deep Q-learning and A3C (short for **Asynchronous Actor-Critic Agents**). Q-learning is an off-policy reinforcement learning algorithm that seeks the best action for the given state. It learns from actions outside the ones mentioned in the current policy by taking random actions. In deep Q-learning, we use a deep neural network to find the optimal Q-value rather than value iteration in regular Q-learning. In this chapter, we will set up a gaming environment powered by reinforcement learning using Project Malmo. Project Malmo is a platform for reinforcement learning experiments built on top of Minecraft.

In this chapter, we will cover the following recipes:

- Setting up the Malmo environment and respective dependencies
- Setting up the data requirements
- Configuring and training a Deep Q-Network (DQN) agent
- Evaluating a Malmo agent

Technical requirements

The source code for this chapter can be found here:
`https://github.com/PacktPublishing/Java-Deep-Learning-Cookbook/blob/master/09_Using_RL4J_for_Reinforcement%20learning/sourceCode/cookbookapp/src/main/java/MalmoExample.java`.

After cloning our GitHub repository, navigate to the `Java-Deep-Learning-Cookbook/09_Using_RL4J_for_Reinforcement learning/sourceCode` directory. Then, import the `cookbookapp` project as a Maven project by importing `pom.xml`.

You need to set up a Malmo client to run the source code. First, download the latest Project Malmo release as per your OS (`https://github.com/Microsoft/malmo/releases`):

- For Linux OS, follow the installation instructions here: `https://github.com/microsoft/malmo/blob/master/doc/install_linux.md`.
- For Windows OS, follow the installation instructions here: `https://github.com/microsoft/malmo/blob/master/doc/install_windows.md`.
- For macOS, follow the installation instructions here: `https://github.com/microsoft/malmo/blob/master/doc/install_macosx.md`.

To launch the Minecraft client, navigate to the Minecraft directory and run the client script:

- Double-click on `launchClient.bat` (on Windows).
- Run `./launchClient.sh` on the console (either on Linux or macOS).

If you're in Windows and are facing issues while launching the client, you can download the dependency walker here: `https://lucasg.github.io/Dependencies/`.

Then, follow these steps:

1. Extract and run `DependenciesGui.exe`.
2. Select `MalmoJava.dll` in the `Java_Examples` directory to see the missing dependencies like the ones shown here:

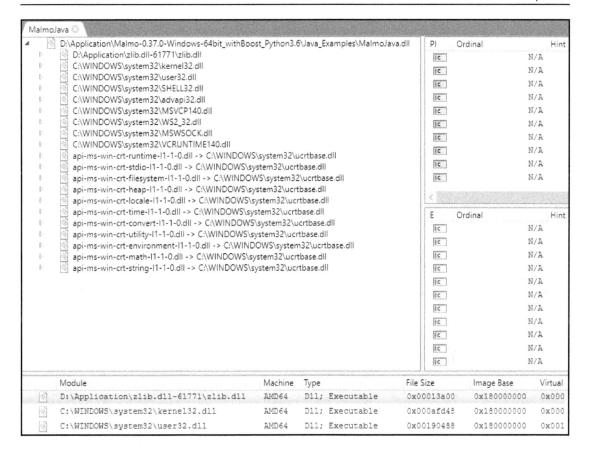

In the case of any issues, the missing dependencies will be marked on the list. You will need to add the missing dependencies in order to relaunch the client successfully. Any missing libraries/files should be present in the PATH environment variable.

You may refer to OS-specific build instructions here:

- https://github.com/microsoft/malmo/blob/master/doc/build_linux.md (Linux)
- https://github.com/microsoft/malmo/blob/master/doc/build_windows.md (Windows)
- https://github.com/microsoft/malmo/blob/master/doc/build_macosx.md (macOS)

If everything goes well, you should see something like this:

Additionally, you need to create a mission schema to build blocks for the gaming window. The complete mission schema can be found in this chapter's project directory at `https://github.com/PacktPublishing/Java-Deep-Learning-Cookbook/blob/master/09_Using_RL4J_for_Reinforcement%20learning/sourceCode/cookbookapp/src/main/resources/cliff_walking_rl4j.xml`.

Setting up the Malmo environment and respective dependencies

We need to set up RL4J Malmo dependencies to run the source code. Just like any other DL4J application, we also need to add ND4J backend dependencies as well depending upon your hardware (CPU/GPU). In this recipe, we will add the required Maven dependencies and set up the environment to run the application.

Getting ready

The Malmo client should be up and running before we run the Malmo example source code. Our source code will communicate with the Malmo client in order to create and run the missions.

How to do it...

1. Add the RL4J core dependency:

```
<dependency>
 <groupId>org.deeplearning4j</groupId>
 <artifactId>rl4j-core</artifactId>
 <version>1.0.0-beta3</version>
</dependency>
```

2. Add the RL4J Malmo dependency:

```
<dependency>
 <groupId>org.deeplearning4j</groupId>
 <artifactId>rl4j-malmo</artifactId>
 <version>1.0.0-beta3</version>
</dependency>
```

3. Add a dependency for the ND4J backend:
   - For CPU, you can use the following:

```
<dependency>
 <groupId>org.nd4j</groupId>
 <artifactId>nd4j-native-platform</artifactId>
 <version>1.0.0-beta3</version>
</dependency>
```

   - For GPU, you can use the following:

```
<dependency>
 <groupId>org.nd4j</groupId>
 <artifactId>nd4j-cuda-10.0</artifactId>
 <version>1.0.0-beta3</version>
</dependency>
```

4. Add Maven dependency for `MalmoJavaJar`:

```
<dependency>
 <groupId>com.microsoft.msr.malmo</groupId>
 <artifactId>MalmoJavaJar</artifactId>
 <version>0.30.0</version>
</dependency>
```

How it works...

In step 1, we added RL4J core dependencies to bring in RL4J DQN libraries in our application. RL4J Malmo dependencies are added in step 2 to construct the Malmo environment and build missions in RL4J.

We need to add CPU/GPU-specific ND4J backend dependencies as well (step 3). Finally, in step 4, we added dependencies for `MalmoJavaJar` (step 4), which acts as a communication interface for the Java program to interact with Malmo.

Setting up the data requirements

The data for the Malmo reinforcement learning environment includes the image frames that the agent is moving in. A sample gaming window for Malmo will look like the following. Here, the agent dies if they step over the lava:

Malmo requires developers to specify the XML schema in order to generate the mission. We will need to create mission data for both the agent and the server to create blocks in the world (that is, the gaming environment). In this recipe, we will create an XML schema to specify the mission data.

How to do it...

1. Define the initial conditions of the world using the `<ServerInitialConditions>` tag:

```
Sample:
<ServerInitialConditions>
<Time>
<StartTime>6000</StartTime>
<AllowPassageOfTime>false</AllowPassageOfTime>
</Time>
<Weather>clear</Weather>
<AllowSpawning>false</AllowSpawning>
</ServerInitialConditions>
```

2. Navigate to `http://www.minecraft101.net/superflat/` and create your own preset string for the super-flat world:

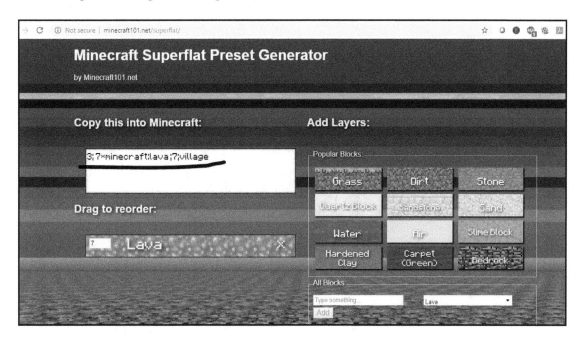

3. Generate a super-flat world with the specified preset string using the `<FlatWorldGenerator>` tag:

```
<FlatWorldGenerator generatorString="3;7,220*1,5*3,2;3;,biome_1"/>
```

4. Draw structures in the world using the `<DrawingDecorator>` tag:

```
Sample:
 <DrawingDecorator>
 <!-- coordinates for cuboid are inclusive -->
 <DrawCuboid x1="-2" y1="46" z1="-2" x2="7" y2="50" z2="18"
type="air" />
 <DrawCuboid x1="-2" y1="45" z1="-2" x2="7" y2="45" z2="18"
type="lava" />
 <DrawCuboid x1="1" y1="45" z1="1" x2="3" y2="45" z2="12"
type="sandstone" />
 <DrawBlock x="4" y="45" z="1" type="cobblestone" />
 <DrawBlock x="4" y="45" z="12" type="lapis_block" />
 <DrawItem x="4" y="46" z="12" type="diamond" />
 </DrawingDecorator>
```

5. Specify a time limit for all agents using the `<ServerQuitFromTimeUp>` tag:

```
<ServerQuitFromTimeUp timeLimitMs="100000000"/>
```

6. Add all mission handlers to the block using the `<ServerHandlers>` tag:

```
<ServerHandlers>
 <FlatWorldGenerator>{Copy from step 3}</FlatWorldGenerator>
 <DrawingDecorator>{Copy from step 4}</DrawingDecorator>
 <ServerQuitFromTimeUp>{Copy from step 5}</ServerQuitFromTimeUp>
 </ServerHandlers>
```

7. Add `<ServerHandlers>` and `<ServerInitialConditions>` under the `<ServerSection>` tag:

```
<ServerSection>
 <ServerInitialConditions>{Copy from step
1}</ServerInitialConditions>
 <ServerHandlers>{Copy from step 6}</ServerHandlers>
 </ServerSection>
```

8. Define the agent name and starting position:

```
Sample:
<Name>Cristina</Name>
<AgentStart>
   <Placement x="4.5" y="46.0" z="1.5" pitch="30" yaw="0"/>
</AgentStart>
```

9. Define the block types using the `<ObservationFromGrid>` tag:

```
Sample:
<ObservationFromGrid>
 <Grid name="floor">
 <min x="-4" y="-1" z="-13"/>
 <max x="4" y="-1" z="13"/>
 </Grid>
</ObservationFromGrid>
```

10. Configure the video frames using the `<VideoProducer>` tag:

```
Sample:
<VideoProducer viewpoint="1" want_depth="false">
<Width>320</Width>
<Height>240</Height>
</VideoProducer>
```

11. Mention the reward points to be received when an agent comes into contact with a block type using the `<RewardForTouchingBlockType>` tag:

```
Sample:
<RewardForTouchingBlockType>
<Block reward="-100.0" type="lava" behaviour="onceOnly"/>
<Block reward="100.0" type="lapis_block" behaviour="onceOnly"/>
</RewardForTouchingBlockType>
```

12. Mention the reward points to issue a command to the agent using the `<RewardForSendingCommand>` tag:

```
Sample:
<RewardForSendingCommand reward="-1"/>
```

13. Specify the mission endpoints for the agent using the `<AgentQuitFromTouchingBlockType>` tag:

```
<AgentQuitFromTouchingBlockType>
  <Block type="lava" />
  <Block type="lapis_block" />
</AgentQuitFromTouchingBlockType>
```

14. Add all agent handler functions under the `<AgentHandlers>` tag:

```
<AgentHandlers>
   <ObservationFromGrid>{Copy from step 9}</ObservationFromGrid>
   <VideoProducer></VideoProducer> // Copy from step 10
   <RewardForTouchingBlockType>{Copy from step
11}</RewardForTouchingBlockType>
   <RewardForSendingCommand> // Copy from step 12
   <AgentQuitFromTouchingBlockType>{Copy from step 13}
</AgentQuitFromTouchingBlockType>
 </AgentHandlers>
```

15. Add all agent handlers to `<AgentSection>`:

```
<AgentSection mode="Survival">
    <AgentHandlers>
       {Copy from step 14}
    </AgentHandlers>
 </AgentSection>
```

16. Create a `DataManager` instance to record the training data:

```
DataManager manager = new DataManager(false);
```

How it works...

In step 1, the following configurations are added as the initial conditions for the world:

- `StartTime`: This specifies the time of day at the start of the mission, in thousandths of an hour. 6,000 refers to noontime.
- `AllowPassageOfTime`: If set to `false`, then it will stop the day-night cycle. The weather and the sun position will remain constant during the mission.
- `Weather`: This specifies the type of weather at the start of the mission.
- `AllowSpawning`: If set to `true`, then it will produce animals and hostiles during the mission.

In *step 2*, we created a preset string to represent the super-flat type that is being used in step 3. A super-flat type is nothing but the type of surface seen in the mission.

In step 4, we drew structures into the world using `DrawCuboid` and `DrawBlock`.

We follow three-dimensional space `(x1,y1,z1)` -> `(x2,y2,z2)` to specify the boundaries. The `type` attribute is used to represent block types. You may add any of the available 198 blocks for your experiments.

In step 6, we add all mission handlers specific to world creation under the `<ServerHandlers>` tag. Then, we add them to the `<ServerSection>` parent tag in step 7.

In step 8, the `<Placement>` tag is used to specify the player's starting position. The starting point will be chosen randomly if it is not specified.

In step 9, we specified the position of the floor block in the gaming window. In step 10, `viewpoint` sets the camera viewpoint:

```
viewpoint=0 -> first-person
 viewpoint=1 -> behind
 viewpoint=2 -> facing
```

In step 13, we specify the block types in which agent movement is stopped once the step is over. In the end, we add all agent-specific mission handlers in the `AgentSection` tag at step 15. Mission schema creation will end at step 15.

Now, we need to store the training data from the mission. We use `DataManager` to handle the recording of training data. It creates the `rl4j-data` directory if it does not exist and stores the training data as the reinforcement learning training progresses. We passed `false` as an attribute while creating `DataManager` in step 16. This means that we are not persisting the training data or the model. Pass `true` if the training data and model are to be persisted. Note that we are going to need the data manager instance while configuring DQN.

See also

- Refer to the following documentation to create your own custom XML schema for the Minecraft world:
    - http://microsoft.github.io/malmo/0.14.0/Schemas/Mission.html
    - http://microsoft.github.io/malmo/0.30.0/Schemas/MissionHandlers.html

Configuring and training a DQN agent

DQN refers to an important class of reinforcement learning, called value learning. Here, we use a deep neural network to learn the optimal Q-value function. For every iteration, the network approximates Q-value and evaluates them against the Bellman equation in order to measure the agent accuracy. Q-value is supposed to be optimized while the agent makes movements in the world. So, how we configure the Q-learning process is important. In this recipe, we will configure DQN for a Malmo mission and train the agent to achieve the task.

Getting ready

Basic knowledge on the following are prerequisites for this recipe:

- Q-learning
- DQN

Q-learning basics will help while configuring the Q-learning hyperparameters for the DQN.

How to do it...

1. Create an action space for the mission:

```
Sample:
 MalmoActionSpaceDiscrete actionSpace =
 new MalmoActionSpaceDiscrete("movenorth 1", "movesouth 1",
"movewest 1", "moveeast 1");
 actionSpace.setRandomSeed(rndSeed);
```

2. Create an observation space for the mission:

```
MalmoObservationSpace observationSpace = new
MalmoObservationSpacePixels(xSize, ySize);
```

3. Create a Malmo consistency policy:

```
MalmoDescretePositionPolicy obsPolicy = new
MalmoDescretePositionPolicy();
```

4. Create an MDP (short for **Markov Decision Process**) wrapper around the Malmo Java client:

```
Sample:
 MalmoEnv mdp = new MalmoEnv("cliff_walking_rl4j.xml", actionSpace,
observationSpace, obsPolicy);
```

5. Create a DQN using `DQNFactoryStdConv`:

```
Sample:
 public static DQNFactoryStdConv.Configuration MALMO_NET = new
DQNFactoryStdConv.Configuration(
 learingRate,
 l2RegParam,
 updaters,
 listeners
 );
```

6. Use `HistoryProcessor` to scale the pixel image input:

```
Sample:
 public static HistoryProcessor.Configuration MALMO_HPROC = new
HistoryProcessor.Configuration(
 numOfFrames,
 rescaledWidth,
 rescaledHeight,
 croppingWidth,
 croppingHeight,
 offsetX,
 offsetY,
 numFramesSkip
 );
```

7. Create a Q-learning configuration by specifying hyperparameters:

```
Sample:
 public static QLearning.QLConfiguration MALMO_QL = new
QLearning.QLConfiguration(
```

```
    rndSeed,
    maxEpochStep,
    maxStep,
    expRepMaxSize,
    batchSize,
    targetDqnUpdateFreq,
    updateStart,
    rewardFactor,
    gamma,
    errorClamp,
    minEpsilon,
    epsilonNbStep,
    doubleDQN
    );
```

8. Create the DQN model using `QLearningDiscreteConv` by passing MDP wrapper and `DataManager:` within the `QLearningDiscreteConv` constructor:

```
Sample:
QLearningDiscreteConv<MalmoBox> dql =
new QLearningDiscreteConv<MalmoBox>(mdp, MALMO_NET, MALMO_HPROC,
MALMO_QL, manager);
```

9. Train the DQN:

```
dql.train();
```

How it works...

In step 1, we defined an action space for the agent by specifying a defined set of Malmo actions. For example, `movenorth 1` means moving the agent one block north. We passed in a list of strings to `MalmoActionSpaceDiscrete` indicating an agent's actions on Malmo space.

In step 2, we created an observation space from the bitmap size (mentioned by `xSize` and `ySize`) of input images(from the Malmo space). Also, we assumed three color channels (R, G, B). The agent needs to know about observation space before they run. We used `MalmoObservationSpacePixels` because we target observation from pixels.

In step 3, we have created a Malmo consistency policy using `MalmoDescretePositionPolicy` to ensure that the upcoming observation is in a consistent state.

A MDP is an approach used in reinforcement learning in grid-world environments. Our mission has states in the form of grids. MDP requires a policy and the objective of reinforcement learning is to find the optimal policy for the MDP. `MalmoEnv` is an MDP wrapper around a Java client.

In step 4, we created an MDP wrapper using the mission schema, action space, observation space, and observation policy. Note that the observation policy is not the same as the policy that an agent wants to form at the end of the learning process.

In step 5, we used `DQNFactoryStdConv` to build the DQN by adding convolutional layers.

In step 6, we configured `HistoryProcessor` to scale and remove pixels that were not needed. The actual intent of `HistoryProcessor` is to perform an experience replay, where the previous experience from the agent will be considered while deciding the action on the current state. With the use of `HistoryProcessor`, we can change the partial observation of states to a fully-observed state, that is, when the current state is an accumulation of the previous states.

Here are the hyperparameters used in step 7 while creating Q-learning configuration:

- `maxEpochStep`: The maximum number of steps allowed per epoch.
- `maxStep`: The maximum number of steps that are allowed. Training will finish when the iterations exceed the value specified for `maxStep`.
- `expRepMaxSize`: The maximum size of experience replay. Experience replay refers to the number of past transitions based on which the agent can decide on the next step to take.
- `doubleDQN`: This decides whether double DQN is enabled in the configuration (true if enabled).
- `targetDqnUpdateFreq`: Regular Q-learning can overestimate the action values under certain conditions. Double Q-learning adds stability to the learning. The main idea of double DQN is to freeze the network after every M number of updates or smoothly average for every M number of updates. The value of M is referred to as `targetDqnUpdateFreq`.
- `updateStart`: The number of no-operation (do nothing) moves at the beginning to ensure the Malmo mission starts with a random configuration. If the agent starts the game in the same way every time, then the agent will memorize the sequence of actions, rather than learning to take the next action based on the current state.

- `gamma`: This is also known as the discount factor. A discount factor is multiplied by future rewards to prevent the agent from being attracted to high rewards, rather than learning the actions. A discount factor close to 1 indicates that the rewards from the distant future are considered. On the other hand, a discount factor close to 0 indicates that the rewards from the immediate future are being considered.
- `rewardFactor`: This is a reward-scaling factor to scale the reward for every single step of training.
- `errorClamp`: This will clip the gradient of loss function with respect to output during backpropagation. For `errorClamp = 1`, the gradient component is clipped to the range *(-1, 1)*.
- `minEpsilon`: Epsilon is the derivative of the loss function with respect to the output of the activation function. Gradients for every activation node for backpropagation are calculated from the given epsilon value.
- `epsilonNbStep`: Th epsilon value is annealed to `minEpsilon` over an `epsilonNbStep` number of steps.

There's more...

We can make the mission even harder by putting lava onto the agent's path after a certain number of actions are performed. First, start by creating a mission specification using the schema XML:

```
MissionSpec mission = MalmoEnv.loadMissionXML("cliff_walking_rl4j.xml");
```

Now, setting the lava challenge on the mission is as simple as follows:

```
mission.drawBlock(xValue, yValue, zValue, "lava");"
 malmoEnv.setMission(mission);
```

`MissionSpec` is a class file included in the `MalmoJavaJar` dependency, which we can use to set missions in the Malmo space.

Evaluating a Malmo agent

We need to evaluate the agent to see how well it has learned to play the game. We just trained our agent to navigate through the world to reach the target. In this recipe, we will evaluate the trained Malmo agent.

Getting ready

As a prerequisite, we will need to persist the agent policies and reload them back during evaluation.

The final policy (policy to make movements in Malmo space) used by the agent after training can be saved as shown here:

```
DQNPolicy<MalmoBox> pol = dql.getPolicy();
 pol.save("cliffwalk_pixel.policy");
```

`dql` refers to the DQN model. We retrieve the final policies and store them as a `DQNPolicy`. A DQN policy provides actions that have the highest Q-value estimated by the model.

It can be restored later for evaluation/inference:

```
DQNPolicy<MalmoBox> pol = DQNPolicy.load("cliffwalk_pixel.policy");
```

How to do it...

1. Create an MDP wrapper to load the mission:

   ```
   Sample:
    MalmoEnv mdp = new MalmoEnv("cliff_walking_rl4j.xml", actionSpace,
   observationSpace, obsPolicy);
   ```

2. Evaluate the agent:

   ```
   Sample:
    double rewards = 0;
    for (int i = 0; i < 10; i++) {
    double reward = pol.play(mdp, new HistoryProcessor(MALMO_HPROC));
    rewards += reward;
    Logger.getAnonymousLogger().info("Reward: " + reward);
    }
   ```

How it works...

The Malmo mission/world is launched in step 1. In step 2, MALMO_HPROC is the history processor configuration. You can refer to step 6 of the previous recipe for the sample configuration. Once the agent is subjected to evaluation, you should see the results as shown here:

```
MalmoExample

  [main] INFO org.deeplearning4j.malmo.MalmoEnv - Mission ended
  Aug 24, 2019 7:18:21 AM MalmoExample loadMalmoCliffWalk
  INFO: Reward: 85.0
  [main] INFO org.deeplearning4j.malmo.MalmoEnv - Waiting for the mission to start
  [main] INFO org.deeplearning4j.malmo.MalmoEnv - Mission ended
  Aug 24, 2019 7:18:24 AM MalmoExample loadMalmoCliffWalk
  INFO: Reward: 81.0
  [main] INFO org.deeplearning4j.malmo.MalmoEnv - Waiting for the mission to start
  [main] INFO org.deeplearning4j.malmo.MalmoEnv - Mission ended
  Aug 24, 2019 7:18:26 AM MalmoExample loadMalmoCliffWalk
  INFO: Reward: 83.0
  [main] INFO org.deeplearning4j.malmo.MalmoEnv - Waiting for the mission to start
  [main] INFO org.deeplearning4j.malmo.MalmoEnv - Mission ended
  Aug 24, 2019 7:18:29 AM MalmoExample loadMalmoCliffWalk
  INFO: Reward: 85.0
  [main] INFO org.deeplearning4j.malmo.MalmoEnv - Waiting for the mission to start
  [main] INFO org.deeplearning4j.malmo.MalmoEnv - Mission ended
  Aug 24, 2019 7:18:32 AM MalmoExample loadMalmoCliffWalk
  INFO: Reward: 85.0
  Aug 24, 2019 7:18:32 AM MalmoExample loadMalmoCliffWalk
  INFO: average: 84.0
```

For every mission evaluation, we calculate the reward score. A positive reward score indicates that the agent has reached the target. At the end, we calculated the average reward score of the agent.

In the preceding screenshot, we can see that the agent has reached the target. This is the ideal target position, no matter how the agent decides to move across the block. After the training session, the agent will form a final policy, which the agent can use to reach the target without falling into lava. The evaluation process will ensure that the agent is trained enough to play the Malmo game on its own.

10
Developing Applications in a Distributed Environment

As the demand increases regarding the quantity of data and resource requirements for parallel computations, legacy approaches may not perform well. So far, we have seen how big data development has become famous and is the most followed approach by enterprises due to the same reasons. DL4J supports neural network training, evaluation, and inference on distributed clusters.

Modern approaches to heavy training, or output generation tasks, distribute training effort across multiple machines. This also brings additional challenges. We need to ensure that we have the following constraints checked before we use Spark to perform distributed training/evaluation/inference:

- Our data should be significantly large enough to justify the need for distributed clusters. Small network/data on Spark doesn't really gain any performance improvements and local machine execution may have much better results in such scenarios.
- We have more than a single machine to perform training/evaluation or inference.

Let's say we have a single machine with multiple GPU processors. We could simply use a parallel wrapper rather than Spark in this case. A parallel wrapper enables parallel training on a single machine with multiple cores. Parallel wrappers will be discussed in Chapter 12, *Benchmarking and Neural Network Optimization*, where you will find out how to configure them. Also, if the neural network takes more than 100 ms for one single iteration, it may be worth considering distributed training.

In this chapter, we will discuss how to configure DL4J for distributed training, evaluation, and inference. We will develop a distributed neural network for the `TinyImageNet` classifier. In this chapter, we will cover the following recipes:

- Setting up DL4J and the required dependencies
- Creating an uber-JAR for training
- CPU/GPU-specific configuration for training
- Memory settings and garbage collection for Spark
- Configuring encoding thresholds
- Performing a distributed test set evaluation
- Saving and loading trained neural network models
- Performing distributed inference

Technical requirements

The source code for this chapter can be found at `https://github.com/PacktPublishing/Java-Deep-Learning-Cookbook/tree/master/10_Developing_applications_in_distributed_environment/sourceCode/cookbookapp/src/main/java/com/javacookbook/app`.

After cloning our GitHub repository, navigate to the `Java-Deep-Learning-Cookbook/10_Developing_applications_in_distributed_environment/sourceCode` directory. Then, import the `cookbookapp` project as a Maven project by importing the `pom.xml` file.

You need to run either of the following preprocessor scripts (`PreProcessLocal.java` or `PreProcessSpark.java`) before running the actual source code:

- `https://github.com/PacktPublishing/Java-Deep-Learning-Cookbook/blob/master/10_Developing_applications_in_distributed_environment/sourceCode/cookbookapp/src/main/java/com/javacookbook/app/PreProcessLocal.java`
- `https://github.com/PacktPublishing/Java-Deep-Learning-Cookbook/blob/master/10_Developing_applications_in_distributed_environment/sourceCode/cookbookapp/src/main/java/com/javacookbook/app/PreprocessSpark.java`

These scripts can be found in the `cookbookapp` project.

You will also need the `TinyImageNet` dataset, which can be found at `http://cs231n.stanford.edu/tiny-imagenet-200.zip`. The home page can be found at `https://tiny-imagenet.herokuapp.com/`.

It is desirable if you have some prior knowledge of working with Apache Spark and Hadoop so that you get the most out of this chapter. Also, this chapter assumes that Java is already installed on your machine and has been added to your environment variables. We recommend Java version 1.8.

Note that the source code requires good hardware in terms of memory/processing power. We recommend that you have at least 16 GB of RAM on your host machine in case you're running the source on a laptop/desktop.

Setting up DL4J and the required dependencies

We are discussing setting up DL4J again because we are now dealing with a distributed environment. For demonstration purposes, we will use Spark's local mode. Due to this, we can focus on DL4J rather than setting up clusters, worker nodes, and so on. In this recipe, we will set up a single node Spark cluster (Spark local), as well as configure DL4J-specific dependencies.

Getting ready

In order to demonstrate the use of a distributed neural network, you will need the following:

- A distributed filesystem (Hadoop) for file management
- Distributed computing (Spark) in order to process big data

How to do it...

1. Add the following Maven dependency for Apache Spark:

```
<dependency>
    <groupId>org.apache.spark</groupId>
    <artifactId>spark-core_2.11</artifactId>
    <version>2.1.0</version>
</dependency>
```

2. Add the following Maven dependency for DataVec for Spark:

```
<dependency>
    <groupId>org.datavec</groupId>
    <artifactId>datavec-spark_2.11</artifactId>
    <version>1.0.0-beta3_spark_2</version>
</dependency>
```

3. Add the following Maven dependency for parameter averaging:

```
<dependency>
    <groupId>org.datavec</groupId>
    <artifactId>datavec-spark_2.11</artifactId>
    <version>1.0.0-beta3_spark_2</version>
</dependency>
```

4. Add the following Maven dependency for gradient sharing:

```
<dependency>
    <groupId>org.deeplearning4j</groupId>
    <artifactId>dl4j-spark-parameterserver_2.11</artifactId>
    <version>1.0.0-beta3_spark_2</version>
</dependency>
```

5. Add the following Maven dependency for the ND4J backend:

```
<dependency>
    <groupId>org.nd4j</groupId>
    <artifactId>nd4j-native-platform</artifactId>
    <version>1.0.0-beta3</version>
</dependency>
```

6. Add the following Maven dependency for CUDA:

```
<dependency>
    <groupId>org.nd4j</groupId>
    <artifactId>nd4j-cuda-x.x</artifactId>
    <version>1.0.0-beta3</version>
</dependency>
```

7. Add the following Maven dependency for JCommander:

```
<dependency>
    <groupId>com.beust</groupId>
    <artifactId>jcommander</artifactId>
    <version>1.72</version>
</dependency>
```

8. Download Hadoop from the official website at `https://hadoop.apache.org/releases.html` and add the required environment variables.

    Extract the downloaded Hadoop package and create the following environment variables:

```
HADOOP_HOME = {PathDownloaded}/hadoop-x.x
 HADOOP_HDFS_HOME = {PathDownloaded}/hadoop-x.x
 HADOOP_MAPRED_HOME = {PathDownloaded}/hadoop-x.x
 HADOOP_YARN_HOME = {PathDownloaded}/hadoop-x.x
```

    Add the following entry to the `PATH` environment variable:

    ${HADOOP_HOME}\bin

9. Create name/data node directories for Hadoop. Navigate to the Hadoop home directory (which is set in the `HADOOP_HOME` environment variable) and create a directory named `data`. Then, create two subdirectories named `datanode` and `namenode` underneath it. Make sure that access for read/write/delete has been provided for these directories.

10. Navigate to `hadoop-x.x/etc/hadoop` and open `hdfs-site.xml`. Then, add the following configuration:

```
<configuration>
    <property>
     <name>dfs.replication</name>
     <value>1</value>
    </property>
    <property>
     <name>dfs.namenode.name.dir</name>
     <value>file:/{NameNodeDirectoryPath}</value>
```

```
      </property>
      <property>
       <name>dfs.datanode.data.dir</name>
       <value>file:/{DataNodeDirectoryPath}</value>
      </property>
    </configuration>
```

11. Navigate to `hadoop-x.x/etc/hadoop` and open `mapred-site.xml`. Then, add the following configuration:

```
<configuration>
  <property>
   <name>mapreduce.framework.name</name>
   <value>yarn</value>
  </property>
 </configuration>
```

12. Navigate to `hadoop-x.x/etc/hadoop` and open `yarn-site.xml`. Then, add the following configuration:

```
<configuration>
  <!-- Site specific YARN configuration properties -->
  <property>
   <name>yarn.nodemanager.aux-services</name>
   <value>mapreduce_shuffle</value>
  </property>
  <property>
<name>yarn.nodemanager.auxservices.mapreduce.shuffle.class</name>
    <value>org.apache.hadoop.mapred.ShuffleHandler</value>
  </property>
 </configuration>
```

13. Navigate to `hadoop-x.x/etc/hadoop` and open `core-site.xml`. Then, add the following configuration:

```
<configuration>
  <property>
   <name>fs.default.name</name>
   <value>hdfs://localhost:9000</value>
  </property>
 </configuration>
```

14. Navigate to `hadoop-x.x/etc/hadoop` and open `hadoop-env.cmd`. Then, replace `set JAVA_HOME=%JAVA_HOME%` with `set JAVA_HOME={JavaHomeAbsolutePath}`.

    Add the `winutils` Hadoop fix (only applicable for Windows). You can download this from `http://tiny.cc/hadoop-config-windows`. Alternatively, you can navigate to the respective GitHub repository, `https://github.com/steveloughran/winutils`, and get the fix that matches your installed Hadoop version. Replace the `bin` folder at `${HADOOP_HOME}` with the `bin` folder in the fix.

15. Run the following Hadoop command to format `namenode`:

    ```
    hdfs namenode –format
    ```

    You should see the following output:

```
Administrator: Command Prompt                                                                          —  □  ×
18/05/23 19:28:05 INFO util.GSet: Computing capacity for map cachedBlocks
18/05/23 19:28:05 INFO util.GSet: VM type       = 64-bit
18/05/23 19:28:05 INFO util.GSet: 0.25% max memory 1000 MB = 2.5 MB
18/05/23 19:28:05 INFO util.GSet: capacity      = 2^18 = 262144 entries
18/05/23 19:28:05 INFO namenode.FSNamesystem: dfs.namenode.safemode.threshold-pct = 0.9990000128746033
18/05/23 19:28:05 INFO namenode.FSNamesystem: dfs.namenode.safemode.min.datanodes = 0
18/05/23 19:28:05 INFO namenode.FSNamesystem: dfs.namenode.safemode.extension     = 30000
18/05/23 19:28:05 INFO metrics.TopMetrics: NNTop conf: dfs.namenode.top.window.num.buckets = 10
18/05/23 19:28:05 INFO metrics.TopMetrics: NNTop conf: dfs.namenode.top.num.users = 10
18/05/23 19:28:05 INFO metrics.TopMetrics: NNTop conf: dfs.namenode.top.windows.minutes = 1,5,25
18/05/23 19:28:05 INFO namenode.FSNamesystem: Retry cache on namenode is enabled
18/05/23 19:28:05 INFO namenode.FSNamesystem: Retry cache will use 0.03 of total heap and retry cache entry expiry time
is 600000 millis
18/05/23 19:28:05 INFO util.GSet: Computing capacity for map NameNodeRetryCache
18/05/23 19:28:05 INFO util.GSet: VM type       = 64-bit
18/05/23 19:28:05 INFO util.GSet: 0.029999999329447746% max memory 1000 MB = 307.2 KB
18/05/23 19:28:05 INFO util.GSet: capacity      = 2^15 = 32768 entries
18/05/23 19:28:10 INFO namenode.FSImage: Allocated new BlockPoolId: BP-1984558503-192.168.77.1-1527078490081
18/05/23 19:28:10 INFO common.Storage: Storage directory C:\hadoop-2.8.0\data\namenode has been successfully formatted.
18/05/23 19:28:10 INFO namenode.FSImageFormatProtobuf: Saving image file C:\hadoop-2.8.0\data\namenode\current\fsimage.c
kpt_0000000000000000000 using no compression
18/05/23 19:28:10 INFO namenode.FSImageFormatProtobuf: Image file C:\hadoop-2.8.0\data\namenode\current\fsimage.ckpt_000
0000000000000000 of size 322 bytes saved in 0 seconds.
18/05/23 19:28:10 INFO namenode.NNStorageRetentionManager: Going to retain 1 images with txid >= 0
18/05/23 19:28:10 INFO util.ExitUtil: Exiting with status 0
18/05/23 19:28:10 INFO namenode.NameNode: SHUTDOWN_MSG:
/************************************************************
SHUTDOWN_MSG: Shutting down NameNode at DESK
************************************************************/
```

16. Navigate to `${HADOOP_HOME}\sbin` and start the Hadoop services:
    - For Windows, run `start-all.cmd`.
    - For Linux or any other OS, run `start-all.sh` from Terminal.

You should see the following output:

17. Hit `http://localhost:50070/` in your browser and verify whether Hadoop is up and running:

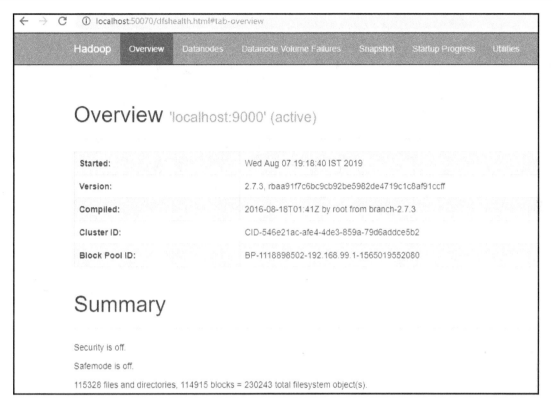

18. Install Spark from `https://spark.apache.org/downloads.html` and add the required environment variables. Extract the package and add the following environment variables:

```
SPARK_HOME = {PathDownloaded}/spark-x.x-bin-hadoopx.x
SPARK_CONF_DIR = ${SPARK_HOME}\conf
```

19. Configure Spark's properties. Navigate to the directory location at `SPARK_CONF_DIR` and open the `spark-env.sh` file. Then, add the following configuration:

```
SPARK_MASTER_HOST=localhost
```

20. Run the Spark master by running the following command:

```
spark-class org.apache.spark.deploy.master.Master
```

You should see the following output:

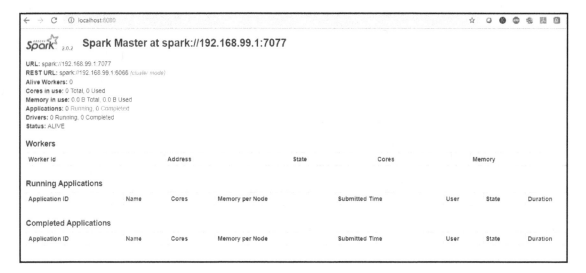

21. Hit `http://localhost:8080/` in your browser and verify whether Hadoop is up and running:

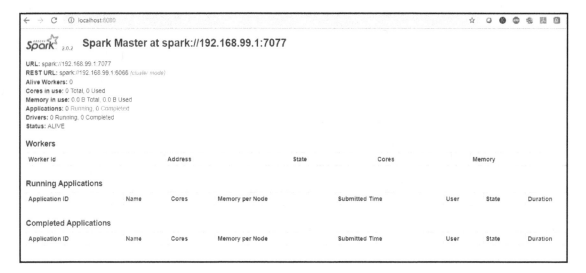

How it works...

In step 2, dependencies were added for `DataVec`. We need to use data transformation functions in Spark just like in regular training. Transformation is a data requirement for neural networks and is not Spark-specific.

For example, we talked about `LocalTransformExecutor` in `Chapter 2`, *Data Extraction, Transformation, and Loading*. `LocalTransformExecutor` is used for `DataVec` transformation in non-distributed environments. `SparkTransformExecutor` will be used for the `DataVec` transformation process in Spark.

In step 4, we added dependencies for gradient sharing. Training times are faster for gradient sharing and it is designed to be scalable and fault-tolerant. Therefore, gradient sharing is preferred over parameter averaging. In gradient sharing, instead of relaying all the parameter updates/gradients across the network, it only updates those that are above the specified threshold. Let's say we have an update vector at the beginning that we want to communicate across the network. Due to this, we will be creating a sparse binary vector for the large values (as specified by a threshold) in the update vector. We will use this sparse binary vector for further communication. The main idea is to decrease the communication effort. Note that the rest of the updates will not be discarded and are added in a residual vector for processing later. Residual vectors will be kept for future updates (delayed communication) and not lost. Gradient sharing in DL4J is an asynchronous SGD implementation. You can read more about this in detail at `http://nikkostrom.com/publications/interspeech2015/strom_interspeech2015.pdf`.

In step 5, we added CUDA dependencies for the Spark distributed training application.

Here are the uber-JAR requirements for this:

- If the OS that's building the uber-JAR is the same as that of the cluster OS (for example, run it on Linux and then execute it on a Spark Linux cluster), include the `nd4j-cuda-x.x` dependency in the `pom.xml` file.
- If the OS that's building the uber-JAR is not the same as that of the cluster OS (for example, run it on Windows and then execute it on a Spark Linux cluster), include the `nd4j-cuda-x.x-platform` dependency in the `pom.xml` file.

Just replace `x.x` with the CUDA version you have installed (for example, `nd4j-cuda-9.2` for CUDA 9.2).

In cases where the clusters don't have CUDA/cuDNN set up, we can include `redist javacpp-` presets for the cluster OS. You can refer to the respective dependencies here: `https://deeplearning4j.org/docs/latest/deeplearning4j-config-cuDNN`. That way, we don't have to install CUDA or cuDNN in each and every cluster machine.

In step 6, we added a Maven dependency for JCommander. JCommander is used to parse command-line arguments that are supplied with `spark-submit`. We need this because we will be passing directory locations (HDFS/local) of the train/test data as command-line arguments in `spark-submit`.

From steps 7 to 16, we downloaded and configured Hadoop. Remember to replace `{PathDownloaded}` with the actual location of the extracted Hadoop package. Also, replace `x.x` with the Hadoop version you've downloaded. We need to specify the disk location where we will store the metadata and the data represented in HDFS. Due to this, we created name/data directories in step 8/step 9. To make changes, in step 10, we configured `mapred-site.xml`. If you can't locate the file in the directory, just create an XML file by copying all the content from the `mapred-site.xml.template` file, and then make the changes that were mentioned in step 10.

In step 13, we replaced the `JAVA_HOME` path variable with the actual Java home directory location. This was done to avoid certain `ClassNotFound` exceptions from being encountered at runtime.

In step 18, make sure that you are downloading the Spark version that matches your Hadoop version. For example, if you have Hadoop 2.7.3, then get the Spark version that looks like `spark-x.x-bin-hadoop2.7`. When we made changes in step 19, if the `spark-env.sh` file isn't present, then just create a new file named `spark-env.sh` by copying the content from the `spark-env.sh.template` file. Then, make the changes that were mentioned in step 19. After completing all the steps in this recipe, you should be able to perform distributed neural network training via the `spark-submit` command.

Creating an uber-JAR for training

The training job that's executed by `spark-submit` will need to resolve all the required dependencies at runtime. In order to manage this task, we will create an uber-JAR that has the application runtime and its required dependencies. We will use the Maven configurations in `pom.xml` to create an uber-JAR so that we can perform distributed training. Effectively, we will create an uber-JAR and submit it to `spark-submit` to perform the training job in Spark.

In this recipe, we will create an uber-JAR using the Maven shade plugin for Spark training.

How to do it...

1. Create an uber-JAR (shaded JAR) by adding the Maven shade plugin to the pom.xml file, as shown here:

```
<plugin>
    <groupId>org.apache.maven.plugins</groupId>
    <artifactId>maven-shade-plugin</artifactId>
    <version>3.2.0</version>
    <executions>
        <execution>
            <phase>package</phase>
            <goals>
                <goal>shade</goal>
            </goals>
            <configuration>
                <transformers>
                    <transformer implementation="org.apache.maven.plugins.shade.resource.ApacheLicenseResourceTransformer" />
                    <transformer implementation="org.apache.maven.plugins.shade.resource.ManifestResourceTransformer">
                        <mainClass>com.javacookbook.app.SparkExample</mainClass>
                    </transformer>
                </transformers>
            </configuration>
        </execution>
    </executions>
</plugin>
```

Refer to the pom.xml file in this book's GitHub repository for more information: https://github.com/PacktPublishing/Java-Deep-Learning-Cookbook/blob/master/10_
Developing%20applications%20in%20distributed%20environment/sourceCode/
cookbookapp/pom.xml. Add the following filter to the Maven configuration:

```
<filters>
    <filter>
     <artifact>*:*</artifact>
     <excludes>
      <exclude>META-INF/*.SF</exclude>
      <exclude>META-INF/*.DSA</exclude>
      <exclude>META-INF/*.RSA</exclude>
     </excludes>
    </filter>
</filters>
```

2. Hit the Maven command to build an uber-JAR for the project:

```
mvn package -DskipTests
```

How it works...

In step 1, you need to specify the main class that should run while executing the JAR file. In the preceding demonstration, `SparkExample` is our main class that invokes a training session. You may come across exceptions that look as follows:

```
Exception in thread "main" java.lang.SecurityException: Invalid signature
file digest for Manifest main attributes.
```

Some of the dependencies that were added to the Maven configuration may have a signed JAR, which may cause issues like these.

In step 2, we added the filters to prevent the addition of signed `.jars` during the Maven build.

In step 3, we generated an executable `.jar` file with all the required dependencies. We can submit this `.jar` file to `spark-submit` to train our networks on Spark. The `.jar` file is created in the `target` directory of the project:

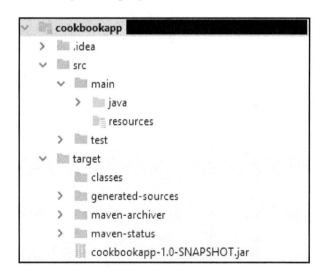

The Maven shade plugin is not the only way to build an uber-JAR file. However, the Maven shade plugin is recommended over other alternatives. Other alternatives may not be able to include the required files from source `.jars`. Some of those files act as dependencies for the Java service loader's functionality. ND4J makes use of Java's service loader functionality. Therefore, other alternative plugins can cause issues.

CPU/GPU-specific configuration for training

Hardware-specific changes are generic configurations that can't be ignored in a distributed environment. DL4J supports GPU-accelerated training in NVIDIA GPUs with CUDA/cuDNN enabled. We can also perform Spark distributed training using GPUs.

In this recipe, we will configure CPU/GPU-specific changes.

How to do it...

1. Download, install, and set up the CUDA toolkit from `https://developer.nvidia.com/cuda-downloads`. OS-specific setup instructions are available at the NVIDIA CUDA official website.

2. Configure the GPU for Spark distributed training by adding a Maven dependency for ND4J's CUDA backend:

```
<dependency>
    <groupId>org.nd4j</groupId>
    <artifactId>nd4j-cuda-x.x</artifactId>
    <version>1.0.0-beta3</version>
</dependency>
```

3. Configure the CPU for Spark distributed training by adding an ND4J-native dependency:

```
<dependency>
    <groupId>org.nd4j</groupId>
    <artifactId>nd4j-native-platform</artifactId>
    <version>1.0.0-beta3</version>
</dependency>
```

How it works...

We need to enable a proper ND4J backend so that we can utilize GPU resources, as we mentioned in step 1. Enable the `nd4j-cuda-x.x` dependency in your `pom.xml` file for GPU training, where `x.x` refers to the CUDA version that you have installed.

We may include both ND4J backends (CUDA/native dependencies) if the master node is running on the CPU and the worker nodes are running on the GPU, as we mentioned in the previous recipe. If both backends are present in the classpath, the CUDA backend will be tried out first. If it doesn't load for some reason, then the CPU backend (native) will be loaded. The priority can also be changed by changing the BACKEND_PRIORITY_CPU and BACKEND_PRIORITY_GPU environment variables in the master node. The backend will be picked depending on which one of these environment variables has the highest value.

In step 3, we added CPU-specific configuration that targets CPU-only hardware. We don't have to keep this configuration if both the master/worker nodes have GPU hardware in place.

There's more...

We can further optimize the training throughput by configuring cuDNN into CUDA devices. We can run a training instance in Spark without CUDA/cuDNN installed on every node. To gain optimal performance with cuDNN support, we can add the DL4J CUDA dependency. For that, the following components must be added and made available:

- The DL4J CUDA Maven dependency:

```
<dependency>
  <groupId>org.deeplearning4j</groupId>
  <artifactId>deeplearning4j-cuda-x.x</artifactId>
  <version>1.0.0-beta3</version>
</dependency>
```

- The cuDNN library files at https://developer.nvidia.com/cuDNN. Note that you need to sign up to the NVIDIA website to download cuDNN libraries. Signup is free. Refer to the installation guide here: https://docs.nvidia.com/deeplearning/sdk/cuDNN-install/index.html.

Memory settings and garbage collection for Spark

Memory management is very crucial for distributed training with large datasets in production. It directly influences the resource consumption and performance of the neural network. Memory management involves configuring off-heap and on-heap memory spaces. DL4J/ND4J-specific memory configuration will be discussed in detail in `Chapter 12`, *Benchmarking and Neural Network Optimization*.

In this recipe, we will focus on memory configuration in the context of Spark.

How to do it...

1. Add the `--executor-memory` command-line argument while submitting a job to `spark-submit` to set on-heap memory for the worker node. For example, we could use `--executor-memory 4g` to allocate 4 GB of memory.

2. Add the `--conf` command-line argument to set the off-heap memory for the worker node:

   ```
   --conf "spark.executor.extraJavaOptions=-
   Dorg.bytedeco.javacpp.maxbytes=8G"
   ```

3. Add the `--conf` command-line argument to set the off-heap memory for the master node. For example, we could use `--conf`
   `"spark.driver.memoryOverhead=-`
   `Dorg.bytedeco.javacpp.maxbytes=8G"` to allocate 8 GB of memory.

4. Add the `--driver-memory` command-line argument to specify the on-heap memory for the master node. For example, we could use `--driver-memory 4g` to allocate 4 GB of memory.

5. Configure garbage collection for the worker nodes by calling `workerTogglePeriodicGC()` and `workerPeriodicGCFrequency()` while you set up the distributed neural network using `SharedTrainingMaster`:

   ```
   new SharedTrainingMaster.Builder(voidConfiguration, minibatch)
      .workerTogglePeriodicGC(true)
      .workerPeriodicGCFrequency(frequencyIntervalInMs)
      .build();
   ```

6. Enable Kryo optimization in DL4J by adding the following dependency to the `pom.xml` file:

```
<dependency>
   <groupId>org.nd4j</groupId>
   <artifactId>nd4j-kryo_2.11</artifactId>
  <version>1.0.0-beta3</version>
 </dependency>
```

7. Configure `KryoSerializer` with `SparkConf`:

```
SparkConf conf = new SparkConf();
 conf.set("spark.serializer",
"org.apache.spark.serializer.KryoSerializer");
 conf.set("spark.kryo.registrator", "org.nd4j.Nd4jRegistrator");
```

8. Add locality configuration to `spark-submit`, as shown here:

```
--conf spark.locality.wait=0
```

How it works...

In step 1, we discussed Spark-specific memory configurations. We mentioned that this can be configured for master/worker nodes. Also, these memory configurations can be dependent on the cluster resource manager.

Note that the `--executor-memory 4g` command-line argument is for YARN. Please refer to the respective cluster resource manager documentation to find out the respective command-line argument for the following:

- **Spark Standalone:** https://spark.apache.org/docs/latest/spark-standalone.html
- **Mesos:** https://spark.apache.org/docs/latest/running-on-mesos.html
- **YARN:** https://spark.apache.org/docs/latest/running-on-yarn.html

For Spark Standalone, use the following command-line options to configure the memory space:

- The on-heap memory for the driver can be configured like so (`8G` -> 8 GB of memory):

```
SPARK_DRIVER_MEMORY=8G
```

- The off-heap memory for the driver can be configured like so:

  ```
  SPARK_DRIVER_OPTS=-Dorg.bytedeco.javacpp.maxbytes=8G
  ```

- The on-heap memory for the worker can be configured like so:

  ```
  SPARK_WORKER_MEMORY=8G
  ```

- The off-heap memory for the worker can be configured like so:

  ```
  SPARK_WORKER_OPTS=-Dorg.bytedeco.javacpp.maxbytes=8G
  ```

In step 5, we discussed garbage collection for worker nodes. Generally speaking, there are two ways in which we can control the frequency of garbage collection. The following is the first approach:

```
Nd4j.getMemoryManager().setAutoGcWindow(frequencyIntervalInMs);
```

This will limit the frequency of garbage collector calls to the specified time interval, that is, `frequencyIntervalInMs`. The second approach is as follows:

```
Nd4j.getMemoryManager().togglePeriodicGc(false);
```

This will totally disable the garbage collector's calls. However, the these approaches will not alter the worker node's memory configuration. We can configure the worker node's memory using the builder methods that are available in `SharedTrainingMaster`.

We call `workerTogglePeriodicGC()` to disable/enable periodic **garbage collector** (**GC**) calls and `workerPeriodicGCFrequency()` to set the frequency in which GC needs to be called.

In step 6, we added support for Kryo serialization in ND4J. The Kryo serializer is a Java serialization framework that helps to increase the speed/efficiency during training in Spark.

For more information, refer to `https://spark.apache.org/docs/latest/tuning.html`. In step 8, locality configuration is an optional configuration that can be used to improve training performance. Data locality can have a major impact on the performance of Spark jobs. The idea is to ship the data and code together so that the computation can be performed really quickly. For more information, please refer to `https://spark.apache.org/docs/latest/tuning.html#data-locality`.

There's more...

Memory configurations are often applied to master/worker nodes separately. Therefore, memory configuration on worker nodes alone may not bring the required results. The approach we take can vary, depending on the cluster resource manager we use. Therefore, it is important to refer to the respective documentation on the different approaches for a specific cluster resource manager. Also, note that the default memory settings in the cluster resource managers are not appropriate (too low) for libraries (ND4J/DL4J) that heavily rely on off-heap memory space. `spark-submit` can load the configurations in two different ways. One way is to use the *command line*, as we discussed previously, while another one is to specify the configuration in the `spark-defaults.conf` file, like so:

```
spark.master spark://5.6.7.8:7077
spark.executor.memory 4g
```

Spark can accept any Spark properties using the `--conf` flag. We used it to specify off-heap memory space in this recipe. You can read more about Spark configuration here: `http://spark.apache.org/docs/latest/configuration.html`:

- The dataset should justify the memory allocation in the driver/executor. For 10 MB of data, we don't have to assign too much of the memory to the executor/driver. In this case, 2 GB to 4 GB of memory would be enough. Allotting too much memory won't make any difference and it can actually reduce the performance.

- The *driver* is the process where the main Spark job runs. *Executors* are worker node tasks that have individual tasks allotted to run. If the application runs in local mode, the driver memory is not necessarily allotted. The driver memory is connected to the master node and it is relevant while the application is running in *cluster* mode. In *cluster* mode, the Spark job will not run on the local machine it was submitted from. The Spark driver component will launch inside the cluster.

- Kryo is a fast and efficient serialization framework for Java. Kryo can also perform automatic deep/shallow copying of objects in order to attain a high speed, low size, and easy-to-use API. The DL4J API can make use of Kryo serialization to optimize the performance a bit further. However, note that since INDArrays consume off-heap memory space, Kryo may not result in much performance gain. Check the respective logs to ensure your Kryo configuration is correct while using it with
the `SparkDl4jMultiLayer` or `SparkComputationGraph` classes.

- Just like in regular training, we need to add the proper ND4J backend for DL4J Spark to function. For newer versions of YARN, some additional configurations may be required. Refer to the YARN documentation for more details: `https://hadoop.apache.org/docs/r3.1.0/hadoop-yarn/hadoop-yarn-site/UsingGpus.html`.

 Also, note that older versions (2.7.x or earlier) will not support GPUs natively (GPU and CPU). For these versions, we need to use node labels to ensure that jobs are running in GPU-only machines.

- If you perform Spark training, you need to be aware of data locality in order to optimize the throughput. Data locality ensures that the data and the code that operates on the Spark job are together and not separate. Data locality ships the serialized code from place to place (instead of chunks of data) where the data operates. It will speed up its performance and won't introduce further issues since the size of the code will be significantly smaller than the data. Spark provides a configuration property named `spark.locality.wait` to specify the timeout before moving the data to a free CPU. If you set it to zero, then data will be immediately moved to a free executor rather than wait for a specific executor to become free. If the freely available executor is distant from the executor where the current task is executed, then it is an additional effort. However, we are saving time by waiting for a nearby executor to become free. So, the computation time can still be reduced. You can read more about data locality on Spark here: `https://spark.apache.org/docs/latest/tuning.html#data-locality`.

Configuring encoding thresholds

The DL4J Spark implementation makes use of a threshold encoding scheme to perform parameter updates across nodes in order to reduce the commuted message size across the network and thereby reduce the cost of traffic. The threshold encoding scheme introduces a new distributed training-specific hyperparameter called **encoding threshold**.

In this recipe, we will configure the threshold algorithm in a distributed training implementation.

How to do it...

1. Configure the threshold algorithm in `SharedTrainingMaster`:

```
TrainingMaster tm = new
SharedTrainingMaster.Builder(voidConfiguration, minibatchSize)
   .thresholdAlgorithm(new
AdaptiveThresholdAlgorithm(gradientThreshold))
   .build();
```

2. Configure the residual vectors by calling `residualPostProcessor()`:

```
TrainingMaster tm = new
SharedTrainingMaster.Builder(voidConfiguration, minibatch)
 .residualPostProcessor(new
ResidualClippingPostProcessor(clipValue, frequency))
 .build();
```

How it works...

In step 1, we configured the threshold algorithm in `SharedTrainingMaster`, where the default algorithm is `AdaptiveThresholdAlgorithm`. Threshold algorithms will determine the encoding threshold for distributed training, which is a hyperparameter that's specific to distributed training. Also, note that we are not discarding the rest of the parameter updates. As we mentioned earlier, we put them into separate residual vectors and process them later. We do this to reduce the network traffic/load during training. `AdaptiveThresholdAlgorithm` is preferred in most cases for better performance.

In step 2, we used `ResidualPostProcessor` to post process the residual vector. The residual vector was created internally by the gradient sharing implementation to collect parameter updates that were not marked by the specified bound. Most implementations of `ResidualPostProcessor` will clip/decay the residual vector so that the values in them will not become too large compared to the threshold value. `ResidualClippingPostProcessor` is one such implementation. `ResidualPostProcessor` will prevent the residual vector from becoming too large in size as it can take too much time to communicate and may lead to stale gradient issues.

In step 1, we called `thresholdAlgorithm()` to set the threshold algorithm. In step 2, we called `residualPostProcessor()` to post process the residual vector for the gradient sharing implementation in DL4J. `ResidualClippingPostProcessor` accepts two attributes: `clipValue` and `frequency`. `clipValue` is the multiple of the current threshold that we use for clipping. For example, if threshold is `t` and `clipValue` is `c`, then the residual vectors will be clipped to the range `[-c*t , c*t]`.

There's more...

The idea behind the threshold (the encoding threshold, in our context) is that the parameter updates will happen across clusters, but only for the values that come under the user-defined limit (threshold). This threshold value is what we refer to as the encoding threshold. Parameter updates refer to the changes in gradient values during the training process. High/low encoding threshold values are not good for optimal results. So, it is reasonable to come up with a range of acceptable values for the encoding threshold. This is also termed as the sparsity ratio, in which the parameter updates happen across clusters.

In this recipe, we also discussed how to configure threshold algorithms for distributed training. The default choice would be to use `AdaptiveThresholdAlgorithm` if `AdaptiveThresholdAlgorithm` provides undesired results.

The following are the various threshold algorithms that are available in DL4J:

- `AdaptiveThresholdAlgorithm`: This is the default threshold algorithm that works well in most scenarios.
- `FixedThresholdAlgorithm`: This is a fixed and non-adaptive threshold strategy.
- `TargetSparsityThresholdAlgorithm`: This is an adaptive threshold strategy with a specific target. It decreases or increases the threshold to try and match the target.

Performing a distributed test set evaluation

There are challenges involved in distributed neural network training. Some of these challenges include managing different hardware dependencies across master and worker nodes, configuring distributed training to produce good performance, memory benchmarks across the distributed clusters, and more. We discussed some of those concerns in the previous recipes. While keeping such configurations in place, we'll move on to the actual distributed training/evaluation. In this recipe, we will perform the following tasks:

- ETL for DL4J Spark training
- Create a neural network for Spark training
- Perform a test set evaluation

How to do it...

1. Download, extract, and copy the contents of the `TinyImageNet` dataset to the following directory location:

   ```
   * Windows:
   C:\Users\<username>\.deeplearning4j\data\TINYIMAGENET_200
    * Linux: ~/.deeplearning4j/data/TINYIMAGENET_200
   ```

2. Create batches of images for training using the `TinyImageNet` dataset:

   ```
   File saveDirTrain = new File(batchSavedLocation, "train");
    SparkDataUtils.createFileBatchesLocal(dirPathDataSet,
   NativeImageLoader.ALLOWED_FORMATS, true, saveDirTrain, batchSize);
   ```

3. Create batches of images for testing using the `TinyImageNet` dataset:

   ```
   File saveDirTest = new File(batchSavedLocation, "test");
    SparkDataUtils.createFileBatchesLocal(dirPathDataSet,
   NativeImageLoader.ALLOWED_FORMATS, true, saveDirTest, batchSize);
   ```

4. Create an `ImageRecordReader` that holds a reference of the dataset:

   ```
   PathLabelGenerator labelMaker = new ParentPathLabelGenerator();
    ImageRecordReader rr = new ImageRecordReader(imageHeightWidth,
   imageHeightWidth, imageChannels, labelMaker);
    rr.setLabels(new TinyImageNetDataSetIterator(1).getLabels());
   ```

5. Create `RecordReaderFileBatchLoader` from `ImageRecordReader` to load the batch data:

```
RecordReaderFileBatchLoader loader = new
RecordReaderFileBatchLoader(rr, batchSize, 1,
TinyImageNetFetcher.NUM_LABELS);
  loader.setPreProcessor(new ImagePreProcessingScaler());
```

6. Use JCommander at the beginning of your source code to parse command-line arguments:

```
JCommander jcmdr = new JCommander(this);
  jcmdr.parse(args);
```

7. Create a parameter server configuration (gradient sharing) for Spark training using `VoidConfiguration`, as shown in the following code:

```
VoidConfiguration voidConfiguration = VoidConfiguration.builder()
 .unicastPort(portNumber)
 .networkMask(netWorkMask)
 .controllerAddress(masterNodeIPAddress)
 .build();
```

8. Configure a distributed training network using `SharedTrainingMaster`, as shown in the following code:

```
TrainingMaster tm = new
SharedTrainingMaster.Builder(voidConfiguration, batchSize)
 .rngSeed(12345)
 .collectTrainingStats(false)
 .batchSizePerWorker(batchSize) // Minibatch size for each worker
 .thresholdAlgorithm(new AdaptiveThresholdAlgorithm(1E-3))
//Threshold algorithm determines the encoding threshold to be use.
 .workersPerNode(1) // Workers per node
 .build();
```

9. Create a `GraphBuilder` for `ComputationGraphConfguration`, as shown in the following code:

```
ComputationGraphConfiguration.GraphBuilder builder = new
NeuralNetConfiguration.Builder()
 .convolutionMode(ConvolutionMode.Same)
 .l2(1e-4)
 .updater(new AMSGrad(lrSchedule))
 .weightInit(WeightInit.RELU)
 .graphBuilder()
 .addInputs("input")
 .setOutputs("output");
```

10. Use `DarknetHelper` from the DL4J Model Zoo to power up our CNN architecture, as shown in the following code:

```
DarknetHelper.addLayers(builder, 0, 3, 3, 32, 0); //64x64 out
 DarknetHelper.addLayers(builder, 1, 3, 32, 64, 2); //32x32 out
 DarknetHelper.addLayers(builder, 2, 2, 64, 128, 0); //32x32 out
 DarknetHelper.addLayers(builder, 3, 2, 128, 256, 2); //16x16 out
 DarknetHelper.addLayers(builder, 4, 2, 256, 256, 0); //16x16 out
 DarknetHelper.addLayers(builder, 5, 2, 256, 512, 2); //8x8 out
```

11. Configure the output layers while considering the number of labels and loss functions, as shown in the following code:

```
builder.addLayer("convolution2d_6", new ConvolutionLayer.Builder(1,
1)
 .nIn(512)
 .nOut(TinyImageNetFetcher.NUM_LABELS) // number of labels
(classified outputs) = 200
 .weightInit(WeightInit.XAVIER)
 .stride(1, 1)
 .activation(Activation.IDENTITY)
 .build(), "maxpooling2d_5")
 .addLayer("globalpooling", new
GlobalPoolingLayer.Builder(PoolingType.AVG).build(),
"convolution2d_6")
 .addLayer("loss", new
LossLayer.Builder(LossFunctions.LossFunction.NEGATIVELOGLIKELIHOOD)
.activation(Activation.SOFTMAX).build(), "globalpooling")
 .setOutputs("loss");
```

12. Create `ComputationGraphConfguration` from the `GraphBuilder`:

```
ComputationGraphConfiguration configuration = builder.build();
```

13. Create the `SparkComputationGraph` model from the defined configuration and set training listeners to it:

```
SparkComputationGraph sparkNet = new
SparkComputationGraph(context,configuration,tm);
 sparkNet.setListeners(new PerformanceListener(10, true));
```

14. Create `JavaRDD` objects that represent the HDFS paths of the batch files that we created earlier for training:

```
String trainPath = dataPath + (dataPath.endsWith("/") ? "" : "/") +
"train";
 JavaRDD<String> pathsTrain = SparkUtils.listPaths(context,
trainPath);
```

15. Invoke the training instance by calling `fitPaths()`:

```
for (int i = 0; i < numEpochs; i++) {
   sparkNet.fitPaths(pathsTrain, loader);
 }
```

16. Create `JavaRDD` objects that represent the HDFS paths to batch files that we created earlier for testing:

```
String testPath = dataPath + (dataPath.endsWith("/") ? "" : "/") +
"test";
 JavaRDD<String> pathsTest = SparkUtils.listPaths(context,
testPath);
```

17. Evaluate the distributed neural network by calling `doEvaluation()`:

```
Evaluation evaluation = new
Evaluation(TinyImageNetDataSetIterator.getLabels(false), 5);
 evaluation = (Evaluation) sparkNet.doEvaluation(pathsTest, loader,
evaluation)[0];
  log.info("Evaluation statistics: {}", evaluation.stats());
```

18. Run the distributed training instance on `spark-submit` in the following format:

```
spark-submit --master spark://{sparkHostIp}:{sparkHostPort} --class
{clssName} {JAR File location absolute path} --dataPath
{hdfsPathToPreprocessedData} --masterIP {masterIP}

Example:
 spark-submit --master spark://192.168.99.1:7077 --class
com.javacookbook.app.SparkExample cookbookapp-1.0-SNAPSHOT.jar --
dataPath hdfs://localhost:9000/user/hadoop/batches/imagenet-
preprocessed --masterIP 192.168.99.1
```

How it works....

Step 1 can be automated using `TinyImageNetFetcher`, as shown here:

```
TinyImageNetFetcher fetcher = new TinyImageNetFetcher();
 fetcher.downloadAndExtract();
```

For any OS, the data needs to be copied to the user's home directory. Once it is executed, we can get a reference to the train/test dataset directory, as shown here:

```
File baseDirTrain = DL4JResources.getDirectory(ResourceType.DATASET,
f.localCacheName() + "/train");
 File baseDirTest = DL4JResources.getDirectory(ResourceType.DATASET,
f.localCacheName() + "/test");
```

You can also mention your own input directory location from your local disk or HDFS. You will need to mention that in place of `dirPathDataSet` in step 2.

In step 2 and step 3, we created batches of images so that we could optimize the distributed training. We used `createFileBatchesLocal()` to create these batches, where the source of the data is a local disk. If you want to create batches from the HDFS source, then use `createFileBatchesSpark()` instead. These compressed batch files will save space and reduce bottlenecks in computation. Suppose we loaded 64 images in a compressed batch – we don't require 64 different disk reads to process the batch file. These batches contain the contents of raw files from multiple files.

In step 5, we used `RecordReaderFileBatchLoader` to process file batch objects that were created using either `createFileBatchesLocal()` or `createFileBatchesSpark()`. As we mentioned in step 6, you can use JCommander to process the command-line arguments from `spark-submit` or write your own logic to handle them.

In step 7, we configured the parameter server using the `VoidConfiguration` class. This is a basic configuration POJO class for the parameter server. We can mention the port number, network mask, and so on for the parameter server. The network mask is a very important configuration in a shared network environment and YARN.

In step 8, we started configuring the distributed network for training using `SharedTrainingMaster`. We added important configurations such as threshold algorithms, worker node count, minibatch size, and so on.

Starting from steps 9 and 10, we focused on distributed neural network layer configuration. We used `DarknetHelper` from the DL4J Model Zoo to borrow functionalities from DarkNet, TinyYOLO and YOLO2.

In step 11, we added the output layer configuration for our tiny `ImageNet` classifier. There are 200 labels in which the image classifier makes a prediction. In step 13, we created a Spark-based `ComputationGraph` using `SparkComputationGraph`. If the underlying network structure is `MultiLayerNetwork`, then you could use `SparkDl4jMultiLayer` instead.

In step 17, we created an evaluation instance, as shown here:

```
Evaluation evaluation = new
Evaluation(TinyImageNetDataSetIterator.getLabels(false), 5);
```

The second attribute (5, in the preceding code) represents the value `N`, which is used to measure the top `N` accuracy metrics. For example, evaluation on a sample will be correct if the probability for the `true` class is one of the highest `N` values.

Saving and loading trained neural network models

Training the neural network over and over to perform an evaluation is not a good idea since training is a very costly operation. This is why model persistence is important in distributed systems as well.

In this recipe, we will persist the distributed neural network models to disk and load them for further use.

How to do it...

1. Save the distributed neural network model using `ModelSerializer`:

```
MultiLayerNetwork model = sparkModel.getNetwork();
 File file = new File("MySparkMultiLayerNetwork.bin");
 ModelSerializer.writeModel(model,file, saveUpdater);
```

2. Save the distributed neural network model using `save()`:

```
MultiLayerNetwork model = sparkModel.getNetwork();
  File locationToSave = new File("MySparkMultiLayerNetwork.bin);
  model.save(locationToSave, saveUpdater);
```

3. Load the distributed neural network model using `ModelSerializer`:

```
ModelSerializer.restoreMultiLayerNetwork(new
File("MySparkMultiLayerNetwork.bin"));
```

4. Load the distributed neural network model using `load()`:

```
MultiLayerNetwork restored =
MultiLayerNetwork.load(savedModelLocation, saveUpdater);
```

How it works...

Although we used `save()` or `load()` for the model's persistence in a local machine, it is not an ideal practice in production. For a distributed cluster environment, we can make use of `BufferedInputStream`/`BufferedOutputStream` in steps 1 and 2 to save/load models to/from clusters. We can use `ModelSerializer` or `save()`/`load()` just like we demonstrated earlier. We just need to be aware of the cluster resource manager and model persistence, which can be performed across clusters.

There's more...

`SparkDl4jMultiLayer` and `SparkComputationGraph` internally make use of the standard implementations of `MultiLayerNetwork` and `ComputationGraph`, respectively. Thus, their internal structure can be accessed by calling the `getNetwork()` method.

Performing distributed inference

In this chapter, we have discussed how to perform distributed training using DL4J. We have also performed distributed evaluation to evaluate the trained distributed model. Now, let's discuss how to utilize the distributed model to solve use cases such as predictions. This is referred to as inference. Let's go over how we can perform *distributed* inference in a Spark environment.

In this recipe, we will perform distributed inference on Spark using DL4J.

How to do it...

1. Perform distributed inference for `SparkDl4jMultiLayer` by calling `feedForwardWithKey()`, as shown here:

```
SparkDl4jMultiLayer.feedForwardWithKey(JavaPairRDD<K, INDArray>
featuresData, int batchSize);
```

2. Perform distributed inference for `SparkComputationGraph` by calling `feedForwardWithKey()`:

```
SparkComputationGraph.feedForwardWithKey(JavaPairRDD<K, INDArray[]>
featuresData, int batchSize) ;
```

How it works...

The intent of the `feedForwardWithKey()` method in step 1 and 2 is to generate output/predictions for the given input dataset. A map is returned from this method. The input data is represented by the keys in the map and the results (output) are represented by values (`INDArray`).

`feedForwardWithKey()` accepts two attributes: input data and the minibatch size for feed-forward operations. The input data (features) is in the format of `JavaPairRDD<K, INDArray>`.

Note that RDD data is unordered. We need a way to map each input to the respective results (output). Hence, we need to have a key-value pair that maps each input to its respective output. That's the main reason why we use key values here. It has nothing to do with the inference process. Values for the minibatch size are used for the trade-off between memory versus computational efficiency.

11
Applying Transfer Learning to Network Models

In this chapter, we will talk about transfer learning methods, which are essential to reuse a model that was previously developed. We will see how we can apply transfer learning to the model created in `Chapter 3`, *Building Deep Neural Networks for Binary Classification*, as well as a pre-trained model from the DL4J Model Zoo API. We can use the DL4J transfer learning API to modify the network architecture, hold specific layer parameters while training, and fine-tune model configurations. Transfer learning enables improved performance and can develop skillful models. We pass learned parameters learned from another model to the current training session. If you have already set up the DL4J workspace for previous chapters, then you don't have to add any new dependencies in `pom.xml`; otherwise, you need to add the basic Deeplearning4j Maven dependency in `pom.xml`, as specified in `Chapter 3`, *Building Deep Neural Networks for Binary Classification*.

In this chapter, we will cover the following recipes:

- Modifying an existing customer retention model
- Fine-tuning the learning configurations
- Implementing frozen layers
- Importing and loading Keras models and layers

Technical requirements

This chapter's source code can be located here: `https://github.com/PacktPublishing/`
`Java-Deep-Learning-Cookbook/tree/master/11_Applying_Transfer_Learning_to_`
`network_models/sourceCode/cookbookapp/src/main/java`.

After cloning the GitHub repository, navigate to the `Java-Deep-Learning-`
`Cookbook/11_Applying_Transfer_Learning_to_network_models/sourceCode`
directory, then import the `cookbookapp` project as a Maven project by importing `pom.xml`.

 You need to have the pre-trained model from `Chapter` 3, *Building Deep Neural Networks for Binary Classification*, to run the transfer learning example. The model file should be saved in your local system once the `Chapter` 3, *Building Deep Neural Networks for Binary Classification* source code is executed. You need to load the model here while executing the source code in this chapter. Also, for the `SaveFeaturizedDataExample` example, you need to update the train/test directories where the application will be saving featurized datasets.

Modifying an existing customer retention model

We created a customer churn model in `Chapter` 3, *Building Deep Neural Networks for Binary Classification*, that is capable of predicting whether a customer will leave an organization based on specified data. We might want to train the existing model on newly available data. Transfer learning occurs when an existing model is exposed to fresh training on a similar model. We used the `ModelSerializer` class to save the model after training the neural network. We used a feed-forward network architecture to build a customer retention model.

In this recipe, we will import an existing customer retention model and further optimize it using the DL4J transfer learning API.

How to do it...

1. Call the `load()` method to import the model from the saved location:

```
File savedLocation = new File("model.zip");
 boolean saveUpdater = true;
 MultiLayerNetwork restored = MultiLayerNetwork.load(savedLocation,
saveUpdater);
```

2. Add the required `pom` dependency to use the `deeplearning4j-zoo` module:

```
<dependency>
 <groupId>org.deeplearning4j</groupId>
 <artifactId>deeplearning4j-zoo</artifactId>
 <version>1.0.0-beta3</version>
 </dependency>
```

3. Add the fine-tuning configuration for `MultiLayerNetwork` using the `TransferLearning` API:

```
MultiLayerNetwork newModel = new TransferLearning.Builder(oldModel)
 .fineTuneConfiguration(fineTuneConf)
 .build();
```

4. Add the fine-tuning configuration for `ComputationGraph` using the `TransferLearning` API:

```
ComputationGraph newModel = new
TransferLearning.GraphBuilder(oldModel).
 .fineTuneConfiguration(fineTuneConf)
 .build();
```

5. Configure the training session using `TransferLearningHelper`. `TransferLearningHelper` can be created in two ways:
   - Pass in the model object that was created using the transfer learning builder (step 2) with the frozen layers mentioned:

     ```
     TransferLearningHelper tHelper = new
     TransferLearningHelper(newModel);
     ```

   - Create it directly from the imported model by specifying the frozen layers explicitly:

     ```
     TransferLearningHelper tHelper = new
     TransferLearningHelper(oldModel, "layer1")
     ```

6. Featurize the train/test data using the `featurize()` method:

```
while(iterator.hasNext()) {
        DataSet currentFeaturized =
transferLearningHelper.featurize(iterator.next());
        saveToDisk(currentFeaturized); //save the featurized date
to disk
        }
```

7. Create train/test iterators by using `ExistingMiniBatchDataSetIterator`:

```
DataSetIterator existingTrainingData = new
ExistingMiniBatchDataSetIterator(new File("trainFolder"),"churn-
"+featureExtractorLayer+"-train-%d.bin");
 DataSetIterator existingTestData = new
ExistingMiniBatchDataSetIterator(new File("testFolder"),"churn-
"+featureExtractorLayer+"-test-%d.bin");
```

8. Start the training instance on top of the featurized data by calling
   `fitFeaturized()`:

```
transferLearningHelper.fitFeaturized(existingTrainingData);
```

9. Evaluate the model by calling `evaluate()` for unfrozen layers:

```
transferLearningHelper.unfrozenMLN().evaluate(existingTestData);
```

How it works...

In step 1, the value of `saveUpdater` is going to be `true` if we plan to train the model at a later point. We have also discussed pre-trained models provided by DL4J's model zoo API. Once we add the dependency for `deeplearning4j-zoo`, as mentioned in step 1, we can load pre-trained models such as VGG16, as follows:

```
ZooModel zooModel = VGG16.builder().build();
 ComputationGraph pretrainedNet = (ComputationGraph)
zooModel.initPretrained(PretrainedType.IMAGENET);
```

DL4J has support for many more pre-trained models under its transfer learning API.

Fine-tuning a configuration is the process of taking a model that was trained to perform a task and training it to perform another similar task. Fine-tuning configurations is specific to transfer learning. In steps 3 and 4, we added a fine-tuning configuration specific to the type of neural network. The following are possible changes that can be made using the DL4J transfer learning API:

- Update the weight initialization scheme, gradient update strategy, and the optimization algorithm (fine-tuning)
- Modify specific layers without altering other layers
- Attach new layers to the model

All these modifications can be applied using the transfer learning API. The DL4J transfer learning API comes with a builder class to support these modifications. We will add a fine-tuning configuration by calling the `fineTuneConfiguration()` builder method.

As we saw earlier, in step 4 we use `GraphBuilder` for transfer learning with computation graphs. Refer to our GitHub repository for concrete examples. Note that the transfer learning API returns an instance of the model from the imported model after applying all the modifications that were specified. The regular `Builder` class will build an instance of `MultiLayerNetwork` while `GraphBuilder` will build an instance of `ComputationGraph`.

We may also be interested in making changes only in certain layers rather than making global changes across layers. The main motive is to apply further optimization to certain layers that are identified for further optimization. That also begs another question: How do we know the model details of a stored model? In order to specify layers that are to be kept unchanged, the transfer learning API requires layer attributes such as the layer name/layer number.

We can get these using the `getLayerWiseConfigurations()` method, as shown here:

```
oldModel.getLayerWiseConfigurations().toJson()
```

Once we execute the preceding, you should see the network configuration mentioned as follows:

```
          "learningRate" : 0.015
        },
        "l1" : 0.0,
        "l1Bias" : 0.0,
        "l2" : 0.0,
        "l2Bias" : 0.0,
        "layerName" : "layer3",
        "legacyBatchScaledL2" : false,
        "lossFn" : {
          "@class" : "org.nd4j.linalg.lossfunctions.impl.LossMCXENT",
          "softmaxClipEps" : 1.0E-10,
          "weights" : [ 0.5699999928474426, 0.75 ],
          "configProperties" : false,
          "numOutputs" : -1
        },
        "nin" : 4,
        "nout" : 2,
        "pretrain" : false,
        "weightInit" : "RELU_UNIFORM",
        "weightNoise" : null
      },
      "maxNumLineSearchIterations" : 5,
      "miniBatch" : true,
      "minimize" : true,
      "optimizationAlgo" : "STOCHASTIC_GRADIENT_DESCENT",
      "pretrain" : false,
      "seed" : 1559410991805,
      "stepFunction" : null,
```

Gist URL for complete network configuration JSON is at `https://gist.github.com/rahul-raj/ee71f64706fa47b6518020071711070b`.

Neural network configurations such as the learning rate, the weights used in neurons, optimization algorithms used, layer-specific configurations, and so on can be verified from the displayed JSON content.

The following are some possible configurations from the DL4J transfer learning API to support model modifications. We need layer details (name/ID) in order to invoke these methods:

- `setFeatureExtractor()`: To freeze the changes on specific layers
- `addLayer()`: To add one or more layers to the model
- `nInReplace()`/`nOutReplace()`: Modifies the architecture of the specified layer by changing the `nIn` or `nOut` of the specified layer
- `removeLayersFromOutput()`: Removes the last n layers from the model (from the point where an output layer must be added back)

 Note that the last layer in the imported transfer learning model is a *dense* layer. because the DL4J transfer learning API doesn't enforce training configuration on imported model. So, we need to add an output layer to the model using the `addLayer()` method.

- `setInputPreProcessor()`: Adds the specified preprocessor to the specified layer

In step 5, we saw another way to apply transfer learning in DL4J, by using `TransferLearningHelper`. We discussed two ways in which it can be implemented. When you create `TransferLearningHelper` from the transfer learning builder, you need to specify `FineTuneConfiguration` as well. Values configured in `FineTuneConfiguration` will override for all non-frozen layers.

There's a reason why `TransferLearningHelper` stands out from the regular way of handling transfer learning. Transfer learning models usually have frozen layers with constant values across training sessions. The purpose of frozen layers depends on the observation being made in the existing model performance. We have also mentioned the `setFeatureExtractor()` method, which is used to freeze specific layers. Layers can be skipped using this method. However, the model instance still holds the entire frozen and unfrozen part. So, we still use the entire model (including both the frozen and unfrozen parts) for computations during training.

Using `TransferLearningHelper`, we can reduce the overall training time by creating a model instance of just the unfrozen part. The frozen dataset (with all the frozen parameters) is saved to disk and we use the model instance that refers to the unfrozen part for the training. If all we have to train is just one epoch, then `setFeatureExtractor()` and the transfer learning helper API will have almost the same performance. Let's say we have 100 layers with 99 frozen layers and we are doing *N* epochs of training. If we use `setFeatureExtractor()`, then we will end up doing a forward pass for those 99 layers *N* times, which essentially takes additional time and memory.

In order to save training time, we create the model instance after saving the activation results of the frozen layers using the transfer learning helper API. This process is also known as featurization. The motive is to skip computations for frozen layers and train on unfrozen layers.

 As a prerequisite, frozen layers need to be defined using the transfer learning builder or explicitly mentioned in the transfer learning helper.

`TransferLearningHelper` was created in step 3, as shown here:

```
TransferLearningHelper tHelper = new TransferLearningHelper(oldModel,
"layer2")
```

In the preceding case, we explicitly specified freezing all of the layers up to `layer2` in the layer structure.

In step 6, we discussed saving the dataset after featurization. After featurization, we save the data to disk. We will need to fetch this featurized data to train on top of it. Training/evaluation will be easier if we separate it and then save it to disk. The dataset can be saved to disk using the `save()` method, as follows:

```
currentFeaturized.save(new File(fileFolder,fileName));
```

`saveTodisk()` is the customary way to save a dataset for training or testing. The implementation is straightforward as it's all about creating two different directories (train/test) and deciding on the range of files that can be used for train/test. We'll leave that implementation to you. You can refer to our example in the GitHub repository (`SaveFeaturizedDataExample.java`): `https://github.com/PacktPublishing/Java-Deep-Learning-Cookbook/blob/master/11_Applying%20Transfer%20Learning%20to%20network%20models/sourceCode/cookbookapp/src/main/java/SaveFeaturizedDataExample.java`.

In steps 7/8, we discussed training our neural network on top of featurized data. Our customer retention model follows `MultiLayerNetwork` architecture. This training instance will alter the network configuration for the unfrozen layers. Hence, we need to evaluate the unfrozen layers. In step 5, we evaluated just the model on the featurized test data as shown here:

```
transferLearningHelper.unfrozenMLN().evaluate(existingTestData);
```

If your network has the `ComputationGraph` structure, then you can use the `unfrozenGraph()` method instead of `unfrozenMLN()` to achieve the same result.

There's more...

Here are some important pre-trained models offered by the DL4J Model Zoo API:

- **VGG16**: VGG-16 referred to in this paper: `https://arxiv.org/abs/1409.1556`.

  This is a very deep convolutional neural network targeting large-scale image recognition tasks. We can use transfer learning to train the model further. All we have to do is import VGG16 from the model zoo:

  ```
  ZooModel zooModel =VGG16.builder().build();
   ComputationGraph network =
  (ComputationGraph)zooModel.initPretrained();
  ```

  Note that the underlying architecture of the VGG16 model in the DL4J Model Zoo API is `ComputationGraph`.

- **TinyYOLO**: TinyYOLO is referred to in this paper: `https://arxiv.org/pdf/1612.08242.pdf`.

  This is a real-time object detection model for fast and accurate image classification. We can apply transfer learning to this model as well after importing from it the model zoo, as shown here:

  ```
  ComputationGraph pretrained =
  (ComputationGraph)TinyYOLO.builder().build().initPretrained();
  ```

  Note that the underlying architecture of the TinyYOLO model in the DL4J model zoo API is `ComputationGraph`.

- **Darknet19**: Darknet19 is referred to in this paper: `https://arxiv.org/pdf/1612.08242.pdf`.

This is also known as YOLOV2, a faster object detection model for real-time object detection. We can apply transfer learning to this model after importing it from the model zoo, as shown here:

```
ComputationGraph pretrained = (ComputationGraph)
Darknet19.builder().build().initPretrained();
```

Fine-tuning the learning configurations

While performing transfer learning, we might want to update the strategy for how weights are initialized, which gradients are updated, which activation functions are to be used, and so on. For that purpose, we fine-tune the configuration. In this recipe, we will fine-tune the configuration for transfer learning.

How to do it...

1. Use `FineTuneConfiguration()` to manage modifications in the model configuration:

```
FineTuneConfiguration fineTuneConf = new
FineTuneConfiguration.Builder()
.optimizationAlgo(OptimizationAlgorithm.STOCHASTIC_GRADIENT_DESCENT
)
 .updater(new Nesterovs(5e-5))
 .activation(Activation.RELU6)
 .biasInit(0.001)
 .dropOut(0.85)
.gradientNormalization(GradientNormalization.RenormalizeL2PerLayer)
 .l2(0.0001)
 .weightInit(WeightInit.DISTRIBUTION)
 .seed(seed)
 .build();
```

2. Call `fineTuneConfiguration()` to fine-tune the model configuration:

```
MultiLayerNetwork newModel = new TransferLearning.Builder(oldModel)
 .fineTuneConfiguration(fineTuneConf)
 .build();
```

How it works...

We saw a sample fine-tuning implementation in step 1. Fine-tuning configurations are intended for default/global changes that are applicable across layers. So, if we want to remove specific layers from being considered for fine-tuning configuration, then we need to make those layers frozen. Unless we do that, all the current values for the specified modification type (gradients, activation, and so on) will be overridden in the new model.

 All the fine-tuning configurations mentioned above will be applied to all unfrozen layers, including output layers. So, you might get errors due to the addition of the `activation()` and `dropOut()` methods. Dropouts are relevant to hidden layers and we may have a different value range for output activation as well. A quick fix would be to remove these unless really needed. Otherwise, remove output layers from the model using the transfer learning helper API, apply fine-tuning, and then add the output layer back with a specific activation.

In step 2, if our original `MultiLayerNetwork` model has convolutional layers, then it is possible to make modifications in the convolution mode as well. As you might have guessed, this is applicable if you perform transfer learning for the image classification model from `Chapter 4`, *Building Convolutional Neural Networks*. Also, if your convolutional neural network is supposed to run in CUDA-enabled GPU mode, then you can also mention the cuDNN algo mode with your transfer learning API. We can specify an algorithmic approach (PREFER_FASTEST, NO_WORKSPACE, or USER_SPECIFIED) for cuDNN. It will impact the performance and memory usage of cuDNN. Use the `cudnnAlgoMode()` method with the PREFER_FASTEST mode to achieve performance improvements.

Implementing frozen layers

We might want to keep the training instance limited to certain layers, which means some layers can be kept frozen for the training instance, so we can focus on optimizing other layers while frozen layers are kept unchanged. We saw two ways of implementing frozen layers earlier: using the regular transfer learning builder and using the transfer learning helper. In this recipe, we will implement frozen layers for transfer layers.

How to do it...

1. Define frozen layers by calling `setFeatureExtractor()`:

```
MultiLayerNetwork newModel = new TransferLearning.Builder(oldModel)
 .setFeatureExtractor(featurizeExtractionLayer)
 .build();
```

2. Call `fit()` to start the training instance:

```
newModel.fit(numOfEpochs);
```

How it works...

In step 1, we used `MultiLayerNetwork` for demonstration purposes. For `MultiLayerNetwork`, featurizeExtractionLayer refers to the layer number (integer). For `ComputationGraph`, featurizeExtractionLayer refers to the layer name (`String`). By shifting frozen layer management to the transfer learning builder, it can be grouped along with all the other transfer learning functions, such as fine-tuning. This gives better modularization. However, the transfer learning helper has its own advantages, as we discussed in the previous recipe.

Importing and loading Keras models and layers

There can be times when you want to import a model that is not available in the DL4J Model Zoo API. You might have created your own model in Keras/TensorFlow, or you might be using a pre-trained model from Keras/TensorFlow. Either way, we can still load models from Keras/TensorFlow using the DL4J model import API.

Getting ready

This recipe assumes that you already have the Keras model (pre-trained/not pre-trained) set up and ready to be imported to DL4J. We will skip the details about how to save Keras models to disk as it is beyond the scope of this book. Usually, Keras models are stored in .h5 format, but that isn't a restriction as the model-import API can import from other formats as well. As a prerequisite, we need to add the following Maven dependency in pom.xml:

```
<dependency>
   <groupId>org.deeplearning4j</groupId>
   <artifactId>deeplearning4j-modelimport</artifactId>
   <version>1.0.0-beta3</version>
</dependency>
```

How to do it...

1. Use `KerasModelImport` to load an external `MultiLayerNetwork` model:

```
String modelFileLocation = new
ClassPathResource("kerasModel.h5").getFile().getPath();
 MultiLayerNetwork model =
KerasModelImport.importKerasSequentialModelAndWeights(modelFileLoca
tion);
```

2. Use `KerasModelImport` to load an external `ComputationGraph` model:

```
String modelFileLocation = new
ClassPathResource("kerasModel.h5").getFile().getPath();
 ComputationGraph model =
KerasModelImport.importKerasModelAndWeights(modelFileLocation);
```

3. Use `KerasModelBuilder` to import an external model:

```
KerasModelBuilder builder = new
KerasModel().modelBuilder().modelHdf5Filename(modelFile.getAbsolute
Path())
 .enforceTrainingConfig(trainConfigToEnforceOrNot);
 if (inputShape != null) {
 builder.inputShape(inputShape);
 }
 KerasModel model = builder.buildModel();
 ComputationGraph newModel = model.getComputationGraph();
```

How it works...

In step 1, we used `KerasModelImport` to load the external Keras model from disk. If the model was saved separately by calling `model.to_json()` and `model.save_weights()` (in Keras), then we need to use the following variant:

```
String modelJsonFileLocation = new
ClassPathResource("kerasModel.json").getFile().getPath();
 String modelWeightsFileLocation = new
ClassPathResource("kerasModelWeights.h5").getFile().getPath();
 MultiLayerNetwork model =
KerasModelImport.importKerasSequentialModelAndWeights(modelJsonFileLocation
, modelWeightsFileLocation, enforceTrainConfig);
```

Note the following:

- `importKerasSequentialModelAndWeights()`: Imports and creates `MultiLayerNetwork` from the Keras model
- `importKerasModelAndWeights()`: Imports and creates `ComputationGraph` from the Keras model

Consider the following implementation for the `importKerasModelAndWeights()` method to perform step 2:

```
KerasModelImport.importKerasModelAndWeights(modelJsonFileLocation,modelWeig
htsFileLocation,enforceTrainConfig);
```

The third attribute, `enforceTrainConfig`, is a Boolean type, which indicates whether to enforce a training configuration or not. Again, if the model was saved separately using the `model.to_json()` and `model.save_weights()` Keras calls, then we need to use the following variant:

```
String modelJsonFileLocation = new
ClassPathResource("kerasModel.json").getFile().getPath();
 String modelWeightsFileLocation = new
ClassPathResource("kerasModelWeights.h5").getFile().getPath();
 ComputationGraph model =
KerasModelImport.importKerasModelAndWeights(modelJsonFileLocation,modelWeig
htsFileLocation,enforceTrainConfig);
```

In step 3, we discussed how to load `ComputationGraph` from the external model using `KerasModelBuilder`. One of the builder methods is `inputShape()`. It assigns input shape to the imported Keras model. DL4J requires the input shape to be specified. However, you don't have to deal with these if you go for the first two methods, discussed earlier, for the Keras model import. Those methods (`importKerasModelAndWeights()` and `importKerasSequentialModelAndWeights()`) internally make use of `KerasModelBuilder` to import models.

12
Benchmarking and Neural Network Optimization

Benchmarking is a standard against which we compare solutions to find out whether they are good or not. In the context of deep learning, we might set benchmarks for an existing model that is performing pretty well. We might test our model against factors such as accuracy, the amount of data handled, memory consumption, and JVM garbage collection tuning. In this chapter, we briefly talk about the benchmarking possibilities with your DL4J applications. We will start with general guidelines and then move on to more DL4J-specific benchmarking settings. At the end of the chapter, we will look at a hyperparameter tuning example that shows how to find the best neural network parameters in order to yield the best results.

In this chapter, we will cover the following recipes:

- DL4J/ND4J specific configuration
- Setting up heap spaces and garbage collection
- Using asynchronous ETL
- Using arbiter to monitor neural network behavior
- Performing hyperparameter tuning

Technical requirements

The code for this chapter is located at `https://github.com/PacktPublishing/Java-Deep-Learning-Cookbook/tree/master/12_Benchmarking_and_Neural_Network_Optimization/sourceCode/cookbookapp/src/main/java`.

After cloning our GitHub repository, navigate to the `Java-Deep-Learning-Cookbook/12_Benchmarking_and_Neural_Network_Optimization/sourceCode` directory. Then import the `cookbookapp` project as a Maven project by importing `pom.xml`.

The following are links to two examples:

- Hyperparameter tuning example: `https://github.com/PacktPublishing/Java-Deep-Learning-Cookbook/blob/master/12_Benchmarking_and_Neural_Network_Optimization/sourceCode/cookbookapp/src/main/java/HyperParameterTuning.java`
- Arbiter UI example: `https://github.com/PacktPublishing/Java-Deep-Learning-Cookbook/blob/master/12_Benchmarking_and_Neural_Network_Optimization/sourceCode/cookbookapp/src/main/java/HyperParameterTuningArbiterUiExample.java`

This chapter's examples are based on a customer churn dataset (`https://github.com/PacktPublishing/Java-Deep-Learning-Cookbook/tree/master/03_Building_Deep_Neural_Networks_for_Binary_classification/sourceCode/cookbookapp/src/main/resources`). This dataset is included in the project directory.

Although we are explaining DL4J/ND4J-specific benchmarks in this chapter, it is recommended you follow general benchmarking guidelines. The following some important generic benchmarks that are common for any neural network:

- **Perform warm-up iterations before the actual benchmark task**: Warm-up iterations refer to a set of iterations performed on benchmark tasks before commencing the actual ETL operation or network training. Warm up iterations are important because the execution of the first few iterations will be slow. This can add to the total duration of the benchmark tasks and we could end up with wrong/inconsistent conclusions. The slow execution of the first few iterations may be because of the compilation time taken by JVM, the lazy-loading approach of DL4J/ND4J libraries, or the learning phase of DL4J/ND4J libraries. This learning phase refers to the time taken to learn the memory requirements for execution.
- **Perform benchmark tasks multiple times**: To make sure that benchmark results are reliable, we need to run benchmark tasks multiple times. The host system may have multiple apps/processes running in parallel apart from the benchmark instance. So, the runtime performance will vary over time. In order to assess this situation, we need to run benchmark tasks multiple times.

- **Understand where you set the benchmarks and why**: We need to assess whether we are setting the right benchmarking. If we target operation a, then make sure that only operation a is being timed for benchmark. Also, we have to make sure that we are using the right libraries for the right situation. The latest versions of libraries are always preferred. It is also important to assess DL4J/ND4J configurations used in our code. The default configurations may suffice in regular scenarios, but manual configuration may be required for optimal performance. The following some of the default configuration options for reference:
    - Memory configurations (heap space setup).
    - Garbage collection and workspace configuration (changing the frequency at which the garbage collector is called).
    - Add cuDNN support (utilizing a CUDA-powered GPU machine with better performance).
    - Enable DL4J cache mode (to bring in cache memory for the training instance). This will be a DL4J-specific change.

We discussed cuDNN in `Chapter 1`, *Introduction to Deep Learning in Java*, while we talked about DL4J in GPU environments. These configuration options will be discussed further in upcoming recipes.

- **Run the benchmark on a range of sizes**: It is important to run the benchmark on multiple different input sizes/shapes to get a complete picture of its performance. Mathematical computations such as matrix multiplications vary over different dimensions.
- **Understand the hardware**: The training instance with the smallest minibatch size will perform better on a CPU than on a GPU system. When we use a large minibatch size, the observation will be exactly the opposite. The training instance will now be able to utilize GPU resources. In the same way, a large layer size can better utilize GPU resources. Writing network configurations without understanding the underlying hardware will not allow us to exploit its full capabilities.
- **Reproduce the benchmarks and understand their limits**: In order to troubleshoot performance bottlenecks against a set benchmark, we always need to reproduce them. It is helpful to assess the circumstance under which poor performance occurs. On top of that, we also need to understand the limitations put on certain benchmarks. Certain benchmarks set on a specific layer won't tell you anything about the performance factor of other layers.

- **Avoid common benchmark mistakes**:
  - Consider using the latest version of DL4J/ND4J. To apply the latest performance improvements, try snapshot versions.
  - Pay attention to the types of native libraries used (such as cuDNN).
  - Run enough iterations and with a reasonable minibatch size to yield consistent results.
  - Do not compare results across hardware without accounting for the differences.

In order to benefit from the latest fixes for performance issues, you need to have latest version in your local. If you want to run the source on the latest fix and if the new version hasn't been released, then you can make use of snapshot versions. To find out more about working with snapshot versions, go to `https://deeplearning4j.org/docs/latest/deeplearning4j-config-snapshots`.

DL4J/ND4J-specific configuration

Apart from general benchmarking guidelines, we need to follow additional benchmarking configurations that are DL4J/ND4J-specific. These are important benchmarking configurations that target the hardware and mathematical computations.

Because ND4J is the JVM computation library for DL4J, benchmarks mostly target mathematical computations. Any benchmarks discussed with regard to ND4J can then also be applied to DL4J. Let's discuss DL4J/ND4J-specific benchmarks.

Getting ready

Make sure you have downloaded cudNN from the following link: `https://developer.nvidia.com/cudnn`. Install it before attempting to configure it with DL4J. Note that cuDNN doesn't come as a bundle with CUDA. So, adding the CUDA dependency alone will not be enough.

How to do it...

1. Detach the `INDArray` data to use it across workspaces:

```
INDArray array = Nd4j.rand(6, 6);
 INDArray mean = array.mean(1);
 INDArray result = mean.detach();
```

2. Remove all workspaces that were created during training/evaluation in case they are running short of RAM:

```
Nd4j.getWorkspaceManager().destroyAllWorkspacesForCurrentThread();
```

3. Leverage an array instance from another workspace in the current workspace by calling `leverageTo()`:

```
LayerWorkspaceMgr.leverageTo(ArrayType.ACTIVATIONS, myArray);
```

4. Track the time spent on every iteration during training using `PerformanceListener`:

```
model.setListeners(new PerformanceListener(frequency, reportScore));
```

5. Add the following Maven dependency for cuDNN support:

```
<dependency>
   <groupId>org.deeplearning4j</groupId>
   <artifactId>deeplearning4j-cuda-x.x</artifactId> //cuda version
to be specified
   <version>1.0.0-beta4</version>
 </dependency>
```

6. Configure DL4J/cuDNN to favor performance over memory:

```
MultiLayerNetwork config = new NeuralNetConfiguration.Builder()
 .cudnnAlgoMode(ConvolutionLayer.AlgoMode.PREFER_FASTEST) //prefer
performance over memory
 .build();
```

7. Configure `ParallelWrapper` to support multi-GPU training/inferences:

```
ParallelWrapper wrapper = new ParallelWrapper.Builder(model)
 .prefetchBuffer(deviceCount)
.workers(Nd4j.getAffinityManager().getNumberOfDevices())
.trainingMode(ParallelWrapper.TrainingMode.SHARED_GRADIENTS)
.thresholdAlgorithm(new AdaptiveThresholdAlgorithm())
 .build();
```

8. Configure `ParallelInference` as follows:

```
ParallelInference inference = new ParallelInference.Builder(model)
 .inferenceMode(InferenceMode.BATCHED)
.batchLimit(maxBatchSize)
 .workers(workerCount)
 .build();
```

How it works...

A workspace is a memory management model that enables the reuse of memory for cyclic workloads without having to introduce a JVM garbage collector. `INDArray` memory content is invalidated once in every workspace loop. Workspaces can be integrated for training or inference.

In step 1, we start with workspace benchmarking. The `detach()` method will detach the specific INDArray from the workspace and will return a copy. So, how do we enable workspace modes for our training instance? Well, if you're using the latest DL4J version (from 1.0.0-alpha onwards), then this feature is enabled by default. We target version 1.0.0-beta 3 in this book.

In step 2, we removed workspaces from the memory, as shown here:

```
Nd4j.getWorkspaceManager().destroyAllWorkspacesForCurrentThread();
```

This will destroy workspaces from the current running thread only. We can release memory from workspaces in this way by running this piece of code in the thread in question.

DL4J also lets you implement your own workspace manager for layers. For example, activation results from one layer during training can be placed in one workspace, and the results of the inference can be placed in another workspace. This is possible using DL4J's `LayerWorkspaceMgr`, as mentioned in step 3. Make sure that the returned array (`myArray` in step 3) is defined as `ArrayType.ACTIVATIONS`:

```
LayerWorkspaceMgr.create(ArrayType.ACTIVATIONS,myArray);
```

It is fine to use different workspace modes for training/inference. But it is recommended you use `SEPARATE` mode for training and `SINGLE` mode for inference because inference only involves a forward pass and doesn't involve backpropagation. However, for training instances with high resource consumption/memory, it might be better to go for `SEPARATE` workspace mode because it consumes less memory. Note that `SEPARATE` is the default workspace mode in DL4J.

In step 4, two attributes are used while creating `PerformanceListener`: `reportScore` and `frequency`. `reportScore` is a Boolean variable and `frequency` is the iteration count by which time needs to be tracked. If `reportScore` is `true`, then it will report the score (just like in `ScoreIterationListener`) along with information on the time spent on each iteration.

In step 7, we used `ParallelWrapper` or `ParallelInference` for multi-GPU devices. Once we have created a neural network model, we can create a parallel wrapper using it. We specify the count of devices, a training mode, and the number of workers for the parallel wrapper.

We need to make sure that our training instance is cost-effective. It is not feasible to spend a lot adding multiple GPUs and then utilizing one GPU in training. Ideally, we want to utilize all GPU hardware to speed up the training/inference process and get better results. `ParallelWrapper` and `ParallelInference` serve this purpose.

The following some configurations supported by `ParallelWrapper` and `ParallelInference`:

- `prefetchBuffer(deviceCount)`: This parallel wrapper method specifies dataset prefetch options. We mention the number of devices here.
- `trainingMode(mode)`: This parallel wrapper method specifies the distributed training method. `SHARED_GRADIENTS` refers to the gradient sharing method for distributed training.
- `workers(Nd4j.getAffinityManager().getNumberOfDevices())`: This parallel wrapper method specifies the number of workers. We set the number of workers to the number of available systems.
- `inferenceMode(mode)`: This parallel inference method specifies the distributed inference method. `BATCHED` mode is an optimization. If a large number of requests come in, it will process them in batches. If there is a small number of requests, then they will be processed as usual without batching. As you might have guessed, this is the perfect option if you're in production.
- `batchLimit(batchSize)`: This parallel inference method specifies the batch size limit and is only applicable if you use `BATCHED` mode in `inferenceMode()`.

There's more...

The performance of ND4J operations can also vary upon input array ordering. ND4J enforces the ordering of arrays. Performance in mathematical operations (including general ND4J operations) depends on the input and result array orders. For example, performance in operations such as simple addition, such as $z = x + y$, will vary in line with the input array orders. It happens due to memory striding: it is easier to read the memory sequence if they're close/adjacent to each other than when they're spread far apart. ND4J is faster on computations with larger matrices. By default, ND4J arrays are C-ordered. IC ordering refers to row-major ordering and the memory allocation resembles that of an array in C:

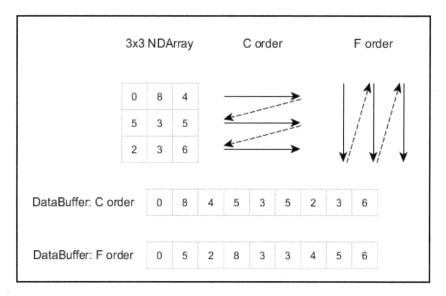

(Image courtesy: Eclipse Deeplearning4j Development Team. Deeplearning4j: Open-source distributed deep learning for the JVM, Apache Software Foundation License 2.0. http://deeplearning4j.org)

ND4J supplies the `gemm()` method for advanced matrix multiplication between two INDArrays depending on whether we require multiplication after transposing it. This method returns the result in F-order, which means the memory allocation resembles that of an array in Fortran. F-ordering refers to column-major ordering. Let's say we have passed a C-ordered array to collect the results from the `gemm()` method; ND4J automatically detects it, creates an F-ordered array, and then passes the result to a C-ordered array.

To learn more about array ordering and how ND4J handles array ordering, go to `https://deeplearning4j.org/docs/latest/nd4j-overview`.

It is also critical to assess the minibatch size used for training. We need to experiment with different minibatch sizes while performing multiple training sessions by acknowledging the hardware specs, data, and evaluation metrics. For a CUDA-enabled GPU environment, the minibatch size will have a big role to play with regard to benchmarks if you use a large enough value. When we talk about a large minibatch size, we are referring to a minibatch size that can be justified against the entire dataset. For very small minibatch sizes, we won't observe any noticeable performance difference with the CPU/GPU after the benchmarks. At the same time, we need to watch out for changes in model accuracy as well. An ideal minibatch size is when we utilize the hardware to its full ability without affecting model accuracy. In fact, we aim for better results with better performance (shorter training time).

Setting up heap spaces and garbage collection

Memory heap spaces and garbage collection are frequently discussed yet are often the most frequently ignored benchmarks. With DL4J/ND4J, you can configure two types of memory limit: on-heap memory and off-heap memory. Whenever an INDArray is collected by the JVM garbage collector, the off-heap memory will be de-allocated, assuming that it is not being used anywhere else. In this recipe, we will set up heap spaces and garbage collection for benchmarking.

How to do it...

1. Add the required VM arguments to the Eclipse/IntelliJ IDE, as shown in the following example:

```
-Xms1G -Xmx6G -Dorg.bytedeco.javacpp.maxbytes=16G -
Dorg.bytedeco.javacpp.maxphysicalbytes=20G
```

For example, in IntelliJ IDE, we can add VM arguments to the runtime configuration:

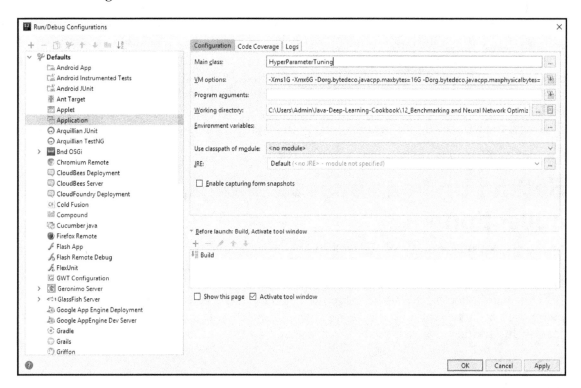

2. Run the following command after changing the memory limits to suit your hardware (for command-line executions):

```
java -Xms1G -Xmx6G -Dorg.bytedeco.javacpp.maxbytes=16G -
Dorg.bytedeco.javacpp.maxphysicalbytes=20G YourClassName
```

3. Configure a server-style generational garbage collector for JVM:

```
java -XX:+UseG1GC
```

4. Reduce the frequency of garbage collector calls using ND4J:

```
Nd4j.getMemoryManager().setAutoGcWindow(3000);
```

5. Disable garbage collector calls instead of step 4:

```
Nd4j.getMemoryManager().togglePeriodicGc(false);
```

6. Allocate memory chunks in memory-mapped files instead of RAM:

```
WorkspaceConfiguration memoryMap = WorkspaceConfiguration.builder()
 .initialSize(2000000000)
 .policyLocation(LocationPolicy.MMAP)
 .build();
 try (MemoryWorkspace workspace =
Nd4j.getWorkspaceManager().getAndActivateWorkspace(memoryMap, "M"))
 {
 INDArray example = Nd4j.create(10000);
 }
```

How it works...

In step 1, we performed on-heap/off-heap memory configurations. On-heap memory simply means the memory that is managed by the JVM heap (garbage collector). Off-heap memory refers to memory that is not managed directly, such as that used with INDArrays. Both off-heap and on-heap memory limits can be controlled using the following VM options in Java command-line arguments:

- −Xms: This defines how much memory will be consumed by the JVM heap at application startup.
- −Xmx: This defines the maximum memory that can be consumed by the JVM heap at any point in runtime. This involves allotting memory only up to this point when it is required.
- −Dorg.bytedeco.javacpp.maxbytes: This specifies the off-heap memory limit.
- −Dorg.bytedeco.javacpp.maxphysicalbytes: This specifies the maximum number of bytes that can be allotted to the application at any given time. Usually, this takes a larger value than −Xmx and maxbytes combined.

Suppose we want to configure 1 GB initially on-heap, 6 GB max on-heap, 16 GB off-heap, and 20 GB maximum for processes; the VM arguments will look as follows, and as shown in step 1:

```
-Xms1G -Xmx6G -Dorg.bytedeco.javacpp.maxbytes=16G -
Dorg.bytedeco.javacpp.maxphysicalbytes=20G
```

Note that you will need to adjust this in line with the memory available in your hardware.

It is also possible to set up these VM options as an environment variable. We can create an environment variable named MAVEN_OPTS and put VM options there. You can choose either step 1 or step 2, or set them up with an environment variable. Once this is done, you can skip to step 3.

In steps 3, 4, and 5, we discussed memory automatically using some tweaks in garbage collection. The garbage collector manages memory management and consumes on-heap memory. DL4J is tightly coupled with the garbage collector. If we talk about ETL, every DataSetIterator object takes 8 bytes of memory. The garbage collector can induce further latency in the system. To that end, we configure **G1GC** (short for **Garbage First Garbage Collector**) tuning in step 3.

If we pass 0 ms (milliseconds) as an attribute to the setAutoGcWindow() method, as in step 4, it will just disable this particular option. getMemoryManager() will return a backend-specific implementation of MemoryManager for lower-level memory management.

In step 6, we discussed configuring memory-mapped files to allocate more memory for INDArrays. We have created a 1 GB memory map file in step 4. Note that memory-mapped files can be created and supported only when using the nd4j-native library. Memory mapped files are slower than memory allocation in RAM. Step 4 can be applied if the minibatch size memory requirement is higher than the amount of RAM available.

There's more...

DL4J has a dependency with JavaCPP that acts as a bridge between Java and C++: https://github.com/bytedeco/javacpp.

JavaCPP works on the basis of the -Xmx value set on the heap space (off-heap memory) and the overall memory consumption will not exceed this value. DL4J seeks help from the garbage collector and JavaCPP to deallocate memory.

For training sessions with large amounts of data involved, it is important to have more RAM for the off-heap memory space than for on-heap memory (JVM). Why? Because our datasets and computations are involved with INDArrays and are stored in the off-heap memory space.

It is important to identify the memory limits of running applications. The following some instances where the memory limit needs to be properly configured:

- For GPU systems, `maxbytes` and `maxphysicalbytes` are the important memory limit settings. We are dealing with off-heap memory here. Allocating reasonable memory to these settings allows us to consume more GPU resources.
- For `RunTimeException` that refer to memory allocation issues, one possible reason may be the unavailability of off-heap memory spaces. If we don't use the memory limit (off-heap space) settings discussed in the *Setting up heap space and garbage collection* recipe, the off-heap memory space can be reclaimed by the JVM garbage collector. This can then cause memory allocation issues.
- If you have limited-memory environments, then it is not recommended to use large values for the `-Xmx` and `-Xms` options. For instance, if we use `-Xms 6G` for an 8 GB RAM system, we leave only 2 GB for the off-heap memory space, the OS, and for other processes.

See also

- If you're interested in knowing more about G1GC garbage collector tuning, you can read about it here: `https://www.oracle.com/technetwork/articles/java/g1gc-1984535.html`

Using asynchronous ETL

We use synchronous ETL for demonstration purposes. But for production, asynchronous ETL is preferable. In production, the existence of a single low-performance ETA component can cause a performance bottleneck. In DL4J, we load data to the disk using `DataSetIterator`. It can load the data from disk or, memory, or simply load data asynchronously. Asynchronous ETL uses an asynchronous loader in the background. Using multithreading, it loads data into the GPU/CPU and other threads take care of compute tasks. In the following recipe, we will perform asynchronous ETL operations in DL4J.

How to do it...

1. Create asynchronous iterators with asynchronous prefetch:

```
DatasetIterator asyncIterator = new
AsyncMultiDataSetIterator(iterator);
```

2. Create asynchronous iterators with synchronous prefetch:

```
DataSetIterator shieldIterator = new
AsyncShieldDataSetIterator(iterator);
```

How it works...

In step 1, we created an iterator using `AsyncMultiDataSetIterator`. We can use `AsyncMultiDataSetIterator` or `AsyncDataSetIterator` to create asynchronous iterators. There are multiple ways in which you can configure an `AsyncMultiDataSetIterator`. There are multiple ways to create `AsyncMultiDataSetIterator` by passing further attributes such as `queSize` (the number of mini-batches that can be prefetched at once) and `useWorkSpace` (a Boolean type indicating whether workspace configuration should be used). While using `AsyncDataSetIterator`, we use the current dataset before calling `next()` to get the next dataset. Also note that we should not store datasets without the `detach()` call. If you do, then the memory used by INDArray data inside the dataset will eventually be overwritten within `AsyncDataSetIterator`. For custom iterator implementations, make sure you don't initialize something huge using the `next()` call during training/evaluation. Instead, keep all such initialization inside the constructor to avoid undesired workspace memory consumption.

In step 2, we created an iterator using `AsyncShieldDataSetIterator`. To opt out of asynchronous prefetch, we can use `AsyncShieldMultiDataSetIterator` or `AsyncShieldDataSetIterator`. These wrappers will prevent asynchronous prefetch in data-intensive operations such as training, and can be used for debugging purposes.

If the training instance performs ETL every time it runs, we are basically recreating the data every time it runs. Eventually, the whole process (training and evaluation) will get slower. We can handle this better using a pre-saved dataset. We discussed pre-save using `ExistingMiniBatchDataSetIterator` in the previous chapter, when we pre-saved feature data and then later loaded it using `ExistingMiniBatchDataSetIterator`. We can convert it to an asynchronous iterator (as in step 1 or step 2) and kill two birds with one stone: pre-saved data with asynchronous loading. This is essentially a performance benchmark that further optimizes the ETL process.

There's more...

Let's say our minibatch has 100 samples and we specify `queSize` as `10`; 1,000 samples will be prefetched every time. The memory requirement of the workspace depends on the size of the dataset, which arises from the underlying iterator. The workspace will be adjusted for varying memory requirements (for example, time series with varying lengths). Note that asynchronous iterators are internally supported by `LinkedBlockingQueue`. This queue data structure orders elements in **First In First Out** (**FIFO**) mode. Linked queues generally have more throughput than array-based queues in concurrent environments.

Using arbiter to monitor neural network behavior

Hyperparameter optimization/tuning is the process of finding the optimal values for hyperparameters in the learning process. Hyperparameter optimization partially automates the process of finding optimal hyperparameters using certain search strategies. Arbiter is part of the DL4J deep learning library and is used for hyperparameter optimization. Arbiter can be used to find high-performing models by tuning the hyperparameters of the neural network. Arbiter has a UI that visualizes the results of the hyperparameter tuning process.

In this recipe, we will set up arbiter and visualize the training instance to take a look at neural network behavior.

How to do it...

1. Add the arbiter Maven dependency in `pom.xml`:

```
<dependency>
   <groupId>org.deeplearning4j</groupId>
   <artifactId>arbiter-deeplearning4j</artifactId>
   <version>1.0.0-beta3</version>
</dependency>
<dependency>
   <groupId>org.deeplearning4j</groupId>
   <artifactId>arbiter-ui_2.11</artifactId>
   <version>1.0.0-beta3</version>
</dependency>
```

2. Configure the search space using `ContinuousParameterSpace`:

```
ParameterSpace<Double> learningRateParam = new
ContinuousParameterSpace(0.0001,0.01);
```

3. Configure the search space using `IntegerParameterSpace`:

```
ParameterSpace<Integer> layerSizeParam = new
IntegerParameterSpace(5,11);
```

4. Use `OptimizationConfiguration` to combine all components required to execute the hyperparameter tuning process:

```
OptimizationConfiguration optimizationConfiguration = new
OptimizationConfiguration.Builder()
  .candidateGenerator(candidateGenerator)
  .dataProvider(dataProvider)
  .modelSaver(modelSaver)
  .scoreFunction(scoreFunction)
  .terminationConditions(conditions)
  .build();
```

How it works...

In step 2, we created `ContinuousParameterSpace` to configure the search space for hyperparameter optimization:

```
ParameterSpace<Double> learningRateParam = new
ContinuousParameterSpace(0.0001,0.01);
```

In the preceding case, the hyperparameter tuning process will select continuous values in the range (0.0001, 0.01) for the learning rate. Note that arbiter doesn't really automate the hyperparameter tuning process. We still need to specify the range of values or a list of options by which the hyperparameter tuning process takes place. In other words, we need to specify a search space with all the valid values for the tuning process to pick the best combination that can produce the best results. We have also mentioned `IntegerParameterSpace`, where the search space is an ordered space of integers between a maximum/minimum value.

Since there are multiple training instances with different configurations, it takes a while to finish the hyperparameter optimization-tuning process. At the end, the best configuration will be returned.

In step 2, once we have defined our search space using `ParameterSpace` or `OptimizationConfiguration`, we need to add it to `MultiLayerSpace` or `ComputationGraphSpace`. These are the arbiter counterparts of DL4J's `MultiLayerConfiguration` and `ComputationGraphConfiguration`.

Then we added `candidateGenerator` using the `candidateGenerator()` builder method. `candidateGenerator` chooses candidates (various combinations of hyperparameters) for hyperparameter tuning. It can use different approaches, such as random search and grid search, to pick the next configuration for hyperparameter tuning.

`scoreFunction()` specifies the evaluation metrics used for evaluation during the hyperparameter tuning process.

`terminationConditions()` is used to mention all termination conditions for the training instance. Hyperparameter tuning will then proceed with the next configuration in the sequence.

Performing hyperparameter tuning

Once search spaces are defined using `ParameterSpace` or `OptimizationConfiguration`, with a possible range of values, the next step is to complete network configuration
using `MultiLayerSpace` or `ComputationGraphSpace`. After that, we start the training process. We perform multiple training sessions during the hyperparameter tuning process.

In this recipe, we will perform and visualize the hyperparameter tuning process. We will be using `MultiLayerSpace` for the demonstration.

How to do it...

1. Add a search space for the layer size using `IntegerParameterSpace`:

```
ParameterSpace<Integer> layerSizeParam = new
IntegerParameterSpace(startLimit,endLimit);
```

2. Add a search space for the learning rate using `ContinuousParameterSpace`:

```
ParameterSpace<Double> learningRateParam = new
ContinuousParameterSpace(0.0001,0.01);
```

3. Use `MultiLayerSpace` to build a configuration space by adding all the search spaces to the relevant network configuration:

```
MultiLayerSpace hyperParamaterSpace = new MultiLayerSpace.Builder()
 .updater(new AdamSpace(learningRateParam))
 .addLayer(new DenseLayerSpace.Builder()
   .activation(Activation.RELU)
   .nIn(11)
   .nOut(layerSizeParam)
   .build())
 .addLayer(new DenseLayerSpace.Builder()
   .activation(Activation.RELU)
   .nIn(layerSizeParam)
   .nOut(layerSizeParam)
   .build())
 .addLayer(new OutputLayerSpace.Builder()
   .activation(Activation.SIGMOID)
   .lossFunction(LossFunctions.LossFunction.XENT)
   .nOut(1)
   .build())
 .build();
```

4. Create `candidateGenerator` from `MultiLayerSpace`:

```
Map<String,Object> dataParams = new HashMap<>();
 dataParams.put("batchSize",new Integer(10));

CandidateGenerator candidateGenerator = new
RandomSearchGenerator(hyperParamaterSpace,dataParams);
```

5. Create a data source by implementing the `DataSource` interface:

```
public static class ExampleDataSource implements DataSource{
  public ExampleDataSource(){
    //implement methods from DataSource
  }
}
```

We will need to implement four methods: `configure()`, `trainData()`, `testData()`, and `getDataType()`:

- The following is an example implementation of `configure()`:

```
public void configure(Properties properties) {
    this.minibatchSize =
Integer.parseInt(properties.getProperty("minibatchSize",
"16"));
  }
```

- Here's an example implementation of `getDataType()`:

```
public Class<?> getDataType() {
  return DataSetIterator.class;
  }
```

- Here's an example implementation of `trainData()`:

```
public Object trainData() {
  try{
  DataSetIterator iterator = new
RecordReaderDataSetIterator(dataPreprocess(),minibatchSize,
labelIndex,numClasses);
  return dataSplit(iterator).getTestIterator();
  }
  catch(Exception e){
  throw new RuntimeException();
  }
  }
```

- Here's an example implementation of `testData()`:

```
public Object testData() {
  try{
  DataSetIterator iterator = new
RecordReaderDataSetIterator(dataPreprocess(),minibatchSize,
labelIndex,numClasses);
  return dataSplit(iterator).getTestIterator();
```

```
    }
    catch(Exception e){
    throw new RuntimeException();
    }
    }
```

6. Create an array of termination conditions:

```
TerminationCondition[] conditions = {
    new MaxTimeCondition(maxTimeOutInMinutes, TimeUnit.MINUTES),
    new MaxCandidatesCondition(maxCandidateCount)
};
```

7. Calculate the score of all models that were created using different combinations of configurations:

```
ScoreFunction scoreFunction = new
EvaluationScoreFunction(Evaluation.Metric.ACCURACY);
```

8. Create `OptimizationConfiguration` and add termination conditions and the score function:

```
OptimizationConfiguration optimizationConfiguration = new
OptimizationConfiguration.Builder()
  .candidateGenerator(candidateGenerator)
  .dataSource(ExampleDataSource.class,dataSourceProperties)
  .modelSaver(modelSaver)
  .scoreFunction(scoreFunction)
  .terminationConditions(conditions)
  .build();
```

9. Create `LocalOptimizationRunner` to run the hyperparameter tuning process:

```
IOptimizationRunner runner = new
LocalOptimizationRunner(optimizationConfiguration,new
MultiLayerNetworkTaskCreator());
```

10. Add listeners to `LocalOptimizationRunner` to ensure events are logged properly (skip to step 11 to add `ArbiterStatusListener`):

```
runner.addListeners(new LoggingStatusListener());
```

11. Execute the hyperparameter tuning by calling the `execute()` method:

```
runner.execute();
```

12. Store the model configurations and replace `LoggingStatusListener` with `ArbiterStatusListener`:

```
StatsStorage storage = new FileStatsStorage(new
File("HyperParamOptimizationStatsModel.dl4j"));
 runner.addListeners(new ArbiterStatusListener(storage));
```

13. Attach the storage to `UIServer`:

```
UIServer.getInstance().attach(storage);
```

14. Run the hyperparameter tuning session and go to the following URL to view the visualization:

```
http://localhost:9000/arbiter
```

15. Evaluate the best score from the hyperparameter tuning session and display the results in the console:

```
double bestScore = runner.bestScore();
 int bestCandidateIndex = runner.bestScoreCandidateIndex();
 int numberOfConfigsEvaluated = runner.numCandidatesCompleted();
```

You should see the output shown in the following snapshot. The model's best score, the index where the best model is located, and the number of configurations evaluated in the process are displayed:

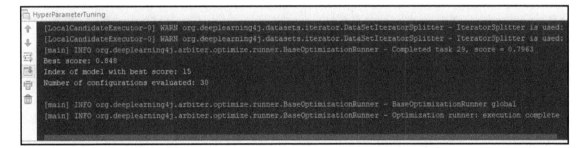

How it works...

In step 4, we set up a strategy by which the network configurations will be picked up from the search space. We use `CandidateGenerator` for this purpose. We created a parameter mapping to store all data mappings for use with the data source and passed it to `CandidateGenerator`.

In step 5, we implemented the `configure()` method along with three other methods from the `DataSource` interface. The `configure()` method accepts a `Properties` attribute, which has all parameters to be used with the data source. If we want to pass `miniBatchSize` as a property, then we can create a `Properties` instance as shown here:

```
Properties dataSourceProperties = new Properties();
 dataSourceProperties.setProperty("minibatchSize", "64");
```

Note that the minibatch size needs to be mentioned as a string: `"64"` and not `64`.

The custom `dataPreprocess()` method pre-processes data. `dataSplit()` creates `DataSetIteratorSplitter` to generate train/test iterators for training/evaluation.

In step 4, `RandomSearchGenerator` generates candidates for hyperparameter tuning at random. If we explicitly mention a probability distribution for the hyperparameters, then the random search will favor those hyperparameters according to their probability. `GridSearchCandidateGenerator` generates candidates using a grid search. For discrete hyperparameters, the grid size is equal to the number of hyperparameter values. For integer hyperparameters, the grid size is the same as `min(discretizationCount,max-min+1)`.

In step 6, we defined termination conditions. Termination conditions control how far the training process should progress. Termination conditions could be `MaxTimeCondition`, `MaxCandidatesCondition`, or we can define our own termination conditions.

In step 7, we created a score function to mention how each and every model is evaluated during the hyperparameter optimization process.

In step 8, we created `OptimizationConfiguration` comprising these termination conditions. Apart from termination conditions, we also added the following configurations to `OptimizationConfiguration`:

- The location at which the model information has to be stored
- The candidate generator that was created earlier
- The data source that was created earlier
- The type of evaluation metrics to be considered

`OptimizationConfiguration` ties all the components together to execute the hyperparameter optimization. Note that the `dataSource()` method expects two attributes: one is the class type of your data source class, the other is the data source properties that we want to pass on (`minibatchSize` in our example). The `modelSaver()` builder method requires you to mention the location of the model being trained. We can store model information (model score and other configurations) in the resources folder, and then we can create a `ModelSaver` instance as follows:

```
ResultSaver modelSaver = new FileModelSaver("resources/");
```

In order to visualize the results using arbiter, skip step 10, follow step 12, and then execute the visualization task runner.

After following the instructions in steps 13 and 14, you should be able to see arbiter's UI visualization, as shown here:

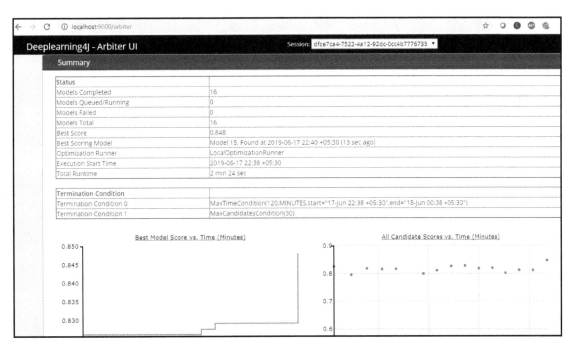

It is very intuitive and easy to figure out the best model score from the arbiter visualization. If you run multiple sessions of hyperparameter tuning, then you can select a particular session from the drop-down list at the top. Further important information displayed on the UI is pretty self-explanatory at this stage.

Other Books You May Enjoy

If you enjoyed this book, you may be interested in these other books by Packt:

Hands-On Deep Learning with Go

Gareth Seneque, Darrell Chua

ISBN: 978-1-78934-099-0

- Explore the Go ecosystem of libraries and communities for deep learning
- Get to grips with Neural Networks, their history, and how they work
- Design and implement Deep Neural Networks in Go
- Get a strong foundation of concepts such as Backpropagation and Momentum
- Build Variational Autoencoders and Restricted Boltzmann Machines using Go
- Build models with CUDA and benchmark CPU and GPU models

Java Deep Learning Projects
Md. Rezaul Karim

ISBN: 978-1-78899-745-4

- Master deep learning and neural network architectures
- Build real-life applications covering image classification, object detection, online trading, transfer learning, and multimedia analytics using DL4J and open-source APIs
- Train ML agents to learn from data using deep reinforcement learning
- Use factorization machines for advanced movie recommendations
- Train DL models on distributed GPUs for faster deep learning with Spark and DL4J
- Ease your learning experience through 69 FAQs

Leave a review - let other readers know what you think

Please share your thoughts on this book with others by leaving a review on the site that you bought it from. If you purchased the book from Amazon, please leave us an honest review on this book's Amazon page. This is vital so that other potential readers can see and use your unbiased opinion to make purchasing decisions, we can understand what our customers think about our products, and our authors can see your feedback on the title that they have worked with Packt to create. It will only take a few minutes of your time, but is valuable to other potential customers, our authors, and Packt. Thank you!

Index